The Search for Faith and Justice in the Twentieth Century

EDITED BY
GENE G. JAMES

A NEW ERA BOOK

PARAGON HOUSE
New York

First edition

Published in the United States by
Paragon House Publishers
90 Fifth Avenue
New York, NY 10011

Copyright © 1987 by Paragon House Publishers
Chapter 14, "The Rational Society and the Future of Religion,"
copyright © 1986 by Richard L. Rubenstein

All rights reserved. No part of this book may be
reproduced in any form without
written permission from the
publisher unless by a reviewer who
wishes to quote brief passages

Library of Congress Cataloging-in-Publication Data

The Search for faith and justice in the twentieth century.

(God, the contemporary discussion series)
"A New ERA book."
Includes index.
1. Religious ethics. 2. Religion and justice.
3. Religion and sociology. I. James, Gene G. II. Series.
BJ1188.S43   1987   291.5'622   86-30352
ISBN 0-913757-78-0
ISBN 0-913757-80-2 (pbk.)

Contents

Introduction GENE G. JAMES	vii
1 Justice I Am: God in the Twentieth Century DEANE WILLIAM FERM	1
2 Faith in God Confronts Collective Evils J. DEOTIS ROBERTS	15
3 The Christian Faith and the Creation of a Just Society from a Filipino Christian Perspective VITALIANO R. GOROSPE	28
4 God, Destiny and Social Injustice: A Critique of a Yoruba Ifa Belief OLUSEGUN GBADEGESIN	52
5 Faith, Justice and Violence in Latin American Liberation Theology GENE G. JAMES	69
6 Is Faith in God Necessary for a Just Society? Insights from Liberation Theology WILLIAM R. JONES	82
7 The Creation of Just Social Order in Islam ABDULAZIZ A. SACHEDINA	97
8 A Buddhist View of Creating a Just Society ILHAN GÜNGÖREN	116
9 A Just Society is Possible Only When the People are Just DOBOOM TULKU	123
10 On the Need of Faith for Justice JAMES GAFFNEY	130

11 Just Society: God's Shadow or Man's Work? SHIVESH C. THAKUR	142
12 Is Faith in God Necessary for the Creation of a Just Society? A Process Perspective GENE REEVES	152
13 Liberalism and Pluralism: Two Values for a Postmodern Christianity JAY McDANIEL	164
14 The Rational Society and the Future of Religion RICHARD L. RUBENSTEIN	178
15 On the Creation of a Good Society THOMAS WALSH	193
Notes on Contributors	213
Index	215

Introduction
GENE G. JAMES

The twentieth century has been a period of unprecedented change, characterized by the growth of science and technology, the development of huge government bureaucracies and multinational corporations, massive transformations of the environment, the breakdown of traditional values and ways of life, violent revolutions, purges, genocide, world wars, ideological conflicts and the threat of total nuclear destruction. These developments have brought about significant changes in the way people conceive faith, justice, and the relationships between them. They have also produced the longing that somehow disunity might be overcome and world community achieved.

The central issue addressed in this volume is whether religious faith is necessary for the creation of just societies and world community. The articles were prepared for the conference "God: the Contemporary Discussion" sponsored by the International Religious Foundation in August 1984. The authors come from a wide range of ethnic and cultural backgrounds and include representatives of the Buddhist, Islamic, Hindu, Jewish, and Christian traditions. There is also great diversity in their theological and philosophical approaches to the issues. To help the reader cope with this diversity, I have provided in the remainder of this introduction, brief summaries of the articles, emphasizing common issues and pointing out the respects in which the authors seem to agree or disagree. These summaries both give an overview of the volume and will assist readers who wish to read only some of the articles. It is my hope that making explicit some of the author's agreements and disagreements will also aid readers to approach the articles more critically.

The first article "Justice I Am: God in the Twentieth Century," by Deane William Ferm, traces the way God has been conceived in mainstream Christian theology since World War II. Ferm argues that the dominant conception of God from the 1970s to the present has been God as Liberator. Political theology, Latin American liberation theology, black theology, feminist theology and Asian liberation theology have all agreed in viewing God as active in history on behalf of the oppressed. The two most important themes in liberation theology, according to Ferm, have been: (a) the issue of *idolatry*, i.e., the way in which theology has been used in the past to justify social injustices, and (b) the claim that to know God is to act justly and vice versa.

The second article "Faith in God Confronts Collective Evils," by the black theologian J. Deotis Roberts, calls attention to the great affluence and poverty that exist side by side in American cities. The causes of this, he argues, are economic greed and racism, which are reinforced by "one dimensional religion" in which personal salvation is the overriding consideration. Roberts finds it strange that "the 'silent majority' has become the 'moral majority' in such a short period of time." In fact, there is "a remarkable silence regarding racism, greed and . . . social, economic and political injustices." Most Christians are oblivious to such problems as sexism, the economic exploitation of people in the third world by U.S. corporations, and the suffering of blacks in South Africa. Although faith in Christ should create concern about these kind of problems, Christians have failed to confront the collective evils of the twentieth century. Roberts believes that to find solutions to these problems, we will have to recognize that we live in a global village, and develop a code of ethics broader than the Christian convenant. This code will have to embody an outlook similar to the cosmopolitanism of the Stoics and affirm the equal dignity of all people. It must draw on the ethical traditions of all the great religions, but not be reducible to any of them. It is the duty of Christians, Roberts urges, to take the lead in developing such a code.

The article by Vitaliano Gorospe, a Jesuit priest and university professor in the Philippines, was written before the fall of the Marcos military dictatorship, and gives an account of the dilemma the Catholic church faced in deciding what political stance to take regarding the events there. The turning point in the church's attitude toward the Marcos regime was the assassination of Benigno Aquino on August 23, 1983. After that event both the bishops and Cardinal Sin became far more outspoken in condemning Marcos and calling for change. Writing at a time when the outcome of opposition to the Marcos government was extremely uncertain, Gorospe endorsed what he called the integrationist approach to the problem. He also pointed out that restoration of free speech and free

Introduction

elections will not by themselves solve the problems in the Philippines unless there is, in addition, a more just distribution of wealth. Gorospe, therefore, concludes by calling on the church to greatly expand its development of self-help basic Christian communities.

The first part of Olusegun Gbadegesin's article describes the December 31, 1983, military coup in his country, Nigeria, and explains why the people welcomed it. Whether or not the new regime will succeed in bringing about a just society, it was clear, he says, that one could not have been achieved under the former regime. In the second part of his paper, he discusses a theological doctrine he thinks has retarded the development of a more just society in Nigeria. This is belief in *Olodumare,* an omnipotent, omniscient Supreme Being who has assigned unchangeable destinies to human beings. Gbadegesin rejects this conception of deity on the grounds that it generates the problem of evil in an insolvable form, is inconsistent with belief in human freedom and responsibility, and justifies the status quo. "Injustice," he says, "cannot be adequately accounted for by appeal to destiny. To blame man's inhumanity to man on destiny is to legitimize despair."

The article by Gene James is a discussion of how faith, justice and violence have been conceived in Latin American liberation theology. A central theme has been that one can know God only by acting justly. Faith requires that one take positive action on behalf of the poor and oppressed. Since this is contrary to the interests of the right and powerful, it is usually met by violence. Although Christians should engage in violence only as a last resort, there are situations in which it is justifiable. One such situation is to overthrow oppressive political regimes which use terror and torture to stay in power. The use of counterviolence in such a situation, liberation theologians argue, is analogous to self-defense in a just war. Christians everywhere have an obligation to examine their life-styles to determine to what extent they contribute to injustice. North Americans especially have an obligation to do this in the context of United States foreign and economic policies toward Latin America. To not do so is to perpetuate injustice.

William R. Jones argues in his article that two of the most important insights of liberation theology are: (1) "any authentic definition of sin in the Judeo-Christian tradition must include esp oppression as a necessary ingredient" (esp is short for economic-social-political), and (2) theological and ontological doctrines frequently function to maintain esp oppression. Oppression, Jones believes, usually has a dual nature. It involves both institutional structures and belief/value systems which justify the structures. Jones agrees with Gbadegesin that the idea of predestination often plays an important role in maintaining oppression. "To perpetuate the unjust society, the oppressor must persuade the oppressed to accept their lot . . . and embrace inequalities as good and/or inevitable." Jones distinguishes *theocentric* from *humanocentric* theism. Theocentric theism interprets everything that happens as predetermined by God. Borrowing a metaphor from the theater, Jones describes it as the view that "God is the playwright, director, producer, star, agent, and critic." This conception of God "relegates the human to the role of spectator or cheerleader for the 'perfect play'." Humanocentric theism, on the other hand, sees humans as having co-responsibility with God for bringing about a just society. This type of theism, therefore, cannot be used to justify the status quo. "The oppressor can no longer point to anything but the human being as the sustaining force behind the unjust society." However, such a doctrine can be a double-edged sword. If appeal to God's will cannot provide an absolute grounding for the status quo, it also cannot provide one for the reformer's vision. Any clash of absolutes with counter-absolutes, Jones argues, "diminishes the authority of absolutes *per se.*" If absolutes come to be seen primarily as legitimation devices, this may lead to moral nihilism. That does not mean that humanocentric theists should abandon their view, but it should make them aware they may be mistaken in believing that faith in God is either necessary or sufficient for moral action. Jones concludes by calling for humanocentric theists to join ranks with other people of good will, such as humanists, to fight oppression, rather than quarrel about doctrinal differences.

    The articles discussed to this point were all written from a Christian perspective. The next three articles were written from the perspective of other world faiths. Abdulaziz Sachedina, a Muslim, discusses the Islamic conception of justice in his article "The Creation of a Just Social Order in Islam." Ilhan Gungoren, a Buddhist layman, who is a native of Turkey, and Doboom Tulku, a Buddist Monk, who is an aide to the Dalai Lama and Director of Tibet House in New Delhi, approach the issue of social justice from their respective commitments to Buddhism.

    Sachedina begins by pointing out that the obligation to create a just social order is as fundamental to Islam as it is to Judaism or Christianity. In fact, it may be even more central since "the Prophet Muhammed was not only the founder of a new religion, but also

Introduction

the guardian of a new social order." Because Muhammed was the leader of a community, he dealt primarily with immediate practical questions regarding social justice. Reflection on problems of justice by Muslims has consequently taken the form of law much more than in Judeo-Christian societies. The idea of a Messiah or Saoshyani who will establish God's kingdom on earth can also be found in Islamic thought. This grew out of the Shi'ite hope that someday a descendant of Muhammed will again rule over the faithful. The Sunnis, on the other hand, have always stressed obedience to the law as interpreted by the current leaders of the community as the means to bring about a just society. Debates regarding justice in Islamic societies, Sachedina states, have, therefore, tended to be politicized. Sachedina also discusses the clash between Asharites, who believe in predestination, and Mutazilites, who argue for free will, and how this has affected debates regarding justice in Islamic cultures.

Ilhan Gungoren maintains in his article, "A Buddhist View of Creating a Just Society," that the most fundamental principle of the universe is the law of causality which not even God can alter. Praying to God to change the course of events is, therefore, futile. Since each of our actions initiates a chain of events that will either harm or benefit others, we are all architects of the future and should take responsibility for our actions. Harmful actions are due to ignorance from which we can free ourselves by following the path of Buddhist enlightenment. This should not be interpreted, as it was by early Theravada Buddhism, as a quest for personal salvation, but as involving the Mahayana doctrine of the Bodhisattva who delays his own salvation to help bring others to Nirvana. This requires the suppression of egoistic desires and cultivation of concern for all living creatures. If everyone did this, a just society would be guaranteed.

A problem many Western thinkers would have with Gungoren's position (and the Asharite doctrine described by Sachedina) is that its determinism seems incompatible with the responsible action required to bring about a just society. If it is true, as he maintains, that the "self is nothing but a product of causal circumstances," and we are "nothing ... but inheritors of past karmas," there would seem to be no way for the individual to resolve to overcome ignorance so as to set out on the path to enlightenment, unless that action were itself predetermined. Gbadegesin and Jones, e.g., would no doubt object to his position on these grounds.

The claim that if everyone were to renounce egoism and cultivate

Buddhist compassion this would insure a just society is the central thesis of Doboom Tulku's article. Indeed, this seems so self-evident to him that he says: "There will be no dispute . . . that if virtuous ideas and deeds prevail among the citizens, creation of a just society is guaranteed." Like Plato in the *Republic,* he believes that if people were just this would automatically be translated into just laws and societies. He goes on to explain in more detail the nature of Buddhist wisdom and compassion, contrasting the kind of wisdom Buddha achieved with the omnipotence attributed to God in the Western tradition.

A fundamental difference between Eastern and Western thinking about justice emerges at this point. Contrary to Tulku's assertion, there are numerous thinkers in the West who would challenge the thesis that the achievement of virtue by all citizens would automatically result in a just society. For example, neither Roberts, who points to the failure of religious people to come to grip with collective evils, nor Jones, who points to the role unjust social structures play in determining human actions, would be likely to accept such a thesis. It would also be rejected by Marxists and most liberation theologians.

The articles by James Gaffney and Shivesh Thakur subject the notions of faith and justice to close analysis. Gaffney begins by pointing out that both terms are ambiguous. He then argues that there are at least three different senses in which faith, as it has been conceived in the West, might be claimed to be necessary for the creation of a just society. Faith might be: (1) a kind of *enlightment* required to envision a just society, (2) an *empowerment* needed to bring about a just society, (3) a *qualification* for participating in such a society. He believes that all three of these ways of conceiving faith are present in the way people talk about conversion experiences as providing insights into new truths, giving a new energy and direction to one's life, and qualifying one to participate in certain activities. Gaffney finds the concept of justice much more problematic than that of faith. He believes there is a radical bifurcation in the way justice has been conceived in the West which is the result of our dual heritage from Israel and Greece. Justice was conceived in the Bible as a type of personal righteousness expressed in acts of love and charity. But, justice as conceived by Aristotle, was a type of proportional equality based on merit. According to this view, what people receive should be proportionate to what they contribute. The problem with this, says Gaffney, is that it "assures not only extreme human inequalities, but utter destitution in the case of

Introduction

those who ... merit nothing because, for whatever reason, they contribute nothing." Given this view of justice, one cannot say that the destitute have a positive right to assistance because that would be to claim more than they deserve. Furthermore, since they do not have a positive right to assistance, no one has a correlative duty to aid them, even though it might be admirable for someone to do so. One consequence of the acceptance of this view of justice by our society, Gaffney argues, is that arguments in favor of the poor must resort to either pity or fear. The only consensus regarding justice we seem to be able to achieve in modern societies, which are characterized by a pluralism of groups with different basic values, is found in liberal theories that merely "strive to reduce ... initial inequalities of persons and groups ... conceived essentially as competitors, leaving the rest to competition itself, apart from emergency care for the graver casualties." But, says Gaffney, one would have "little hope of lasting justice for a married couple or family which was unable or unwilling to agree about what the members loved, to establish fundamental common values and an order of priorities respecting them." We have, therefore, never ceased longing for the kingdom God promised in the Bible, in which all humanity will be one loving family. If we ever attain such a state, he concludes, it will not be the result of reasoning about justice, but the outcome of faith which enlightens, empowers, and qualifies us for it.

One of the central theses of Shivesh Thakur's article "Just Society: God's Shadow or Man's Work?" is that one of our problems in thinking about the idea of justice is failure to realize it has always been an evolving concept. This makes it impossible to define it so as to encompass all its historical usages. Thakur, nevertheless, believes that it is possible "to specify a 'cluster' of identifying marks or properties, such that if an alleged case of a just society fails to exemplify a reasonable number ... in reasonably adequate proportions, we may have no hesitation in rejecting the claim." "In the first place a just society must be based on the 'rule of law' ..., it will not be a society in which anything goes." Secondly, there must be some degree of equality of citizens—equality before the law, equality of opportunity, etc. A just society will, therefore, attempt to minimize accidents of birth by doing such things as providing special education for the handicapped, etc. A just society will also respect the rights of its citizens to "freedom of thought, speech and action, limited only by the requirement that such liberties must not infringe the ... rights of other members of the society." "Finally, a just society incorporates some system for equal distribution of primary goods, as far as possible." By 'primary goods' is meant such things as food, housing, and medical care.

Turning to the issue whether faith in God is necessary for the creation of a just society, Thakur points out that there is no necessary or analytic connection between any of the key terms. He then argues, contrary to Gaffney, that faith in God is not necessary to either envision or create a just society. Only modern societies, in his opinion, have even come close to being just societies. Furthermore, this has been the result of rationality, not piety. Kant, Hume, Mill, and Marx, who more than anyone else, worked out the theories of justice modern societies have attempted to implement, says Thakur, "were singularly unenthusiastic about God." In fact, history shows that belief in God has been detrimental to the development of a just society. "There have not been many examples in history of just societies, but there have been quite a few of cruel and unjust ones, all or most of which were religion and/or God-based." He believes that one reason for this has been that the concept of human rights seems incompatible with the idea of divine grace. "The goal of eliminating or minimizing natural disadvantage or natural inequalities," he asserts, "will surely look suspect in a theocratic society; for such a society will . . . assume that God must have some purpose in creating these . . . in the first place." It is, therefore, no accident that progress toward social justice has most often occurred in societies in which belief in God is weak.

Gene Reeves' article is written from the perspective of process theology. He maintains that faith has been conceived in the West in two distinct ways: as intellectual assent or belief, and as attitudes or values determining a person's outlook on life. If faith is understood in the second way, and defined as a "primordial experience of one's life as meaningful," then Reeves believes this type of faith underlies all major world religions, no matter how much they differ at other levels. One need not be a theist to have this kind of faith. If they experience life as meaningful then "surely atheists and Theravada Buddhists . . . are not without human faith." It is even possible to define the concept of God in such a way that these thinkers can be said to believe in God. "By insisting that the primary or appropriate function or use of the term 'God' is to refer to that in reality . . . which grounds our assurance of the worth of our existence, we can make genuinely intelligible how it is that our common faith is compatible with the creative process which is reality itself." Faith, in the sense of believing that one can contribute to the creative process, is necessary for any long-range action.

Introduction

Cooperative action requires in addition that we have "some common purpose or ideal which transcends our individual self-serving purposes." "This does not imply," Reeves maintains, "that there must be agreement about the substance of such an encompassing ideal." In fact, "because every finite individual's conception of the good will be biased by that individual's limited perspectives . . . no individual can know the larger good." If community good is viewed this way, then it will be impermissible for any individual or group to attempt to force their conception of good on others. Nor need there be any agreement about basic values. Reeves, therefore, rejects Gaffney's model of a just society as a family in which there is agreement about common values. He believes that there are at least two dangers in accepting such a model: (1) "one might have a family in which the members are obedient to some vision of justice relative to the members of the family but which is unjust relative to the wider community," (2) family values may be used to justify patriarchy and authoritarianism. Reeves concludes that love does not require common values, merely respect for the dignity and autonomy of others. Unlike the theocratic conception of God criticized by Thakur, Reeve's theological perspective seems to be consistent with a theory of human rights. The humanocentric theism discussed by Jones would also seem to escape Thakur's criticism.

Jay McDaniel's article is written from a perspective he describes as either process/liberation or process/political theology. Like Reeves, he distinguishes between faith as belief and faith as commitment. Drawing on the work of Paul Tillich, he defines faith in God in terms of ultimate concern. He then points out that one may have faith in God in the sense that one believes God exists, without taking God as one's ultimate concern. One may also dedicate one's life to creative good, without believing that God exists. McDaniel next argues that whether or not atheists and Theravada Buddhists, who are working to bring about social justice, realize it, their actions "involve an unthematized faith in what Christians call God." Furthermore, it is legitimate for Christians to attempt to convince them of this, provided the Christians are committed to religious pluralism and are free from arrogance.

Richard Rubenstein argues in "The Rational Society and the Future of Religion" that the dominant characteristic of the modern world is the progressive rationalization of human activities. By 'rationalization' he means value-free calculation of the most efficient means to obtain a goal regardless of the social consequences.

For example, use of machinery and specialized labor are two of the ways in which economic productivity and distribution have been rationalized. Two of the consequences of this rationalization of the economy, Rubenstein maintains, have been a rapid growth of population and widespread unemployment. Marx believed that the problems created by the capitalist economic system would lead to its overthrow. There are two primary reasons this has not happened. The first is that governments have intervened to correct some of the worst problems. A second, equally important, reason is that millions of people have been killed by wars and genocide in the last two centuries. Not only capitalist, but communist societies, have been committed to rationalizing the economy. One of the most horrendous consequences of rationalization, in fact, occurred in the Soviet Union where an estimated 22,000,000 people died in Stalin's endeavor to modernize agriculture. Rubenstein believes that such a consequence was to be expected because "when morally neutral, functional rationality is used to create an economic and social order, such rationality ultimately becomes the handmaiden of power." Although the excesses have not been as great in capitalist economic systems, because the relationships between people are impersonal and instrumental, there is "a fundamental tension between the requirements of a pure market economy and the values necessary to maintain a community." Communities require a certain amount of self-limitation and altruism, but no rationale can be given for these values in a market economy. Consequently, in times of severe economic competition and widespread unemployment, community values erode. This is especially likely to be true in national states characterized by ethnic diversity. Social Darwinism and Neo-Malthusian ideologies become popular with the privileged classes. Thus Rubenstein concludes that genocide is a permanent possibility of modern societies. Since it is rationalization which has produced this situation, he also concludes that "a purely secular, rationalistic approach to our social problems is unlikely to produce the collective altruism our situation demands." He believes that only religion has been successful in the past in "establishing an enduring universe of moral obligation that transcends ethnicity and class." This does not mean that religion does not also have a dark side. But in Rubenstein's opinion "the worse excesses of religious conflict cannot compare in brutishness or mass destructiveness to the excesses of those political movements of the twentieth century which have regarded themselves as wholly liberated from all religiously defined moral constraints." Our only hope for the future, in his opinion, is that a worldwide faith will emerge.

Thomas Walsh argues in the last article that because contemporary liberal theories of justice are concerned exclusively with rights and law, and not with such matters as the meaning of life, proper goals for human beings and character formation, it is possible for a society to achieve a high level of justice, and, nevertheless, be an impoverished society in which contact between human beings is impersonal, uncaring, and most people live meaningless lives. Walsh maintains that the key figure in the development of liberal theories of justice was Kant because he was the first thinker for whom "moral law is characterized by universalization and independence from ... the good." In Kant's ethical theory "morality is severed from telos, utility, and human purpose." Contemporary theorists such as John Rawls hold a similar position. Rights and obligations are conceived of as grounded in generic features of human beings apart from their character, commitments or communities. They are "derived by removing oneself ... from the particular historical situation, ... from one's particular commitments, and imagining oneself in an 'original position' free from the constraints of history." Justice is seen in modern capitalistic societies as a set of rules or principles that do not presuppose any conception of the good and can thus be used to adjudicate conflicts between people and groups pursuing particular conceptions of the good. Justice, says Walsh, is consequently reduced to the moral relations which hold "between strangers who share no common vision of the good life." Marxist theories which reduce justice to equality of economic distribution have resulted in equally uncaring societies. But, while liberal societies are "relatively non-interventionist," Marxist societies are "interventionist." In their pursuit of economic justice, they have created systems of cultural and political domination which may be described as "a virtual tyranny of justice."

Although Walsh does not think that faith in God is necessary for the creation of a just society, he believes that it is necessary for the creation of a good society. His vision of the good society is the Unification ideal of a community of believers modeled on the family. The development of such a society, he believes, will require the revival of a teleological-virtue-ethics of the type advocated by Alasdair MacIntyre. Walsh admits that modeling society on the family has often led in the past to a kind of tribalism; but he believes that this was due to failure to consider all humankind a family. He also concedes that societies modeled on the family have frequently attempted to impose their conceptions of the good on those who are unreceptive. However, Walsh does not advocate abandoning doctrines of human rights which prevent this. His hope is for a society in which love for others, and respect for their rights, are combined.

The major themes developed in the volume may now be summarized. Gaffney, Rubenstein, and Walsh maintain that only religious commitment can give rise to the virtues required for a just and loving society. Unlike Tulku, who also believes this, they emphasize the need for tradition and community to instill virtue. Roberts, Gorospe, and Sachedina seem to agree. However, Roberts stresses the reform that will have to be undertaken to achieve such a society. Reeves and McDaniel also believe that religious commitment is necessary to achieve a just and loving society, but do not think this commitment need involve belief in the traditional Judeo-Christian God. The liberation theologians discussed by Ferm and James maintain that acting justly is a necessary ingredient of faith in God. They also draw our attention to the resistance engendered by attempts to reform society, and point out the need for religious people to take a stand on the issues of violence and counterviolence. Thakur and Jones reject the thesis that religious faith is necessary for the creation of a just and loving society. They emphasize that religious belief has often been used to justify unjust societies. This is also true of Gbadegesin who joins Jones in rejecting the kind of determinism defended by Gungoren. Gaffney's claim that social practices in contemporary democratic societies are based on the Aristotelian conception of justice as proportional equality based on merit is rejected by Thakur who cites the commitment of these societies to overcome accidents of birth. However, none of the authors seem to reject Robert's claim that the dominant forces in the modern world are economic greed and racism. If this is true, and I do not think any thoughtful person would deny it, we are still a long way from achieving just societies and world community. Rubenstein's thesis that even the most advanced modern societies harbor the possibility of genocide, therefore, unfortunately seem to be descriptive of our current situation.

Gene G. James

1
Justice I Am: God in the Twentieth Century
DEANE WILLIAM FERM

The purpose of this essay is to trace what has happened to God in the twentieth century. Of course, I don't quite mean what I have just written. I doubt that God has changed much during these four score years; what has changed is our conception of God. So what I mean to survey is how mainstream American theologians have changed in their ideas as they have tried to conceive of ultimate reality or God. Of course, the developments I shall discuss have probably had little or no impact on most of the people who sit in church pews Sunday after Sunday. Oh yes, these people have become more tolerant of the views of others; they have come to accept Christian pluralism. But this has not really affected their notion of what God is like. I have in mind here mainstream Protestant theologians—how their minds have changed with respect to God. My contention is that the question of God and the question of justice have become one and the same question, that this fusion is the most important contribution of the various forms of liberation theology, and that it is also the reaffirmation of an important dimension of biblical faith.[1]

Although I want to focus attention on changing perspectives of God over the past forty years, I shall first refer briefly to the situation in American theology before this period. Despite their obvious differences theologians earlier in this century agreed pretty much on both the existence and nature of God. God was considered to be transcendent, personal, loving, just, merciful, sovereign and so on. Where American theologians disagreed was concerning how this God was known. And here American Protestant theology can be divided into roughly three parts. (I am, to be sure, painting this portrait with a very broad brush!) Each division represents a different response to the intellectual upheaval epitomized by the scientific revolution.

On the one hand, liberalism is the response which sought to

come to terms with the modern world, to reinterpret the Christian faith according to the modern scientific worldview. Faith should be compatible with reason and experience. There is continuity among different areas of truth. God is the Source of truth. *That* God created the world and everything therein is more important than *how* God created it. God and human beings are co-partners in building a just social order. God's nature is conceived primarily as love. The love of God and neighbor is the essence of the Christian gospel. Liberalism placed a lot of confidence in our human ability to learn a lot about God.

On the other hand, conservatism embodied a very different response to the modern world. Conservatism proclaimed a set of propositions about God and Jesus, which remain the same regardless of how the world changes, propositions conservatives believe are sanctioned by God's revelation in the Bible. Here the overriding feature of God is sovereignty. God is transcendent, personal, just, righteous, loving and so on, but above all God is sovereign. God is in command. God is God and humans are humans and never the twain shall meet-except as God decides. And God, on God's initiative, has revealed the divine nature uniquely and decisively through Jesus Christ, the second person of the Trinity, who was born of a virgin, was raised from the dead and will come again. Conservatives affirmed a propositional view of God which remains forever the same. God is soverign, whatever the modern world thinks. And the Bible is the unique source of God's truth.[2]

Third—and in between liberalism and conservatism—we have neo-orthodoxy. Begun as a protest against liberalism, neo-orthodoxy became much more than an affirmation of conservatism. Neo-orthodoxy represents a deliberate attempt to return to the basic teachings of the early reformers, especially Martin Luther and John Calvin. It envisioned a new kind of orthodoxy; hence, the term neo-orthodoxy. Neo-orthodox theologians believed that liberalism had perverted the Christian faith in its eagerness to accommodate itself to the modern world. Neo-orthodoxy traces its beginnings as a self-conscious movement to Karl Barth (1886–1968), the Swiss theologian, who in 1918 published a commentary on the book of Romans in the New Testament. He urged a return to the original Lutheran doctrine of salvation, not by works or human initiative, but by faith in God's mercy. This plea won a warm response among European theologians who after World War I had lost confidence in human self-sufficiency. Neo-orthodox theologians accepted the usual attributes of God—personal, loving, just—and for them the key word is transcendence, the discontinuity between God and humanity. As Karl Barth put it:

> It is not the right human thoughts about God which form the content of the Bible, but the right divine thoughts about men. The Bible tells us not how we should talk with God but what he says to us; not how we find the way to him, but how he has sought and found the way to us.[3]

Neo-orthodoxy accepted the results of modern biblical research. This is the primary point at which its advocates differed from the conservatives. Some of them denied certain doctrines which conservatives considered crucial, for example, the virgin birth and the second coming of Jesus. But they did insist on the supernatural unique status of the Bible as the source of God's truth.

What I want to stress is that, although the emphases are different, all three approaches—liberalism, conservatism and neo-orthodoxy—agreed that God is loving, sovereign, transcendent and just. Furthermore, although all three approaches and their variants continued to have representatives in the mainstream theological community through the 1950s, the dominant feature was the continuing strength of neo-orthodoxy. I attended Yale Divinity School in the early 1950s, and in contemporary American theology at that time the superstars were Karl Barth, Emil Brunner and the American Reinhold Niebuhr (1894–1970). Niebuhr had originally been a liberal who, as a pastor in Detroit, had become disenchanted with liberalism's optimistic view of human nature. In the 1920s he began to see that sin is embodied in human pride, and that to be realistic, human beings must acknowledge how corrupt individuals and especially societies can be. Niebuhr came to believe that human hope lies in the transcendent God. Barth, Brunner and Niebuhr and their disciples continued to dominate American theology through the 1950s.

However, during the 1950s two other theologians came into prominence which gradually changed the theological scene, calling into question the general theological consensus concerning the nature and attributes of God: Paul Tillich (1886–1965) and Dietrich Bonhoeffer (1906–1945). Paul Tillich entitled his autobiography *On The Boundary,* which is a good description of his theological stance. Tillich lived on the boundary between faith and doubt, theology and philosophy, revelation and reason, the church and the world. In this way Tillich kept open the lines of communication with the unbeliever who had difficulty with traditional views of the Christian faith, but who continued to struggle with the basic question of human meaning. Important for our purposes is Tillich's reference to God as the "being beyond being" who cannot be adequately defined or categorized. For Tillich, faith becomes not so much the affirmation of God's personality, love, justice, sovereignty and the like, but rather, faith becomes "the courage to be," i.e., the courage to affirm being despite the threat of non-being. Consider these words of Tillich written in the 1940s:

> The Protestant message cannot be a direct proclamation of religious truths as they are given in the Bible and in tradition, for the situation of the modern man of today is precisely one of doubt about all this and about the Protestant church itself. The Christian doctrines, even the most central ones—God and Christ, church and revelation—are radically questioned . . . They cannot in this form be the message of the church to our time . . . It cannot be required of the man of today that he first accept theological truths, even though they should be God and Christ. Wherever the church in its message makes this a primary demand, it does not take seriously the situation of the man today and has no effective defense against the challenge of many thoughtful men of our day who reject the message of the church as of no concern for them.[4]

Here we have a Christian theologian of great prominence in the mainstream who calls into question even the doctrine of God, insisting that in our efforts to win over the modern seeker we cannot begin with the existence of God, but must begin with the human struggle for meaning. Tillich did not question God's importance, but he did shake human confidence in the ability to know God. Doubt becomes an essential ingredient of faith.

Dietrich Bonhoeffer also had a growing influence on American theology in the late 1950s. Bonhoeffer, who had taught at Union Theological Seminary in New York City in the early 1940s, had returned to Germany, was imprisoned by the Nazis and executed only days before the Americans liberated the prison where he had been incarcerated. Bonhoeffer's writings became the rallying point for a whole new breed of theologians. Although his writings obviously dated to the period before 1945, American translations did not appear for the most part until the middle 1950s. Bonhoeffer never had the opportunity to write a systematic theology. As a result he often presented his ideas in cryptic fashion. Consider these sentences from his *Letters and Papers From Prison:*

Justice I Am: God in the Twentieth Century

We are proceeding toward a time of no religion at all; men as they are simply cannot be religious any more.

God is teaching us that we must live as men who can get along very well without him.[5]

What does this mean? We cannot be religious any more? God tells us that we should get along without God? Bonhoeffer considered himself a Christian, but at the least these comments and others like them raised questions about the traditional view of God.

I suggest that, although through the 1950s neo-orthodoxy continued to reign as the dominant American theological school, cracks in this theology had begun to appear as Tillich, Bonhoeffer and their disciples increased in influence. By the early 1960s the edifice of neo-orthodoxy crumbled.

So what happened in the early 1960s? The answer is that drastic changes in American society took place. William McLoughlin refers to this shift as the Fourth Great Awakening.[6] Sidney Ahlstrom suggests:

The decade of the 1960s was a time, in short, when the old foundations of national confidence, patriotic idealism, moral traditionalism, and even of historic Judeo-Christian theism, were awash.[7]

The secular spirit—the age of Sputnik and amazing advances in human technology—began to pervade society in general and the churches in particular. I mean here by the secular spirit the conviction that the only real world for humankind is that of the here-and-now, a world to be known essentially through the natural sciences. Anything beyond this world is in principle unknowable or illusory. A spirit of buoyant confidence in human technology and invention prevailed. Why turn to an unknown God when human beings are quite capable of taking care of themselves? President John F. Kennedy epitomized this new attitude in his presidential address of 1963 when he concluded by saying that "God's work on this earth must truly be our own."

Furthermore, the Roman Catholic ecumenical council Vatican II of the early 1960s—and, in particular, Pope John XXIII—had ushered in a new spirit of cooperation among religious groups, especially on social issues. In these new and positive encounters between Protestants and Catholics, doctrinal issues were often shunted to the sidelines in favor of problems of mutual concern that could be tackled together. After all, doctrine divides; service unites.

For many individuals within the different churches theology became an ecumenical concern of social involvement. Later in the 1960s, racism and the Vietnam War became rallying points for Protestant and Catholic clergy and laity. Increasingly, God came to be considered not so much the object of human speculation or the source of divine revelation but the Great Liberator from human oppression, the primary instigator for social change.

This new secularism had a profound impact on the meaning of God. An indication of the demise of neo-orthodoxy and the subsequent disappearance of the traditional view of God's transcendence is the recognition given the late Anglican bishop John Robinson's little book *Honest to God,* published in 1963. This book, which is largely a popularization of some themes from Tillich and Bonhoeffer, suggests a view of God more in tune with the growing secular spirit. God is not "out there" but "within" the deepest expression of human love which is divine. What is so significant about this little book is not only its immense popularity, but also its complete neglect of Barth, Brunner and Niebuhr. Another timely book was Harvey Cox's *The Secular City* (1965). Here Cox argues that God is the primary Agent for social change, and that the meaning of God has been so misused that "perhaps for a while we shall have to do without a name for God."[8]

The most publicized theological movement of the middle 1960s was, of course, known as the "death of God." These particular theologians differed as to why they joined in writing God's obituary. For some it was inadequate language; how can one speak of the Transcendent in this secular age? For others it was the experience of the absence of God; God is no longer real in our own experience. And for still others it was the problem of evil; how can one continue to believe in a loving God after Auschwitz? These thinkers agreed that since God was dead, the human race must take complete responsibility for this world.

By the end of the 1960s the death-of-God theology had died, primarily because this movement had capitulated to the secular spirit. Other theologians began to ask: what is so final about this here-and-now world? As the philosopher George Santayana used to say, the one who becomes married to the present generation becomes a widower in the next generation. If we become completely enamored by the secular spirit, then secular things become all important. But what if the world includes "more than" the secular? How would we even begin to know the "more than" if our meth-

Justice I Am: God in the Twentieth Century

ods do not permit such knowledge? Although it may be difficult to conceive of the reality of the Transcendent or God, for increasing numbers of people it became even more difficult to comprehend a world devoid of some greater purpose, some intrinsic meaning, i.e., God.

By the end of the 1960s the secular spirit began to wane and theology followed suit. As the underlying national mood began to shift from action to introspection, from liberalism to conservatism, from the spirit of McGovern to the spirit of Reagan, from the secular to the spiritual, theological concerns reflected a significant though ambivalent transition. On the one hand, some theologians—continuing the notion of God as the Great Liberator from human oppression—related that theme to their major area of social concern: economic exploitation, racism and sexism, to mention three such concerns. So we have developing in the 1970s many different forms of liberation theology: Latin American, black and feminist among others. But on the other hand, other theologians, responding to the conservative trend, sought to articulate a more traditional yet more open evangelical faith, which appears very much like a resurgence of neo-orthodoxy. And following this swing from action to introspection we have the growing strength of the charismatic movement, which stresses the experience of God over intellectual content. Let us take a brief look at these two prominent trends of the 1970s.

Latin American liberation theology focuses on the plight of the poor and oppressed and views God as the Liberator who shows a preferential treatment for the poor and oppressed. Consider these words from Latin American liberation theologian Victorio Araya:

> [T]he key question in the world of the exploited . . . is increasingly less 'Does God exist?' and more 'Is God really on the side of those who are struggling for justice against oppression?' God, the God of the covenant, is experienced as a strategic ally in their struggle. What is at stake is not an ontological issue—does God exist—but rather a concrete, historical issue: the death of the poor . . . belief in God entails taking a stand for liberation and against exploitation.[9]

For these theologians God is not a transcendent Being, so much as God is an immanent activist fully involved in the social, economic and political struggle.

Black theology colors God black and sees God as actively involved in overcoming the sin of racism. Here is how American black theologian James Cone expresses it:

The task of Black Theology, then, is *to analyze the black man's condition in the light of God's revelation in Jesus Christ with the purpose of creating a new understanding of black dignity among black people, and providing the necessary soul in that people, to destroy white racism.*[10]

God is on the side of the blacks in a kind of affirmative action program.

Feminist theology understands God or the Goddess to be fighting for liberation from sexism. Here is how Rosemary Ruether defines feminist theology in her latest book *Sexism and God-Talk*:

The critical principle of feminist theology is the promotion of the full humanity of women. Whatever denies, diminishes, or distorts the full humanity of women is, therefore, appraised as not redemptive. Theologically speaking, whatever diminishes or denies the full humanity of women must be presumed not to reflect the divine.[11]

The Goddess has as her goal the liberation of women from all forms of oppression.

To be sure, there is tremendous variety in all three of these forms of liberation theology, but what they have in common is an underlying concern, not for *who* God is, but for *how* God acts. In short, the verb is more important than the noun. God's *doing* is more important than God's *being*.

The other basic theological trend in the 1970s, which is different from liberation theology, is the growth of a new form of evangelicalism. In his influential book *Why Conservative Churches Are Growing* (1972), Dean Kelley suggests that these churches are growing because their members are serious about their faith, they know what they believe, they do not apologize for their convictions, and they do not confuse their loyalties with the beliefs and attitudes of the rest of society. For these theologians God is real, sovereign, transcendent and just. They object to the recent trend in theology—nicknamed "yo yo" theology—which worships change as though the primary purpose of theology is to be relevant. According to these thinkers it is most important to be relevant to the sovereign God who was, is and ever shall be, world without end.

What is new among these evangelical theologians of the 1970s is that they no longer object to the historical-critical method of studying the Bible and, equally important, they have a deepened commitment to the social dimension of the Christian faith. As evangelical scholar Richard Quebedeaux notes, today's leading evangelical theologians are turning to those neo-orthodox theologians so prominent in the 1940s and 1950s who were shunned by their evangelical predecessors, theologians such as Karl Barth, Emil Brunner and Reinhold Niebuhr. Quebedeaux notes:

> The works of these theologians are studied and taught sympathetically in evangelical seminaries. Evangelical scholars are writing an ever increasing number of articles and books paying high tribute to them ... Neo-orthodoxy, carried and nurtured by evangelical theology may prove to be stronger and more durable.[12]

These same evangelicals also stress the conviction that knowing God means doing justice and they are urging their followers to have a greater concern for the poor and oppressed. At this point liberation theologians and many evangelical theologians are finding common ground.

So where do we go from here? How shall we conceive of God in the years to come? I have three suggestions to make as we enter into the middle eighties. First, increasing religious pluralism will expand our view of God. Asian Christian theologian C. S. Song suggests a new view of history with which I agree.

> History must be liberated. But from whom? From us, of course. History must be liberated from Jews, Christians, Hindus or Muslims, in order that a new history may come into existence—a history not cut in pieces by Jews, Christians or Buddhists, but a history which is the realm of divine-human meaning ... No religious system, however great, can contain God.[13]

Stanley Samartha of India sums up the new attitude toward other religions by asserting:

> There is no reason to claim that the religion developed in the desert around Mount Sinai is superior to the religion developed on the banks of the river Ganga.[14]

Whereas earlier in this century the major problem for the Christian religion was how to come to terms with the scientific revolution, today the major problem is how to come to terms with the other major living religions of the world. Our views of God will expand.

Secondly, as our concepts of God expand, we will become less sure of ourselves as we speak of God. The more we know, the more we realize that we do not know. An increasing importance will be attached to the notion of idolatry, the worship of false gods, a conviction so dominant today in Latin American liberation theology. In the introduction to the book *The Idols of Death and the God of Life* we find these words:

> The central question in Latin America today is not atheism—the ontological question of whether or not God exists.... The central question is idolatry—a worship of the false gods of the system of oppression. Even more tragic than atheism is the faith and hope that is put in false gods.... Much to the contrary of what might be supposed, false gods not only exist today, but are in excellent health.[15]

Too often we have used God to justify racism, sexism, poverty, hunger and other forms of human oppression. These false gods will come under increasing attack and rightly so.

Third and finally, what do we have left when it comes to God? What kind of God can we believe in without being idolatrous? We must always be aware of idolatry since we are human and cannot stuff God into any human container. How can we say something about God without claiming too much—and yet say enough? If I were to pick out one concept with which to speak of God that is meeting with growing approval today among different theological perspectives, it would be the concept of justice. To know God is to do justice. What does God require of us but to do justice? I find this affirmation of God as justice to be at the heart of biblical faith and also at the heart of the various forms of liberation theology today. And I also find this concept imbedded in the core of much current evangelical thinking.

Consider these biblical affirmations:

> Justice will go before you,
> and the glory of Yahweh behind you.
> (Isaiah 58:8)

> The people will see your justice,
> and all the kings your glory.
> (Psalm 97:6)

> The heavens proclaim his justice,
> The Most High for his glory.
> (Isaiah 61:3)

> Everyone who does justice is born of God.
> (I John 4:7)

> This is the distinction between the children of God and the children of the devil: Anyone who does not do justice is not of God, nor is anyone who does not love his brother.
> (3 John 11)

Justice I Am: God in the Twentieth Century

> Then the righteous will answer Jesus, "Lord, when did we see thee hungry and feed thee, or thirsty and give thee drink? And when did we see thee a stranger and welcome thee, or naked and clothe thee? And when did we see thee sick and in prison and visit thee?" And the King will answer them, "Truly, I say to you, as you did it to one of the least of these my brethren, you did it to me."
> (Matthew 25:37-40)

To do justice is to know God. To do justice is to follow Jesus. The Hebrew word *yada* means both "to know" and "to love." Justice and love are mutually indispensable; one cannot have one without the other.

This affirmation of God as justice, and therefore on the side of the poor and oppressed, has been an important theme for Christian theologians in this century. Take, for example, these words that Karl Barth has included in a discussion of the righteousness of God in Volume Two of his *Church Dogmatics:*

> [T]he human righteousness required by God and established in obedience—the righteousness which according to Amos 5:24 should pour down as a mighty stream—has necessarily the character of a vindication of right in favour of the threatened innocent, the oppressed poor, widows, orphans and aliens. For this reason, in the relations and events in the life of His people, God always takes His stand unconditionally and passionately on this side and on this side alone: against the lofty and on behalf of the lowly; against those who already enjoy right and privilege and on behalf of those who are denied and deprived of it.[16]

We find this same emphasis on God and justice in the recent writings of evangelical scholars. Consider Ron Sider who calls one of his recent books *Cry Justice* and declares that "the one who discloses himself as boundless love also reveals himself as truth, holiness and justice."[17] And in his book *Evangelicals and Development: Toward A Theology of Social Change* (1981), Sider notes a growing concern on the part of evangelicals for the biblical teaching that stresses concern for the poor, the hungry and the oppressed.

This theme of "God equals justice" is the key to understanding the various forms of liberation theology. Liberation from various forms of oppression—economic exploitation, political oppression, racism, sexism and so on—is another way of saying that the reason God desires liberty and justice for all is that God *is* liberty and justice. This theme of justice is particularly potent in third world liberation theology, which is often accused—wrongly, I believe—of a kind of horizontalism that seems to lose sight of transcendence and otherness. But the problem here is one of focus. It is clear that in his writings Gustavo Gutierrez stresses liberation from economic, social and political oppression, but he also attaches two other meanings to the term 'liberation': liberation in the sense of individuals having the freedom to achieve their own destiny, and liberation in the Christian context of identifying with Christ as the great Liberator. This is why he can write in his latest book *We Drink From Our Wells:*

Liberation is an all-embracing process that leaves no dimension of human life untouched, because when all is said and done it expresses the saving action of God in history.[18]

Minjung theology emanating from South Korea is one significant example of an indigenous liberation theology that zeroes in on justice. Minjung can be translated "downtrodden people" or "the oppressed." Here theology means the merger of the worldly and the heavenly, the expansion of the human spirit, and the demand for justice in the social order. Transcendence is not reference to some other metaphysical order, but a deepening of the here-and-now, the historical expansion of human justice. And the Messiah is the one "who comes from the bottom" to incarnate justice in human lives. In the words of Suh Nam-dong:

In the post-Christian era, the minjung church and minjung theology attempt to deal simultaneously with the purification of the person, which is the realm of freedom, and the humanization of the social structure, which is the realm of necessity. It is, as Kim Chi-ha perceives, "the unification of God and revelation."[19]

So we come to the question: Is faith in God necessary to the creation of a just society? And my answer is that to have faith in God is to work for a just society. Conversely, to work for a just society is to have faith in God. To know God is to do justice. Despite the changing conceptions of God in the twentieth century God is still God. Justice is still justice. Although we humans have changed through the years in how we think of God, and although our conceptions of God have more often than not been idolatrous, yet God as justice still reigns and beckons us to follow. In his book *Hunger For Justice: The Politics of Food and Faith,* Jack Nelson writes of the millions of starving people in this world—starving for both justice and food. In conclusion, I want to quote one passage from this book which illustrates my theme: that the question of the existence of God and the question of the sovereignty of justice are one and the same.

According to Jesus and the prophets, to love and to know God is to love and do justice to one's neighbor. The radical message for which the Son of God was crucified, and the prophets killed or exiled, is that the God of the Bible cannot be known or loved directly. Love and knowledge of God are mediated through one's neighbor. This does not mean that prayer and worship are not important. On the contrary, prayer is essential if we are to discern the will of God, and worship testifies to the transcendence of God. However, without a concrete commitment to a justice that alters the condition of one's neighbor, both prayer and worship are empty rituals that glorify false gods. . . . If we are to know God, we cannot short-circuit our commitment to alter the condition of our neighbor, nor can we be indifferent to the structures that oppress them. The struggle for human liberation, our own and that of Third World peoples, involves a commitment to social justice and a return to authentic biblical faith.[20]

NOTES

1. For the purposes of this essay I mean by justice equal opportunities, rights and dignity for every individual; and that justice and love are mutually complementary.
2. Fundamentalism would, of course, be included here under the rubric of conservatism, but fundamentalists normally hold a much more literal view of scripture than some conservatives. But in their conception of God conservatives and fundamentalists can be placed in the same camp.
3. Karl Barth, *The World of God and the World of Man* (Chicago: Pilgrim Press, 1982), 43.
4. Paul Tillich, *The Protestant Era* (Chicago: The University of Chicago Press, 1963), 202.
5. Dietrich Bonhoeffer, *Letters and Papers From Prison* (New York: The Mac-Millan Co., 1953; paperback edition, 1962), 162, 219.
6. William McLoughlin, *Revivals, Awakenings, and Reform: An Essay on Religion and Social Change in America, 1607–1977* (Chicago: The University of Chicago Press, 1978), 1.
7. Sidney Ahlstrom, *A Religious History of the American People,* Vol. 2 (New York: Doubleday, 1975), 600.

8. Harvey Cox, *The Secular City* (New York: The MacMillan Co., 1965), 267.
9. Victorio Araya G., "The God of the Strategic Covenant," in *The Idols of Death and the God of Life* edited by Pablo Richard et al., (Maryknoll, New York: Orbis Books, 1983), 104.
10. James Cone, *Black Theology and Black Power* (New York: The Seabury Press, 1969), 117.
11. Rosemary Ruether, *Sexism and God-Talk* (Boston: The Beacon Press, 1983), 18–19.
12. Richard Quebedeaux, *The Worldly Evangelicals* (New York: Harper and Row, 1978), 100.
13. C. S. Song in *Southeast Asia Journal of Theology* 19 (2), (1978), 22.
14. Stanley Samartha, in "The Lordship of Jesus Christ and Religious Pluralism," *Christ's Lordship and Religious Pluralism,* edited by Gerald H. Anderson and Thomas F. Stransky, (Maryknoll, New York: Orbis Books, 1981), 32.
15. Pablo Richard, 1.
16. Karl Barth, *Church Dogmatics,* Vol. II, *The Doctrine of God* (Edinburgh: T & T Clark, 1957, Reprint, 1964), 386.
17. Ronald Sider, *Cry Justice* (New York: Paulist Press, 1980), 1.
18. Gustavo Gutierrez, *We Drink From These Wells* (Maryknoll, New York: Orbis Books, 1983), 166.
19. The Commission on Theological Concerns of the Christian Conference in Asia, ed., *Minjung Theology* (Maryknoll, New York: Orbis Books, 1980), 166.
20. Jack Nelson, *Hunger for Justice. The Politics of Food and Faith* (Maryknoll, New York: Orbis Books, 1980), 190–191.

2
Faith in God Confronts Collective Evils
J. DEOTIS ROBERTS

The Problem

The problem of evil in a world created by a good God is not a new issue. It is as old as the human mind's reflection on ultimate things. The word 'theodicy' has been used to name this problem in philosophy and theology. The problem of evil and God has often been discussed from a conceptual, mainly a metaphysical point of view. It has usually involved ethical questions, but these issues have centered in theoretical concerns. I wish to approach the problem from the vantage point of undeserved human suffering. My discussion will be aware of "animal pain" as a reality, but my objective is to confront forthrightly the existence of suffering based upon inhumanity. What accountability does God have, as Creator, in the suffering which human beings inflict upon each other? This issue arises for theists—it does not necessarily occur to humanists. If man is on his own, then the culpability of the divine in human suffering need not arise. But on the other hand, if God is a Creator and provident God, the question is inescapable.

It would appear that a limited number of Euro-American theologians have just discovered what Moltman calls the "crimes of history." Previously, they had mainly viewed sin and evil in very personal terms or as natural evils. But the death camps of Hitler's Germany raised to a level of visibility a problem which had been ignored. Now, the same issues are raised in any consideration of slavery or colonialism. And yet the pacesetters in Western theology overlooked this crucial theme. Neither should we overlook sexism and poverty. The issue of human suffering on a grand scale is with us in the United States, Central America, the Middle East, and especially in South Africa today.

A series of theological programs now approach the question of suffering as a political, sociological and economic concern. The issue is no longer circumscribed to the realm of the person and psychological aspects of faith. Political theology, liberation theology, holocaust theology, black theology, and some African and Asian theologies, all seek to develop a theological perspective which takes seriously group suffering and systemic evils. But as powerful as this company of thinkers may be, the ecclesiological and theological mainstream seems almost ambivalent to the cries of the oppressed. This places an undue burden upon those few theologicans who seek to think theologically in solidarity with the suffering masses. This task is, however, so important and urgent, that those who are involved do not have the luxury of awaiting approval by respectable theologians in the American mainstream.

Nero is said to have fiddled while Rome burned. As the oppressed seek to eke out a survival, theologians as well as church leaders are obsessed with fine points of doctrine and ideological differences which have little to do with making life more human. With Reaganomics, the moral majority and the electronic church leading the United States in a direction which promises widespread human suffering, denominations are preoccupied with the divinity of Christ, the inerrancy of scripture and creation versus evolution. They are busy fiddling. Someone said California is either sliding, shaking or burning. This is predictive of the leadership of the former governor of the state in reference to the state of the nation—sliding, shaking, burning. The fiddling goes on, but so does the burning. The American national administration appeals to the well-off and flirts with military solutions to human problems.

This brief discussion will not suffice to cover in detail such an immense issue as wholesale mass suffering, an enigma within a mystery. It will attempt to deal only with suffering resulting from human culpability. We are limiting our discussion to the area where there is human responsibility related to free moral agency. The reason humans are responsible and free is a theological problem of some moment. Could not God have made humans unresponsible and unfree, morally speaking? Doesn't God possess the power to contradict logic and ethics as understood by finite minds?

But wouldn't it be risky to go this route? To transcend logic and ethics does not and should not require contradiction. We should have a sense that God embodies the best that we know as finite persons, and yet baffles our ability to fully comprehend. In other words, we know in part, but we do know. We see through a glass darkly, but we do see. Theology should direct us to the place where

Faith in God Confronts Collective Evils

faith possesses reasonableness and certitude, even if certainty is not within our grasp. Our concern for the alienation of human suffering should not lead us to question the moral integrity of the very source of the faith to overcome suffering. There needs to be an understanding of human suffering and God which strengthens confidence in the One worthy of trust.[1]

Human Suffering and Pain. Pain is inevitable as a part of our creaturely existence. Humans experience what we may describe as "animal pain." We live in a physical body in a natural environment. The physical work is often harsh—it is indifferent to the moral or spiritual state of human beings. The fact that we dwell in a natural environment, usually goverened by law, means that the violation of a physical law leads directly to punishment. Violation of natural law may be due to ignorance as well as transgression. Every infraction of natural law is met instantly with swift and exacting penalty. There is no "grace" or "mercy" in nature. It is accurate to recall that nature is "red in tooth and claw." There is a "thingness" about nature. Animal pain is unrelated to the moral and spiritual quest.

Furthermore, there are times when nature loses her harmony and the cosmos becomes a violent chaos. Earthquakes, tornadoes, floods, diseases are just some examples of natural disorder. Once again human beings are victims of what seems to be the anger, even the wrath, of a natural order bereft of its usual order. Again, there is an amorality or a moral indifference mainfest when nature abandons her own sense of balance or harmony. Accident, disease and death make no distinctions among humans. When nature strikes out in fury, she is relentless and indiscriminate in her devastation. Those who happen to be at the wrong place at the wrong time are injured or destroyed without exception. We refer to this as the experience of pain.

Natural evils or disorders are difficult to understand and even more difficult to accept. Even though we may have logical and scientific explanations for much natural disorder, we have a tendency to ascribe moral interpretations to the experience of "animal pain." This confuses rather than clarifies the issue. As long as we realize that nature is only a relatively established "order," we can allow for exceptions. We can often determine the effects by causes. Even when nature goes wild, unusual causes explain unusual effects. It is more difficult to deal with moral evil, for it immediately raises the issue of responsiblity. Christians have a sharpened problem because they dare to believe in a Creator—God who is said to be all good and all powerful. Furthermore, God is assumed to have created the world "out of nothing." Where, then, does evil come from? There is no preexistent "stuff" as in Plato's *Timaeus,* no Plotinian "matter" or Hindu "maya." God is said to have created the world and described it as good.

This complicates the argument that sin as moral evil results from the wrong choice. I fail to see how the sexual act can be a proper way out of this quandary. If sex is inherently evil, how then can it be also the means to blessedness? Furthermore, sin seems to be more radical in its nature than the abuse of sex. Sexual perversion and abuse appear to be more of an effect than a cause of moral evil. The question of source, of choice between good and evil, pushes the issues back prior to Adam and Eve's transgression. It is clear that sin and evil involve more than the abuse of sex in personal life. But it is when we take a look at sinful social structures that we are overwhelmed by the complexity of evil. Greed is a deadly sin that is at least as perverse as lust. And yet greed, like lust, is more effect than cause. The question, from whence comes evil remains an intellectual puzzle. For instance, the "moral majority" would eradicate sins associated with *lust,* but they are "the silent majority" when it comes to *greed*. We need to take a careful look again at what medieval theology referred to as the seven deadly sins. It might also help to look at the Ten Commandments and the Sermon on the Mount with some social sins in mind.

As we look at human suffering resulting from inhumanity, greed causes as much havoc in public ethics as lust does in personal ethics. In the case of pimping and prostitution *lust* and *greed* reinforce each other. Marital infidelity usually illustrates lust more than greed, though they are often combined. But it is possible for a person to be a paragon of virtue in faithfulness to family ideals and values, and yet be the perpetrator of great misery for thousands of humans through economic exploitation. In fact, this sponsorship of widespread suffering of other races, individuals and families may be carried out for the sake of an enriched family life. For the sake of the comfort of one's own family, one may be an agent of destruction of other families, not because of lust but because of greed. I would not place a greater or lesser value on these deadly sins, but I wish to make the point that in the realm of ethics, there are no easy answers. There are only hard questions. We do, however, have principles which direct us forward.[2]

Evil and God. The question of Job is an unanswered question.

Faith in God Confronts Collective Evils

The answer is still a *childlike* faith. I do not refer here to a *childish* faith. Even in the maturity of our conviction as Christians we are awed by the complexity and mystery of evil. We dare to believe that God is a creator-spirit and that he is a Benevolent-Provider. Our trust in the meaning of life is supported by a faith in a Supreme Person who is the source of all that is loving and just. But not only do we believe that God is good, we believe that there is sufficient ability in God's Being to sustain the best ideals and values we know in history and human experience.[3]

There is no logical way out of the dilemma that God is both all-good and all-powerful. One attribute reinforces the other, and both are essential for a well-balanced divine personality. This we hold true in spite of the widspread existence and persistence of sin and evil. If God is all-good and *will not* put an end to moral evil, we have a problem. If he is anxious to eradicate evil and *cannot*, whence his omnipotence? Both the desire to have goodness triumph and the ability to bring it to pass are the twin affirmations of theistic faith. If there is a logical answer to this mystery, it is only the logic of faith. Christians have found their faith-solution in the Cross-Resurrection of Jesus. Evil is not explained logically, it is transmuted spiritually. It is faced and it is conquered. The experiential answer is the sufficiency of God's grace—to enable and sanctify. The manifestation of grace in the experience of the believer is likewise a paradox. We live a life of freedom and yet in openness to God's enabling grace which works in and through that same freedom. Human beings can be agents of good as well as evil.

Co-Creators and Co-Laborers. Though we cannot account for the origin of evil, we are painfully aware of its radical nature and destructive power in personal and social relations. Much of the evil, resulting in mass suffering, can be attributed to the abuse of freedom. In the face of knowledge and freedom to choose and act nobly, we deliberately choose a lesser good. Collective evils are more difficult to explain and to overcome. We find moral individuals in an immoral society. It is awesome to analyze sinful social structures. Consequences of sins and evils may be passed on in the context of history and the social environment. How do we place guilt, responsibility, and the means to overcome such evils?

Much moral evil can be explained through God's self-limitation in order to create beings, who are both free and morally responsible. Much suffering is present in our personal and social lives because of the perversion of our nature. Freedom is abused and we have not been responsive or responsible as co-creators with God. We are endowed to scale angelic heights, but we have sunk to diabolical depths. Much of the answer we seek is in the recovery of the creative purpose of human life in the design of God.

Quest for Liberation in an Unjust World

In *A Tale of Two Cities,* Charles Dickens speaks of "the best of times and the worst of times." I found these insights helpful as I pondered the request to write this article. Our city, our nation, and indeed the world, is a tale of two cities: black and white, males and females, rich and poor. And in a real sense this is at once the best of times and the worst of times. Viewed from the perspective of Christian faith, times of great adversity may be our finest hour of commitment to the values and goals that matter most. Our faith in God is a resource which enables us to make creative use of suffering.

The Human Condition. I shall get to the Third World, eventually, but I will begin with the First World. I have walked the streets of Calcutta. The horsemen of the Apocalypse roam freely around the streets of that city; but I would not have the deep compassion I feel for people in Calcutta unless I identified with the plight of the black poor in the cities of America.

Some time ago, as I drove a daughter to Spelman College, we stopped at a drug store. It was the day when government checks were being deposited. On one side of the street was a bank. Diagonally across the street from the bank was a drug store. We observed a large number of elderly persons who cluttered the streets, sidewalks, stores and banks. I had just left my own parents in North Carolina and along the way, I had spent some time in Washington. The plight of the black, elderly poor occupied my thoughts. While my young daughter appeared satisfied with my groping reflections—she is of tender years—I would not communicate to her the fellow-feeling and solidarity in suffering which crowded my mind and spirit. Beyond the sheer compassion I felt, I pondered the effects which the conservative, national, political regime has upon the plight of the elderly. I asked myself who will bind up these wounds?

A little later the same day a young lady called me at home. She is a close friend of my oldest daughter. This young lady, though black, has become a highly successful model in New York City. She indicated that she was visiting a friend at Atlanta University Center and would like to have lunch with me. In a pre-lunch conversation

Faith in God Confronts Collective Evils

in my office, to my surprise, she described her success with complete detail and abandon. At twenty-four she seemed to feel that she was entitled to all this. She did not know that her success outstripped her achievement, that natural beauty fades and that this is often a long life. And then I was even more startled when she said, in a tone of voice which anticipated my approval: "God gives me everything I ask for!" I was tempted to put on the mantle of a preacher or prophet and expose the deficiencies of her God of Success. But I realized that she needed her God, even though too small. She moves daily in a world of human exploitation where her best friends are often sophisticated call girls. Her upbringing and her religious faith have brought comfort and direction to her life. A devastating confrontation would not have helped. Therefore, I found a way to remind her that others who are equally devout are not as successful as she has been in the affairs of this world. In a subtle way I pushed her to seek a deeper understanding of God and his ways of dealing with us humans.

These two illustrations should open your mind. As we look around our cities, we have great evidence of prosperity: large hotels, skyscrapers and church edifices of great magnificence. There is a climate of progress, expansion in many areas of life. But, concurrent with all this affluence is unemployment, hunger, poor housing—grasping poverty. Many people in our midst live from day to day on the edge of survival. It is not sufficient that we contrast this with deprivation in some Third World country. What we see in cities throughout the United States is poverty in the midst of plenty. We are talking about Lazarus receiving, as it were, the crumbs from Dives's table.

I am concerned about our inhumanity in relation to persons who are black, poor, female, aged, in all towns and cities in this country.[4] Racism and economic greed stalk our nation. We are haunted by the results of our national sins. Racism and poverty are the trojan horses within the walls of our cities. Our greatest dangers are within our own nation. If there were no crises abroad, we would still be in trouble. Our internal national sins of racism and greed are the seeds for our own destruction. How will we deal with unjust and inhuman conditions? What about our criminal justice system? Look at the Wilmington Ten! Ben Chavis was a doctoral student of mine. North Carolina is my home state. What about the immorality of law—injustices meted out from judicial benches? We must be concerned about police brutality. In the *Atlanta Constitution* a twenty-three year-old black man was shown being beaten by a white police officer while two other officers held him. In Los Angeles a black woman, Eula Love, was shot to death in the presence of her small children. The matter would have gone unnoticed if the black ministers and their followers had not decided that we have had enough. The Gathering, made up of hundreds of black ministers in Los Angeles, has become a powerful force for monitoring these situations.

Our prison system is crowded with young, black, intelligent, and often gifted men and women. We not only warehouse our aged, we are doing the same with our youth—especially black, poor youth. The society, the courts, and the prisons are destroying the flower of our black youth. This systematic incarceration and dehumanization of generation after generation of black males impacts upon black women and children. The perpetuation of this situation makes the replenishment of candidates for a life of crime, violence, imprisonment, a self-fulfilling prophecy. Spiraling welfare rolls, juvenile delinquency, illegitimacy, pimping, prostitution, drug addition, alcoholism are among the inevitable consequences of this vicious cycle assured by racism—American's national sin.

When are we going to break into this circle with an affirmation of our common humanity under God? We must consider what racism does to the psyche of black people. It triggers self hatred and dislike for those who look like us; for we are often guided by the distorted image of blacks in the white mind. How else can we explain the high incidence of homicide among young black males? At the same time, racism produces a superior self-image in whites. Even poor whites exalt themselves above the most affluent and successful blacks, on the basis of skin color alone. Racism is a cancerous growth which is tearing our nation apart.

Toward Some Solutions

One-dimensional religion is the answer of some Christians. Personal salvation is the solution to everything. Soul salvation is the answer. This is undergirded by a sentimental "Jesusology" and biblical inerrancy. There is nothing wrong with spiritual formation, the deepening of the inner life or a radical personal conversion. But this answer is inadequate because the conception of both sin and salvation is limited. The trouble with the simple gospel is that it is unaware of, or ill-equipped to deal with, the difficult questions human beings face in this world. It is rather easy for this type of gospel to become demonic when it is preached to people who are undergoing gross suffering, deprivation and injustices. If one is privileged, this gospel can also serve diabolical ends. When the Christian God is understood as the author of success and pride of race, religion becomes destructive both to its advocates and its victims.

Religion can be one-dimensional in a this-worldly form. In this form it is difficult to distinguish it from secular humanism. In this instance there is a loss of transcendence—the skies are empty. Humans consider themselves self-sufficient. They seek to bring about an ideal order without dealing with human sinfulness (both personal and corporate) and they cut off the relationship with God. Where there is no sin there is no need for the forgiving grace and power of God.

In some sense the tragedy of Jonestown with the appeal to "have nots," and the victims of racial injustices, illustrates what happens when human beings put their intimate trust in some earthly "messiah." A young woman who declared, "my mother died at Jonestown," described how her mother was transformed from a saintly to an obscene person in that movement.

The Church Growth Thesis approach builds upon the American success story. In the name of Christian love, it advocates that the most loving thing to do is to establish homogeneous unit churches, where each race, class, ethnic group will worship and fellowship with its own kind of people. This would abolish efforts to create interracial congregations. We would not, e.g. attempt to bring Spanish speaking people into our fellowship. The easiest, most natural manner of dealing with our human relations problems becomes the most Christian. We ignore social justice issues and the need for unity-in-diversity in the body of Christ. This cannot be the appropriate response to the sins of racism and greed in a pluralistic society.

The Moral Majority. It is interesting that the "silent majority" has become the "moral majority" in such a short period of time. A few years ago, black church persons were assailed because they dared to advocate the moral and social implications of the gospel. Now we are told that the gospel is literally manifested in the American traditional way of life. Free enterprise, competition in business, democracy, the work ethic, etc. are taken directly from inerrant scripture. There is, however, a remarkable silence regarding racism, greed and all social, economic and political injustices. I am suspicious when persons who have denied the ethical implications of the gospel, all of a sudden become instant experts. The limitations and one-sidedness of their interpretations are apparent. The exposure of this gospel through the mass media should give all of us real concern. How shall we counter this multi-million dollar brainwashing of the very people who need to know the gospel as liberation? These answers are too simple because they have not dealt seriously with the question.

Solutions on the International Front

We live in a global village. Technology and economic factors have made it so. Interdependence has made us one in destiny. Racism at home and militarism abroad will not save America. There is a relationship between exports, imports and our national economy. The connection between imports of cars from Japan and the near collapse of the automobile industry is apparent. We need to compare an almost zero unemployment rate in some countries with unemployment in Detroit. This reality is very destructive for the black and poor people who are the last hired and first fired. There is a realtionship between the amorality of transnational corporations as they control the economy of poor nations and many problems here at home. These financial giants defy the sanctions of governments against them—even by our own President and the Congress. Their lobbyists are so powerful that they are able to have their way regardless of the concerns of politicians and preachers alike. Guns and ammunition are a multi-billion dollar business operation worldwide.

Imperialism has replaced colonialism in the Third World. Neo-colonialism is present in psychological and economic forms. Many people still have an inferiority complex *vis-à-vis* Western peoples. The inferiority-superiority complex of colonialism is aggravated by the persistent power of racism at home and abroad. Many Christian denominations are still building their missionary movements upon the sinking sands of racism and colonialism. With the rising tide of liberation-consciousness, time is running out. But many minds still need to be "de-colonized." Again, we are deeply involved in the economic exploitation of traditional peoples in the Third World. We have enlisted our economic resources in support of the rich and powerful few against the weak and suffering masses. South Africa is

Faith in God Confronts Collective Evils

a real test for capitalism and democracy. There racism and colonialism are still alive and well. Our banks, businesses, and even our churches are under the judgment of God in South Africa.

There is a close relationship between our situation at home and our image abroad. We have not learned that our "big stick" diplomacy does not and cannot work. Here too we have "a tale of two cities." The two-thirds world is uncomfortably non-white, poor and non-Christian. There is a strong sense of fellow-feeling among the "have-nots" on planet earth. We do not have sufficient wealth or military power to prevail in a world where two-thirds of the human family are against us.

National Pride/Human Rights. Reinhold Niebuhr, a prophet-theologian, wrote of America's *Three Prides:* the pride of race, the pride of wealth and the pride of power. Unless we are unable to do away with these prides, they will become the Trojan horses within our gates—and we will self-destruct. Add to this the real ideological, military, and socio-economic challenge of Marxism. Our only hope is to make our way of life more humane.

Under the Carter administration there was much talk about human rights. There is some real question about the practice of human rights—especially at home. A case in point: Why didn't Jimmy Carter use the moral influence of his office to resolve the unjust decision against the Wilmington Ten? Was he a victim of the common fallacy of trying to do abroad what needs to be done first at home?

There is a strange phenomenon among Christians. I have found that some Christian bodies are very much concerned about world hunger, but they show little if any concern about hunger on their doorsteps. Recently, I attended a planning session on global solidarity in theological education. It was reported that a certain seminary had built its program of study around world hunger. Its leaders felt they had solved the problem of international theological education. Having spent several months at this seminary, I had to report that they made a false claim—they were doing little about addressing human relations problems on their campus, in the city where they are located, or in their state. How, I asked, could they become a model for an international program of theological education?

Our approach to human rights must be broader than the Christian covenant. It must be interfaith, interreligious, interethnic and intercultural. It must be based upon mutual respect for the equal dignity of people, something like the cosmopolitanism of the Stoics which influenced the development of the natural law/natural rights tradition in the West. Our dignity must now be inherent in our humanity. This affirmation could be undergirded by the ethics from the great religions, but not dependent upon them for its validity. According to our confession, Christians should lead the way.

Implications for Theological Education and Ministry

A theological education program and a ministry based, as many are, upon the psychological model, is not adequate for our tasks. As priests, we must console the disturbed. As prophets, we must disturb the consoled. Human liberation from personal and social evils must become our *motif* for doing theology. The driving force of our ministry must center around making life more human. Our personal quest as ministers and laypersons in the Christian movement must be to find out where God is at work in the world and join Him.[5]

Summary and Conclusion

In these pages I have indulged in theological reflection, raised several issues and proposed some decisions and actions concerning human suffering in its mass dimensions. I have affirmed faith in God. My faith has not only persisted as I have examined this most difficult test of faith in God, it has deepened. There is no easy or final answer to the theodicy question, but each Christian has to live with it and no serious theologian can bypass it. I have provisional perspectives. My faith is grounded in the God who raised Jesus from the dead.

Since humans are free and responsible and much mass suffering stems from human sins, i.e., racism, greed, sexism, etc., I place heavy emphasis upon human beings as co-workers with God for the triumph of goodness in the world. It follows that much attention is given to the process of placing the gospel into social context. The close look given to both national and international problems, in the light of a gospel of freedom, is the result. As faith in God confronts collective evils and mass human suffering, we humans,

Faith in God Confronts Collective Evils

especially Christians, as fellow-sufferers and co-laborers, must work with God for beneficent ends.

Thy kingdom come,
Thy will be done,
On earth as it is in heaven.

NOTES

1. My reading of Gutierrez and other Latin American Liberation Theologians together with my conversations with Soelle, Moltmann and Metz have sharply focused my attention upon collective evils and mass suffering. Conversation with fellow black theologians as well as African and Asian theologians has made my solidarity with the oppressed more profound. I especially invite the reader to examine Johann Baptist Metz, *Faith in History and Society,* translated by David Smith (New York: Seabury, 1980). See especially Part II, Chapter 6, 100–118. Gustavo Gutierrez, *A Theology of Liberation,* (New York: Orbis, 1973) is *must* reading.

2. See James Cone, *God of the Oppressed* (New York: Seabury, 1975), 163–194.

3. We cannot gainsay the crucial importance of those who have helped us to hold on to faith in God in the face of awesome personal suffering. See Arthur C. McGill, *Suffering: A Test of Theological Method* (Philadelphia: Westminster, 1982), 112–130. Cf. Rabbi Harold S. Kushner, *When Bad Things Happen to Good People* (New York: Schocken Books, 1981), 113–131.

4. Colin B. Archer, a Bahamian studying in the United States, has written an informed and theologically astute book on the American situations (U.S.). It is entitled *Poverty: The Church's Abandoned Revolution* (Nassau: Colmar Publications, 1980). See especially Chapter II, 6–34, and Chapter IV, 44–54.)

5. While my responses to the problems discussed in this essay are based on much reflection they are only the effort of one churchperson and theologian. The views expressed here are written elsewhere in greater detail. See my *Roots of the Black Future: Family and Church* (Philadelphia: Westminster, 1980), and *Black Theology Today: Liberation and Contextualization.* Toronto Studies in Theology, Volume 12 (New York: Edwin Mellen Press, 1984). The latter work emphasizes political and social theology, 127–178.

3
The Christian Faith and the Creation of a Just Society from a Filipino Christian Perspective
VITALIANO R. GOROSPE

Introduction

Religion and Justice. Why is there so much injustice, corruption and violence in the Philippines, which claims to be the only Christian nation in Asia? If the assassination of Senator Benigno S. Aquino, Jr. shocked the whole world, is it because it took place in a country whose people and leadership are predominantly Catholic? The Philippines is suffering from its worst economic, political, and moral crisis in recent history. What is the Catholic church, the church of the majority of the Filipino people, doing in all this? There are no simple answers to these complex nagging questions. This paper is a modest attempt to shed some light on the role of the Christian religion in effecting social change and prompting justice.

Most of the great world religions have laid claim to their own importance in creating a more just society. All religious faiths share in some vision of a truly just and humane society. But history and social science have also shown that institutionalized religions have had their share of guilt in preserving an unjust status quo or in contributing to injustice in the world. As for Christianity, while it is true that many Christians have failed to live up to the social demands of the Christian faith and to fight against poverty and injustice, it is likewise true that a more mature understanding and responsible practice of the Christian faith can contribute much to the creation of a just society.

The Philippine Context and the Christian Perspective. Instead of dealing with the abstract question whether faith in God is necessary to the creation of a just society, this paper takes the Philippine context of poverty and injustice and addresses itself to two interrelated questions: (1) From a *theological* viewpoint, what does *the* Christian faith have to say about the present Philippine situation of injustice? (2) From a *sociological* viewpoint, what is the role of the church in the creation of a more just Philippine society? The first question involves a re-examination of the social justice message of the Christian faith as it applies to the Philippine context. Christianity does not exist as a pure ideal. It is embodied in the church. Only through the church has the social message of the Christian gospel been kept alive through the centuries. Hence, the second question explores the role of the church in the Philippines in the creation of a more just Philippine society.

Although this paper is limited to the Philippine context and to a Christian theological and sociological perspective, *mutatis mutandis*, it is hoped that it will inspire others to reflect on and act in their own situation from their own religious and cultural perspectives.

Filipino Religious Faith and the Christian Faith. At the outset, it is important to take into account the distinction between *Filipino* religious faith and *the* Christian faith, between "popular" and "official" Christianity. The former is the subjective faith of the majority of the Filipino people as embodied in the practical beliefs, practices, and rituals of Filipino popular Christianity. The latter is the objective content of the faith as found in the official Christian creed, code, and cult. Often the social message of the Christian gospel as found in the Bible and official church teaching—for example, the social teaching of John Paul II during his visit to the Philippines and the pastoral letters of the Catholic bishops' conference of the Philippines—does not reach a large number of those who practice "the religion of the people."[1]

The Christian Faith and Justice in Philippine Society

The first part of this paper re-examines the Christian faith's message on justice as found in the Bible and in its doctrine of creation, original sin, and the paschal mystery, all of which find new relevance to the creation of a just society and application to the situation of injustice in the Philippines.

Justice in the Bible. The biblical idea of justice can be described as fidelity to a threefold relationship to *Yahweh,* to neighbor, and to the land.[2] It is based on the covenant relationship between *Yahweh* and His people (Exodus 19:3–6). The justice of *Yahweh* was his saving power and fidelity to his role as Lord of the Covenant (Psalms 95, 97, 103:6). *Yahweh* revealed himself as the liberator and defender of the poor and oppressed when he liberated his people from slavery in Egypt. The covenant on Mount Sinai demanded monotheistic worship and the Torah demanded justice especially for the widow, the orphan, the poor, and the stranger (Exodus 22:21–23). Thus, the just Israelite was faithful to *Yahweh,* to his neighbor, and to the land (Job 31). According to J. Philip Wogaman, in his book *Christians and the Great Economic Debate,* the Christian faith, which concerns our relationship to God, people, and the material world, provides the ultimate framework for forming moral values regarding socioeconomic-political realities.[3] Wogaman's Christian social vision is deeply rooted in the biblical tradition.

When the ancient Israelite ideal of interdependence and equality was replaced by a class society of the rich and the poor, the threefold response of the Bible to the situation of inequality and injustice at that time was through legislation, prophecy, and wisdom literature (the division of the Old Testament books).[4] The prophets were the social conscience of Israel. They denounced the social evils that destroyed the threefold relationship to *Yahweh,* neighbor, and the land, and pointed out that true religion and worship meant justice for the poor and oppressed.

The words of the prophets are applicable to the situation of the Philippines today. The prophet Amos condemns slavery (2:6–8); scandalous extravagance (4:1–3, 6:4–7); luxurious houses, bribery, corrupt courts (5:10–15); cheating and profiteering (8:4–6). He spurns feasts and sacrifices if justice does not abound like a mountain stream (5:21–24). Likewise the prophet Isaiah condemns external rituals, false idols at the expense of justice (1:11–17, 2:6–8); luxurious living (3:12–15); greedy landlords (4:1–3); unjust statutes and oppressive decrees (10:1–4). True fasting is doing justice to the poor and oppressed (58:1–12). The strong words of the prophet Joshua still ring true today:

Thus says the Lord: "Do what is right and just. Rescue the victim from the hand of the oppressor. Do not wrong or oppress the resident alien, the orphan, or the widow, and do not shed innocent blood in this place . . . woe to him who builds his house on wrong, his terraces on injustice; who works his neighbor without pay and gives him no wages . . . because he dispensed justice to the weak and the poor, it went well with him. Is this not true knowledge of me?" says the Lord. But your eyes and heart are set on nothing except on your own gain, on shedding innocent blood, on practicing oppression and extortion. (22:3, 13, 16, 17)

The justice of God is fully revealed in the person, life, and teaching of Jesus Christ who made present God's kingdom of justice and love. The advent of God's kingdom in Jesus is the coming of God's justice in Jesus whose mission is "to bring glad tidings to the poor, to proclaim liberty to captives, recovery of sight to the blind and release to prisoners" (Luke 4:18). Luke's social gospel for the poor shows Jesus' special concern for the *anawim* (the oppressed and outcasts) (Luke 1–3, 2, 4, 6, 8, 10, 12, 14, 16, 18–19). Jesus' fellowship was with tax collectors, outcasts, the poor and marginalized to the extent that he identified whatever is done to the least of our fellowmen as done to him (Matthew 25:40). Jesus' call to discipleship was an invitation to continue his mission of justice (Luke 5:28; 19:1–10). Jesus' teaching on eschatological justice (Luke 1:51–53; 6:20; 14:12–21; 16:19–31; Matthew 25:31–46) and his critique of riches in Luke's rich man, poor man stories (Luke 12:16–21; 16:19–31; 18:18–38) remain critically important today.

What difference does it make to the poor and to Christians, if the Bible says that God is on the side of the poor and oppressed? It means that to be a Christian today is to be on the side of the poor and powerless. A Christian preferential option for and solidarity with the poor is clearly biblical in its inspiration and ultimately should be motivated by the Christian faith. The social message of the Bible can criticize and judge the present Philippine situation of injustice. But in the past, Filipino Christians have tended to spiritualize, privatize, or moralize the biblical message of justice.

Creation. A renewed understanding of the Christian doctrine of creation can help liberate the Filipino people from fatalism and superstition, as well as from the exploitation of natural resources and environmental pollution. In the past, uncritical Filipino popular beliefs in creation and the traditional value of trust in God led to a *bahala na* attitude, a fatalistic resignation to the present situation of poverty and injustice which was an escape from social responsibility; to excessive incredulity in faith healers and mediums; and to superstitious expectations that God will resolve all problems. The Christian faith can purify, and liberate Filipino popular religiosity from fatalistic and superstitious attitudes.

A fresh look at the Bible shows that creation is not simply a once-upon-a-time event, but the beginning of God's continuing involvement in the world and its history. The creation stories in Genesis do not give a cosmology or pseudo-scientific account of the origin of the world, but contain a religious message: (a) everything pertaining to the world has its origin (past), ground (present), and final goal (future) in God, (b) everything created by God's beneficent love is good, and (c) the whole creation is for the sake of man.[5] The *initial* creation of Genesis *continues* in the *present* and refers to the *future* when the final creation of the "new heaven and new earth" (Revelation 21:1) will take place.[6] Creation then is an ongoing process in which man as co-creator has the responsibility of cooperating with God's work to create a new person and a new community.

The biblical doctrine of creation affirms that God alone has sovereign dominion over man and the rest of creation. In the Old Testament *Yahweh* is the God who *saves* and *creates,* but in the New Testament it is Jesus Christ who *redeems* and *creates*. Both St. Paul and St. John make the startling revelation that the world was created *through* Jesus Christ and *for* him and will be renewed and recapitulated *in* him (I Corinthians 8:6; II Corinthians 5:19; Colossians 1:15–18; Ephesians 1:3–10; John 1:1–3). God's command to humans to have dominion over the earth means not only human control over the forces of nature but, more significantly, a vocation as active co-creator, co-lord, and co-provider, and responsible stewardship over God's work of creation.

The Christian theology of creation stresses the total dependence of everything on God, as well as the unity and interrelatedness of God, nature and human beings.[7] Hindu India developed a lovely image to describe the relationship between God and his creation. God "dances" his creation. He is the dancer, his creation is the dance. The moment the dancer stops, the dance ceases to exist. A reexamination of select Old Testament texts (Job 38 and 39: Psalms 8 and 104) reveals the intrinsic value of all creatures and their interdependence on one another and on God.[8] The biblical faith of God being one with humanity and humanity being one with itself and with nature is not alien to Asian thought and experience. Asian religions and cultures show a deep reverence for and stress on harmony with nature. The non-conservation of natural resources and the exploitation and pollution of nature by modern science and technology is largely due to a loss of the biblical and Asian sense of nature as God's gift to human beings. If we no longer care about the poor and the needy or about future generations, we will cease to care about the earth. The words of the prophet Hosea point to the relation between creation and justice. *Yahweh's* "grievance against the inhabitants of the land" is because "there is no fidelity, no mercy . . . therefore the land mourns and all that dwells in it languishes . . . even the fish of the sea perish" (Hosea 4:1–3). Unless we perceive the relationship between humanity and nature, we will not advert to the link between human justice and ecological responsibility, between injustice and environmental pollution. An example in the Philippines is the Bataan nuclear plant, a plague that poisons the people of Morong.

The biblical message of creation provides the Christian faith's vision of *human dignity, work, liberation* and *development*. First, humans are created in the image and likeness of God. *Imago dei*, which is humanity, is the Christian basis of human dignity. Moreover, the Christian mystery of the incarnation—God becoming one of us—has raised the dignity of human beings to that of adoptive sonship—we are all children of one Father, God. Today we no longer see the image of God in modern people. The poor and oppressed in the Third World have become nonpersons. Our creative task is to restore the image of God in humanity. Secondly, human work has dignity because it is a participation in God's creative work. Against the modern alienation of the exploited worker, the Christian doctrine of creation teaches that work is creative and self-creating. Technological culture has made human work easier and faster but the conditions of modern agribusiness and industry have also exploited the worker and alienated the worker from his or her work. The workers in the sugar plantations in Negros and in the Kawasaki smelter plant in Mindanao are examples of human exploitation and degradation. Third, total and integral human liberation and development, which is an effective *process* to correct poverty, injustice, oppression and violation of human rights, is the creation of both God and man. It is the responsibility of all, especially those in power. *Gloria dei est vivens homo*. The more we realize ourselves as persons and God's image, the more we build a just and fraternal society, the brighter the glory of the Creator shines in us.

Original Sin. In contemporary Christian theology, original sin is both the sinful situation into which every person is born, as well as the involuntary inclination to evil in every person *prior* to personal choice or sin (Genesis 3; Romans 7:15–25).[9] Thus, original sin has two dimensions: the *external* aspect which is the sinful environment all around us or "the sin of the world" (John 1:29), and the *internal* aspect or disordered appetites which lead us to sin and to connive with the sins of others. Captive to sin, people are powerless to liberate themselves; they need the liberating, healing grace of Jesus Christ. Just as sin and death entered through one person, so grace and life came through Jesus Christ (Romans 5:12–18). Although original sin is the root of both *personal* and *social* sin, in the new understanding of the Christian doctrine of original sin, there has been a significant shift of emphasis to *social* sin embodied in *unjust* structures as the concrete manifestation of original sin today.

Original sin is concretely manifested in the Philippine situation of immorality and corruption, injustice and violence, that is, in structures of social sin.[10] Social sins are: (a) structures that oppress human dignity, violate human rights, and impose gross inequality (e.g., in the Philippine context, presidential decrees that suppress freedom of speech and assembly, allow arbitrary arrests and indefinite detention in the name of "national security"), (b) situations that promote and facilitate individual acts of selfishness (e.g., nepotism or "cronyism," that is, the relatives and friends of the president have a monopoly of agribusinesses, banks, and mass media, and enjoy excessive privileges, and (c) the complicity and silent acquiescence of persons who do not take responsibility for social injustice (e.g., government-controlled media hiding or distorting the truth about the assassination of Senator Benigno S. Aquino and its aftermath).

Structures have a vast potential for good or evil. This sociological insight confirms the biblical insight that social sin is institutionalized poverty, injustice, violence, discrimination, and apathy. Philippine society is marked by structures of social sin not only on the national level but also on a global level.[11] A structural and historical social analysis of Philippine society reveals that it is dominated by external neo-colonialism and internal colonialism (through domestic capitalism and feudalism), both supported by a government that uses repressive measures which keep the majority of the people in a state of poverty and dependence.[12]

What then are the implications of the contemporary emphasis on original sin as social sin for the creation of a more just society? If original sin is both internal inclination to sin and external situation, then there is need of a *double liberation:* personal conversion from sin or change of heart is not enough; there is need of liberation from unjust and sinful structures. Structures of injustice and inequality *can* be changed but only through *cooperation in community*. However, in dismantling unjust structures and substituting others, one cannot eradicate all injustice. The Christian doctrine of original sin is a realistic reminder that there is no perfect society and that we should distrust absolutes and ideologies that promise a perfectly just society. Any concrete proposal for a more just society must seriously take into account not only human greed but the sinfulness of the human situation.

The Paschal Mystery. The essence of the Christian faith is the

The Christian Faith and the Creation of a Just Society

paschal mystery, that is, the suffering, death, and resurrection of Jesus Christ for the redemption of humanity and its liberation from sin and death, and his final exaltation as Lord of heaven and earth (Philippians 2:9–11; Romans 1:4). The paschal mystery also says something about our responsibility to build a more just society as co-redeemers and co-healers with Christ, the divine savior and liberator of the poor and oppressed.

First, the mystery of the crucified and risen Christ is the lesson of life, the lesson of history, the lesson of the Christian gospel paradox that new life can come only through suffering and death (Matthew 16:25; Mark 8:35; Luke 9:24; John 12:24–25). The paschal mystery then is the Christian basis and motivation of the unselfish, self-sacrificing service of one's fellowmen, of a preferential commitment to the poor. Love of neighbor has a paschal nature: it is a kind of dying to oneself in order to live for others (Romans 14:7–8). Today, the struggle for truth, freedom, justice and peace involves conflict, suffering, even the sacrifice of one's own life.

Second, in the wake of the Aquino assassination, the Filipino people turned to the religious symbol of the paschal mystery as a way of finding the mystery of goodness in the mystery of evil. The paschal mystery in Filipino popular religiosity takes the form of the *pasyon* (passion of Christ), the most popular religious book, which is chanted during Lent. The religious poor in the Philippines see in the *pasyon* a picture of their everyday life of hardship and suffering; yet in Philippine history there have been religio-political individuals and groups who saw in the colonial situation of oppression and injustice a permanent *pasyon* condition of Philippine society that they strove to change by social reform, or if need be, by revolution.[13] Paradoxically, while the Spaniards used the *pasyon* to Christianize and colonize the Filipino people, the Filipino revolutionaries used the *pasyon* as an instrument of the Philippine revolution. It is remarkable that the various revolts against Spanish and American oppression were motivated not by any Marxist consciousness of class conflict and struggle, but by the Christian consciousness that the gospel is good news to the poor and powerless, and demands, by way of suffering and sacrifice, the liberation of captives. Like Christ who suffered and died, and in the end, triumphed over death and his enemies, thus entering into his glory, the Filipino revolutionaries envisioned the masses suffering and dying, but they knew that victory would be assured; in the end, they would overthrow their oppressors and win freedom and independence. Today, under the present Marcos regime, this revolutionary potential of the paschal mystery is seen by many heroic Filipino men and women in the sacrificial death of Christ as the price of salvation from tyranny and liberation from all forms of oppression and injustice. Hence, the popular Filipino image of Christ of the paschal mystery has become the religious symbol of the suffering, death, and resurrection of the Filipino people.

Third, the paschal mystery points to *nonviolence* as the Christian way to social change and the creation of a more just society.[14] In his life and teaching, Christ taught forgiveness and love of enemies (Matthew 5:38–45). Christ's choice of dying on the cross, the "just man" of the Bible become victim of human violence, is proof that active nonviolence is the gospel ideal and a Christian option. It was the paschal mystery that inspired Senator Aquino to fight for freedom and justice, national reconciliation and peace through nonviolent means. Surely too, Gandhi's *ahimsa* and *satyagraha* were Christian in spirit.

Finally, the paschal mystery is a prophetic event that promises not only economic development and material progress, but a total liberation including the more important religious and spiritual dimensions. Asia may be materially poor but it is spiritually rich. Perhaps this is the distinct contribution that Asia can make to the rich developed nations, which despite their scientific and technological progress, may be spiritually bankrupt.

What kind of *spirituality* is needed today for action on behalf of social justice? In the view of an Asian theologian, the new mission of the Asian churches demands a double baptism: in the Jordan of Asian religiosity and on the Calvary of Asian poverty.[15] Applying this double requirement of spirituality to the Philippine context, the church must not only share in the paschal condition of a suffering people, but also share in the "spirituality" of the "religious poor." In practice this means service, sharing of goods and profits, simplicity of life-style, solidarity with the poor, and subversion—in the sense of changing unjust structures through nonviolent means, or at least not profiting from or conniving with these sinful structures.

The Church and Justice in Philippine Society

In view of the present national crisis in the Philippines which the martial law regime has brought about, Part Two of this paper explores from a sociological viewpoint the role of the Catholic church, the church of the majority of Filipinos, in bringing about social change and in creating a more just Philippine society.

Two preliminary remarks are necessary. First, although the discussion is limited to the Catholic church, it goes without saying that other Christian churches and non-Christian groups in the Philippines are also actively involved in the struggle for human rights and justice. Second, although the discussion focuses on the church as an *institution* and on the social teaching of the Catholic bishops' conference of the Philippine, the church is also a *community* that includes all members, especially lay persons, and is by no means to be identified with the Catholic hierarchy. From the viewpoint of the Christian faith and especially since Vatican II, the church is the entire people of God, the community of believers in Jesus Christ.

The Social Teaching of the Philippine Church. The most striking aspect of the Philippine church since Vatican II has been the heightened awareness, on the part of the Catholic bishops, clergy, religious, and educated Filipino Christians in general, of the social thrust of the Christian gospel. This is clearly a worldwide phenomenon, amply documented by the Catholic church's official teaching.[16] In 1971 the Roman synod of bishops declared that "action on behalf of justice and participation in the transformation of the world . . . [are] a constitutive dimension of the preaching of the gospel, . . . of the church's mission for the redemption of the human race and its liberation from every oppressive situation."[17] This declaration is significant because it brings out clearly the Christian truth that the promotion of justice is an essential part of, though not identical with, the mission of the church, and that an integral part of the witness of the Christian faith today especially requires the promotion of justice. Since the imposition of martial law in 1972, the Catholic church hierarchy in its annual pastoral letters has consistently focused on social justice issues. So did the addresses of Pope John Paul II during his 1981 visit to the Philippines.

In his speeches to the Filipino people, Pope John Paul II addressed himself to the grave social problems relating to land, work, ideologies and violence. He rejected Marxist collectivism, capitalist liberalism, and the national security state. In particular, in his speech to the president, the Pope, in strong and unequivocal terms, stated that "even in exceptional situations that may at times arise, one can never justify any violation of the fundamental dignity of the human person or of the basic rights that safeguard this dignity."[18]

The Philippine bishops in their 1982 pastoral letter on "social justice," reiterate the papal social teaching and guidelines.[19] They point out the key to the church's social teaching is *human dignity*, with application especially to stewardship of the land and the dignity of human work, as well as the rights of workers. They state anew that the church's mission includes total human development, preference for the poor, and the practice of love and justice. This involves the integration of personal and social morality, the formation of a critical Christian conscience, and the development of a Christian social analysis of the Philippine situation. While pointing to various serious problems in the Philippines as "the roots and causes of violence" and admitting that the use of violence is not absolutely ruled out, the Philippine bishops in their *Exhortation Against Violence* (1979) emphasize that "the option for nonviolence must be respected . . . as a Christian pattern of action."[20] In their call for peace and reconciliation in *A Dialogue for Peace* (1983), they point to poverty, corruption, questionable government projects, militarization, and a climate of fear that stifles dissent, as *roots* of the present situation leading to arbitrary arrests and detentions. The Philippine bishops exhort the people to vigilance; priests and religious to a preferential option for the poor; the government officials and the military to go to the roots of the present situation, insure due process of law and allow legitimate dissent; and the bishops to service of the people.[21]

Since the imposition of martial law, it is clear that the Philippine bishops, more than ever before, have exercised a prophetic role in protesting against injustice and the violation of basic human rights. There is then no lack of official social teaching on the part of the Catholic bishops' conference of the Philippines; yet what is crucial is not only the communication and implementation of this social teaching but also how effective it is in bringing about significant social change.

The Response of the Church to the Philippine Situation Today. The present economic and political crisis in the Philippines is best described, in the words of businessman Jaime Ongpin, as the legacy of ten years of martial law. We have inherited "a system of one-man rule that is not only virtually uncontrolled but is *in fact* aided and abetted by a legislature which is inutile, a judiciary which is subservient, a military which has been perverted, and a press which is intimidated, not to mention, a central bank which does not know how to count."[22]

A brief background to the present national crisis is called for. In the past, the response of the church to the imposition of martial law in

1972 was that of "critical collaboration." This can be gleaned from the Philippine bishops' pastoral letters, as well as from their statements as groups or as individuals.[23] The bishops spoke on human rights violations with regard to martial law, the plebiscite on the new constitution, the various referenda and national assembly elections, population and family life, abortion, tribal minorities, the Mindanao situation, and due process. They also reiterated the church's social teaching on human development, education for justice, and violence and peace.

With regard to the stand of the church during the martial law regime, two comments are necessary. First, it must be pointed out that, at any time, the Philippine bishops were divided, precisely over the very issue of martial law itself. This division was related to differing views of the church, differing theological positions or lack of them, differing conceptions of their own roles as bishops, as well as the fact that at that time many bishops failed to appreciate the real aim of the martial law government which was to impose a national security state. Second, the bishops' reactions to injustice, violations of human rights and to government abuses were truly *reactions* prompted by crisis situations.

August 21, 1983, the infamous day Senator Benigno S. Aquino, Jr. was assassinated, is a kind of historical landmark for discussing the response of the Philippine church to the present national crisis. What that tragic death did was to bring to the national consciousness of an angry and outraged people the sad state of affairs gripping the nation. It also highlighted the possible role of the church in the ensuing economic and political crisis—a crisis of credibility in the Marcos government.

Can the Philippine Church become a Political Force? According to a study made by Philippine sociologist John Carroll, there is no doubt that the Catholic church in the Philippines can be a very strong influential *cultural, social,* and *moral* force.[24] First, more than eighty percent of the population is Catholic and is more or less in contact with its social message. Through its thousands of priests, religious sisters and brothers, lay teachers, church leaders and workers, through its churches, schools, and other institutions, through its print and radio media, the church has a gigantic communications network capable of carrying its social message to every town and barrio in the Philippines.

Second, at a time when other institutions have lost credibility, the church has enhanced its moral credibility with the people, especially with the urban and rural poor in some areas, and with victims of injustice. Not only has the church been traditionally involved in health and education programs, community development and organization, social welfare and relief (especially in the rural areas), but in the last fifteen years, with the help of church-related special-purpose organizations, it has conspicuously stood for the rights of poor settlers, tribal minorities, political detainees, small farmers, workers, and fishermen. Providing a framework and integrating all these various social apostolates and activities of the church is the *basic Christian communities* movement which augurs well for social change. Finally, the church is also a "transitional" organization with international linkages, which can assist it in many ways.

Why then has the church not become a political force despite its immense social and moral power? The Philippine church, although no longer the conservative force that it was in the past, has not become a consistent force for social change due to certain limiting factors. First, there have been differences among the bishops, and between some bishops and the more activist priests, religious and laypersons, precisely with regard to the role of the church in social and political areas. Secondly, because of their social class origin, the clergy tend to be more at home with the middle class than with the poor, and the bishops and the higher clergy tend to be linked with the economic and political elite. And pressure has also come from Rome and the Apostolic Nuncio to avoid "political" involvement that could lead to confrontation with the government or "divisions within the church." Tension within the church has increased in areas where activists are ideologically oriented and linked to or sympathetic with underground groups of the left. Finally, a large part of the population has minimal or only occasional contact with the church (there is only one priest for 8,706 Catholics) and the popular religiosity of the people remains a conservative force.

These divisions within the church, together with its traditional respect for freedom of conscience, point to its weakness as a political force in the sense that the church cannot adopt a precise political position and require that all its members support it. Even if the church were to adopt a particular position, it would have difficulty in urging it effectively on the people, for the Christian faith is one, but it allows many options and different commitments.

To sum up, there are hopeful signs that the Philippine church might play an indirect political role in the future. The Catholic hierarchy has made efforts to defend human rights and has had some success in mitigating military abuses. Since about 1977, the bishops have become more outspoken and have focused on the social and economic roots of the rising discontent and escalating violence. Although this may be a reaction to pressures from "below" or from "the left," and to the worsening crisis in Philippine society as a result of corruption in the government and its lack of credibility, it nevertheless, reflects a growing consensus on the part of the official church as to its role in the concrete Philippine situation. In the first six months of 1983, church and state relations became more tense as the bishops and Jaime Cardinal Sin became more critical of the government.

Towards National Reconciliation and Peace. Shortly before and after the Aquino assassination, two specific messages communicated by the official church to the people are worth noting. The first came from the prominent archbishop of Manila, Cardinal Sin, who stands for national reconciliation and peace through dialogue and nonviolent means. At the 1983 annual bishops-businessmen's Conference for Human Development, Cardinal Sin formulated his vision of the proper roles of the church, state, and the people in the promotion of justice and human development.[25] First, he insisted on the right and duty of the church to be one with the people in the face of oppression by the state. That is why "the national problem is between the state and the people," not between the state and the church as such. After presenting the basic values on which a more just Philippine society could develop, Cardinal Sin proposed a "Council of Reconciliation" composed of representatives of the church, the government, and the private sector, to help the president formulate policies based on consensus. Up to this date, the president has done nothing about this proposal. Again in his homily at the Aquino funeral mass, the Cardinal did not abandon the theme of peace and national reconciliation. In his "National Prayer for Peace," read daily over radio *Veritas,* the Cardinal made it clear that genuine national reconciliation must be based on truth, freedom and justice. Finally, in a speech delivered in Bacolod, the Cardinal pointed out that the source of the nationwide protest was neither political nor economic but *moral*—that is, the need for *moral* reforms in the government. He criticized the government for becoming more progressively isolated from the people by its refusal to cooperate in the process of reconciliation based on justice.

The second important communication from the bishops' conference, "Reconciliation Today," was issued on 27 November 1983, the birthday of Senator Aquino. Returning to the themes of their

1983 pastoral letter, "A Dialogue for Peace," the bishops emphasize reconciliation as an alternative to both continuing injustice and revolutionary violence. According to the bishops, reconciliation "can take place only in truth, sincerity, freedom and justice." The bishops call for "social transformation" and on "those who have the power to summon up the necessary will to give us a more just and peaceful society."[26]

Inasmuch as these statements of Cardinal Sin and the Philippine bishops pointed to a widening gap between the people and the regime, and called for major and difficult reforms, they could hardly have been welcome by the government. It is clear that the Cardinal and the bishops are calling for a change in the socioeconomic-political order through conversion of heart and change of moral values. But values are not self-implementing and the question arises whether the Philippine church has a concrete strategy by which a more just social order can be created.

A Strategy for Social Change. In the history of social thought there are two fundamental approaches to social change: the *integration* and *coercion* theories. The first holds that society is organized around *shared values* and the common good, and that social change occurs through evolution in these values or through efforts to bring social institutions more into line with them. The second looks at society essentially as a structure of *power* in which social change is brought about through changes in the balance of power; those who hold power use it to impose upon society those "values" that will serve to legitimize and justify their position. Each of the two theories accounts for part of social reality, but neither explains it entirely.

From the viewpoint of social theory, Cardinal Sin and the Philippine bishops are more in conformity with the integration than the coercion theory. Fully aware that Philippine society is *in fact* not effectively organized for the realization of shared values and the common good, they are calling for reorganization of Philippine society to be brought about by an appeal to moral values, conversion of heart and the cooperation of all social classes, rather than through class conflict. From a moral and theological point of view, the bishops' position is within the tradition of Catholic social thought, but from the viewpoint of social theory, sociologist Carroll finds that the approach embodied in the position of the Cardinal and the bishops is not fully adequate, either as an analysis of the Philippine situation and a guide to action, or as representative of Catholic social thought. As an analysis, it presents the problems of violence, corruption, social injustice, etc. as moral *deviations* to be corrected by good will on all sides. It fails to give sufficient emphasis to some of the insights of the coercion theory: the opposition of social and class interests which affect one's perception of the common good, the fundamental problem of the concentration of power and wealth in society. In the coercion theory, the problems of society are not just deviations from a moral ideal, but are structured and predictable. Hence, the solution lies in a change of unjust structures so that wealth and power may be distributed more equitably. These insights, though less central to Catholic social thought as shared values and the common good, are nevertheless found there (e.g., the right to organize a union, the right to strike, and other rights that involve social tension and conflict).

These sociological insights of the coercion theory recall our theological discussion of *social sin* or *structural* injustice. Filipino Christians should seriously ask whether and to what extent the economic, political, educational, and religious institutions of Philippine society are so organized as to preserve the status quo and the interests of the dominant elite. Are Philippine cultural institutions—family, schools, the church—inculcating those values principally which serve to support an unjust system? Can values be changed without a prior change in unjust structures and institutions? Is social change possible without conflict with those who control these institutions?

This line of thinking can also help the church to avoid the danger of seeing the present national crisis in exclusively political and economic terms, i.e., how to get the political and economic systems back on the tracks. This very middle-class point of view may have been behind the protests of the Makati-based businessmen, who were merely concerned with the restoration of freedom (i.e., the issue of presidential succession, free and honest elections, a free press and an independent judiciary, *without* considering the fundamental problem of the distribution of power and wealth in Philippine society). The past seventy years of relatively free elections have done nothing to change the distribution of wealth and power. Thus, an exclusive emphasis on *freedom,* at the expense of an equally determined and concrete emphasis on *equality,* may only enhance the freedom of the wealthy and powerful to accumulate more power and wealth.

Sociologist Carroll proposes a more adequate approach, which he calls "Christian realism." This approach looks at society as *both* a system for the realization of certain shared values *and* a structure by which more powerful groups impose their own points of view and promote their own interests at the expense of the common good. Philippine society today seems to conform to the coercion model more closely than at any time in its history. Over time the Filipino people have lost control of the power to decide their own future. Gradually, economic and political power became concentrated in the hands of a few. National institutions such as free elections, separation of powers, free press, labor and peasant organizations have been subverted so that those who wield power use it arbitrarily for their own benefit. Power tends to generate more power. Thus, power tends to be concentrated and the nation's income tends to "trickle upward."

The problem then is to restore the control of power to the people. In Carroll's analysis, this will not come about by an appeal to moral principles *alone* but through a combination of *both* pressure from below *and* creative ideas, plus moral suasion directed at those who wield economic and political power. The pressure from below would come from the organized poor, supported by the newly awakened middle classes who are committed to genuine *social* change. The moral suasion would come largely from the official church and would be directed at basic issues, such as a balance of freedom and equality and respect for basic human rights, including the right of the poor to organize and exert pressure. It would be aimed at a *positive response* from those who hold power to pressure from below, the kind of response that leads to reconciliation and social change without resorting to violence and armed revolution.

A Challenge to the Philippine Church. There is in the Philippines today a united front from the left that offers a program and strategy to "restore democracy" in the country. They emphasize *sectoral* organizing, are open to violence, and politicize every issue (i.e., they relate it to the "U.S.-Marcos dictatorship"). It is outside the scope of this paper to discuss why the church cannot support this view from the left.[27] Suffice it to say that the church has a vision of man and society based on the Christian faith that is contradicted by the present Philippine situation, is different from that of Marxist collectivism, capitalist liberalism, or the national security state,[28] and goes beyond the middle class view that the solution to the present economic and political crisis consists principally in the restoration of freedom and democracy.

The institutional church, as an important cultural and social force in Philippine society, cannot remain "neutral" when fundamental issues are at stake. This is *not* the same thing as saying that the church is a partisan political force. The church cannot be involved in partisan politics but must take a stand when human dignity and basic human rights are violated. If the Christian faith has a lot to say about justice in the world, then its embodiment in the Philippine context, the institutional church, has something to say on the fundamental issues facing the Filipino nation today: on human dignity and the need to safeguard it in the process of sociopolitical change and economic development; on human rights, including the right to organize, to participate in decision making, to express dissent; on the need not only for a return to the rule of law and to personal and public moral integrity, but also for a more equitable distribution of power and wealth and for structural changes which will bring about a reasonable balance between freedom and equality; on national autonomy and freedom from foreign domination; and on the most appropriate way of bringing about social change. The Christian doctrine of original sin is a forceful reminder that the Marxist vision of a perfectly just society here and now is just as illusory as "pie in the sky by and by when you die."

These Christian themes are part of the cultural or doctrinal heritage of the church and have been communicated more or less explicitly by the Catholic hierarchy and the speeches of Pope John Paul II. But much more can be done to make them an integral part of the Christian message as carried by the national communications system of the church to many parts of the country, especially to the urban and rural poor. Many more bishops could be actively involved with the bishops-businessmen's conference, which has been doing serious studies on key issues facing the nation.

The articulation of values and the building of consensus constitute part of the *cultural* underpinning of a political system; they can also constitute the type of moral suasion and pressure to effect social change. But values are non-self-implementing and become effective in Philippine society only when embodied in organizations that constitute part of the *social* underpinning of political systems. The church itself is one such organization, which has been very instrumental in articulating key issues and defending human rights. The church has also a tradition of promoting local organizations and programs whereby the urban and rural poor may be able to solve their more basic problems. And the people themselves have come to look up to the church in meeting their urgent problems of peace and order, livelihood, land rights, abuses by the military and the new people's army, etc.

In the first part of this paper, the point was made that unjust structures can be changed through *cooperation in community*. No better strategy for organizing the people at the grassroots level has been tried so far with as much hope of success as the *Basic Christian Communities* (BCC) movement. The BCC promises to be the best structure for value-formation, communication, and action. In the BCC cells, groups of neighbors are encouraged to articulate their own reactions to the gospel message, and to reflect on its meaning for their lives, to analyze their problems and needs, to become aware of their rights, and to communicate both to the members of other cells and to the authorities. From this new style communication at the base of the social pyramid, it is possible that subtle changes in power relationships may be emerging as the barrio people acquire self-confidence and the determination to confront together "outside" forces that have been dominating their lives. If this be the case, and the BCC movement can survive attempts at suppression by the military and manipulation by the left, then it may be that the work of the church in promoting these small communities will have greater long-range impact in bringing about a more just society in the Philippines than any number of episcopal statements.

However, none of this rules out the possibility of the church playing the role of intermediary or go-between among contending groups at the local and national levels. The members of these groups are for the most part Christian laypersons who have made different political options. Precisely because the church does not have a detailed political program, and cannot support a particular candidate or party, but remains on the level of objectives and principles, it may be in a position to provide a forum of dialogue and promote national reconciliation across a broad band of the political system.

The Transcendence of the Church: Faith in God and Man. In the second part of this paper, the sociological focus has been on the church as a sociocultural institution. But from a philosophical and theological viewpoint, the church is specifically a *religious* institution and is distinguished from any other sociocultural institution by its orientation to a *transcendent* reality—God. Herein lies the significance of the question: Is faith in God necessary for the creation of a just society? Whether one takes this question in theory or in practice, the answer cannot but have grave practical consequences for justice in the world. If one denies or ignores God, then he or she will have difficulty understanding the transcendent reality of the church, let alone, the challenge to the Philippine church to create a more just society through moral suasion and nonviolent opposition.

In trying to build a more just Philippine society, the church cannot afford to abandon its transcending orientation and identify its salvific mission with the promotion of justice alone. Nor can the church afford to neglect the religious and spiritual dimension of its mission of human liberation and development. To do so would be both to give up its own identity and to destroy its *social* effectiveness. The challenge to the Philippine church today is to develop a spirituality of action on behalf of justice, that encompasses *both elements*: a deep faith and commitment to *humanity*, suffering and oppressed, and a deep faith and commitment to *God*. From the perspective of the Christian faith within the Philippine context, the challenge to the Filipino Christian is a double commitment to the suffering and oppressed Filipino poor, and to the Christ of the paschal mystery. This challenge to the church becomes real for the Filipino Christian only on the basis of a double *experience*: a deep experience of *God* in prayer, and a lived experience of Filipino *humanity* victimized and degraded by the selfishness of one's fellow humans and the unjust structures of Philippine society. The price of such a spirituality is very high for individuals as well as for the church as an institution. Unlike current ideologies, neither the Christian gospel nor the church offers any "money-back guarantee" that moral pressure and nonviolent opposition will bring about change. But if they do not, there is still a role for the church to "be with" and "suffer" with the people as exemplified by the martyrdom of Father Godofredo Alingal, S.J., in the Philippines, and of Archbishop Oscar Romero and the four American Catholic missionaries in San Salvador.[29]

Summary and Conclusion

The purpose of this paper was to reflect from both a theological and sociological perspective on the relation between the Christian faith and the creation of a just society within the Philippine context.

The first part discussed the *theological* question: What does *the* Christian faith have to say about the present Philippine situation of gross inequality and injustice? Christians today do have a rich biblical and doctrinal heritage to draw from that bears on the promotion of justice and the construction of a just social order. The reality of justice in the Bible as fidelity to God, neighbor, and land provides the ultimate Christian framework for judging socio-economic political realities. A contemporary understanding of the Christian doctrines of creation, original sin, and the paschal mystery finds new relevance and application to the creation of a more just society, and provides a theology of human liberation and development within the Philippine context.

The second part discussed the *sociological* question: What is the role of the Catholic church in the Philippines in bringing about a more just Philippine society? There is no lack of official social teaching on the part of the Catholic bishops' conference in the Philippines, but more can be done to communicate this social message effectively to Filipino Christians. In spite of its socio-cultural power and moral credibility, the Catholic church, due to certain limitations, cannot be a direct, partisan political force, but may assume a growing indirect, nonpartisan political role in the future. From a sociological viewpoint, the response of the Catholic hierarchy to the present national crisis is not adequate either as an analysis or a guide to action, and is not representative of Catholic social thought. It is more in line with the integration rather than the coercion model. A more adequate and realistic approach to social change and the creation of a more just Philippine society must combine the best insights of both social theory models; that is, social change can come about through a combination of pressure from below and moral suasion directed to those who wield economic and political power. An appeal to moral conversion and moral values is not sufficient; there is also a need to change unjust structures of power to bring about a balance of freedom and equality. The church in the Philippines has a Christian social vision of man and society, and therefore has something to say about the fundamental issues facing the nation. The response to values can be effective only if these values are embodied in organizations which promote justice. In the long run the movement to organize basic Christian communities shows great promise in bringing about a more just Philippine society.

But there is more to the church than being just another socio-cultural institution. As a religious institution it is oriented towards the transcendent reality of God. Therefore, from a religious viewpoint, among the many challenges to the Philippine church there stands out the challenge to develop a spirituality of action on behalf of justice that requires faith in God and man. Within the Philippine context this requires a double commitment to Christ of the paschal mystery and to the suffering and oppressed Filipino people.

In conclusion, the Christian faith has a vision of God, man and society that can contribute much to the creation of a just society. Even though it is true that there is no specifically Christian socio-economic analysis of society nor a concrete Christian program for social change, the Christian faith offers a hope over and above problems of social change, and a transcendence that goes beyond death itself. In the Philippine context, besides the prophetic role of carrying the social message of the Christian gospel to the people, and of protesting against injustice and the violation of human rights, the Catholic church can assume a greater role in building a more just Philippine society through a specific strategy and structure for nonviolent but revolutionary social change.

NOTES

1. "Let the People Be: Popular Religion and the Religion of the People," *Pro Mundi Vita Bulletin* 61 (July 1976): 1–31. A more recent and provocative paper on the distinction between official Christianity and Filipino popular religiosity is Rita H. Mataragnon's "God of the Rich, God of the Poor," in *God and Global Justice: Religion and Poverty in an Unequal World*, edited by Frederick Ferré and Rita H. Mataragnon (N.Y.: Paragon House, 1985), 139–159.

2. This section on the Bible is based mainly on John R. Donahue, S.J., "Biblical Perspectives on Justice," in *The Faith That Does Justice*, edited by John C. Haughey, S.J. (N.Y.: Paulist Press, 1977), 68–112.

3. J. Philip Wogaman, *Christians and the Great Economic Debate* (London: SCM Press Ltd., 1977).

4. Herman Hendrickx, *The Bible on Justice* (Quexon City: JMC Press, 1978).

5. Pieter Smulders, "Creation," *Sacramentum Mundo: An Encyclopedia of Theology*, Vol. 2, 27–28. See also Zachary Hayes, *What are They Saying about Creation* (N.Y.: Paulist Press, 1980).

6. John Reumann, *Creation and New Creation: The Past, Present, and Future of God's Creative Activity* (Minneapolis: Augsburg Publishing House, 1973).

7. Charles Birch, "Creation, Technology, and Human Survival," *Theology Digest* 27 (Fall 1979):203–206. Cf. also his "Nature, Humanity and God in Ecological Perspective," in *Faith and Science in an Unjust World*, Vol. 1, edited by Roger L. Shinn (Geneva: WCC, 1980), 62–73.

8. Rold Rendtorff, "Subdue the Earth: Man and Nature in the Old Testament,"

Theology Digest 27 (Fall 1979):213–216. See also John Carmody, *Ecology and Religion: Toward a New Christian Theology of Nature* (N.Y.: Paulist Press, 1983), who gives a synthesis of biblical doctrines, 84–99.

9. Brian O. McDermott, S.J., "The Theology of Original Sin: Recent Developments," *Theological Studies* 38 (September 1977):508–512. See also Edward Yarnold, S.J., *The Theology of Original Sin*, Theology Today Series 28 (The Mercier Press, 1971).

10. Richard P. McBrien, *Catholicism*, Vol. 2 (Minneapolis: Winston Press, 1980), defines social sin as "a situation in which the very organization of some level of society systematically functions to the detriment of groups or individuals in society. The sinfulness consists in the way social relationships are contrived or allowed to exist. Sometimes people of good will administer those systems. They are caught up in them. Although they may bear no personal guilt, the *situation* is sinful nonetheless." Peter J. Henriot, S.J., "The Concept of Social," *Catholic Mind* 71 (October 1980):38–53, gives an excellent summary of the development of the concept of social sin in Catholic social thought.

11. Peter J. Henriot, S.J., "A Theology of Action for Social Justice: Applications in the Global Context," *Catholic Mind* 71 (December 1973):31–45.

12. Romeo Intengan, S.J., *A Survey of Theology of Liberation in the Philippine Context* (Quezon City: Ateneo de Manila University Press, 1980).

13. Reynaldo C. Ileto, *Pasyon and Revolution: Popular Movements in the Philippines, 1840–1910* (Quezon City: Ateneo de Manila University Press, 1981). See also Vitaliano R. Gorospe, S.J., "Sources of Filipino Moral Consciousness," *Philippine Studies* 25 (1977):291–301.

14. Vitaliano R. Gorospe, S.J., "Towards the Christian Option and Praxis of Active Non-Violence," *Life Forum* 15 (June 1983):7–18.

15. Aloysius Pieris, S.J., "Asia's Non-Semitic Religions and the Mission of the Local Churches," *The Month* (March 1982):87–89.

16. "The Church in the Modern World of Vatican II," Medellin Conference of 1968; "Justice in the World" of the 1971 Synod of Bishops; "On the Development of Peoples" in 1967, of Paul VI; the Puebla Conference in 1979; and the latest *Laborem Exercens* in 1981, of John Paul II.

17. 1971 Roman Synod of Catholic Bishops, *Justice in the World* (Manila: St. Paul Publications, 1971), 8.

18. *John Paul II in the Philippines: Addresses and Homilies*, edited by Pedro S. Achutegui, S.J. (Quezon City: Cardinal Bea Institute, 1981). The quote is John Paul II's address to the president and nation on page 28.

19. The Catholic Bishops' conference of the Philippines (Henceforth, CBCP), "On Social Justice," *CBCP Monitor* 3(2) (February 1982):19–26.

20. CBCP, "Exhortation Against Violence," (1979), *Boletin Ecclesiastico de Filipinas* 53 (November–December 1979):521–526.

21. CBCP, "A Dialogue for Peace," (1983). *Boletin Ecclesiastico de Filipinas* 59 (May–June 1983):277–282.

22. Jaime V. Ongpin, "A Report on the Political Situation," paper presented to the

The Christian Faith and the Creation of a Just Society

Makati Business Club plenary session, 29 February 1984, Makati, Metro Manila.

23. Felix Casalmo, *The Vision of a New Society* (Manila, 1980) is a documented study of the response of the Catholic bishops to the violation of human rights during martial law (1972–1982). The author is a fictitious name and the press is withheld for security reasons.

24. This sociological section of the paper is an abbreviated and edited version plus this author's supplementary comments of a study by John J. Carroll, S.J., "The Church: A Political Force?," *Human Society* monograph 28 (Manila: HDRD, 2215 Pedro Gil Street, 1984).

25. Jaime L. Cardinal Sin, "Church and State Commitment to Human Development," speech delivered at the general assembly of the Bishops-Businessmen's Conference for Human Development on 12 March 1983.

26. CBCP, "Reconciliation Today," *Boletin Ecclesiastico de Filipinas* 60 (March–April 1984):248–251.

27. Romeo Intengan, S.J., "Christians for Socialism and the Question of Christian–Marxist Relations: A Practical Philippine Perspective," *Teaching All Nations* (1977):192–201, discovers from firsthand experience that many arguments proposed in favor of a Christian–Marxist collaboration in the Philippines are misleading and defective. However, the weaknesses among Filipino Christians that may lead to such a dangerous alliance must be solved by a kind of service that stresses the serious and disciplined study, contact with the concrete situation, detachment from unjust structures, and confidence in the power of the Christian gospel.

28. Arthur F. McGovern, *Marxism: An American Christian Perspective* (N.Y.: Orbis Books, 1980) gives a scholarly critique of Marxism, capitalism, and the national security state.

29. The story of hundreds of martyrs in the struggle for human rights in Latin America that brings the Catholic church into conflict with U.S. policy is told passionately but objectively by Penny Lernoux, *Cry of the People* (N.Y.: Penguin Books, 1980).

4
God, Destiny and Social Injustice: A Critique of a Yoruba Ifa Belief
OLUSEGUN GBADEGESIN

In the early hours of December 31, 1983, Nigerians woke to the sound of martial music on their transistors. It was as strange as it was exciting. Apparently there had been an army takeover of a government that had been thought of by the West as a successful experiment in democracy in Africa. For Western theorists, it must have been a sad change. For many Nigerians however, the news was welcomed with mixed feelings. On the one hand, military involvement in politics is an aberration, and many Nigerians know this. On the other hand, it was a welcome relief after a four-year period of the most despicable acts of injustice ever perpetrated on Nigerians by an administration—civil or military. For many, therefore, this New Year's eve political drama was a significant landmark in the struggle to create a just society. It rekindled the faith of many in the existence of a God of justice. For some, like the newspaper columnist Ray Ekpu, it showed that God is a Nigerian!

Why all the excitement about an unconstitutional change of government? This innocent question reveals one fundamental fact about man and society. It is that the reality of social injustice cannot be fully appreciated unless it is directly experienced. However, with some imagination, one may have a fairly adequate understanding of what others directly experience. The important thing to note is that social injustice pertains to empirical state of affairs. It is not just a concept. It is a characterization of the real practical world of many human beings. A denial of a fundamental right is an injustice. An unprovoked assault on a weaker person is an injustice. The existence of two separate sets of laws, one applying to the rich and the other to the poor, is an injustice. A closer look at the dimensions of injustice in the Nigerian social life may help bring its meaning and significance into sharper focus. The Yoruba belief in predestination and its implication for the phenomenon of social injustice will then be examined. Finally, the role of man, the place of faith, and the legitimacy of struggle in the creation of a just society will be addressed. First, however, there is need to highlight, even if only briefly, the antecedents of December 31, 1983, to have a fairly adequate understanding of the present situation and the despair and impatience which it has generated in Nigerians.

Dimensions of Social Injustice

Social life in precolonial Africa has been variously described. Some regard it as a haven of justice—a proverbial paradise on earth—where there was virtually no exploitation, oppression or class distinctions. There was, on this view, a harmonious relationship between the various sectors of traditional society, reducing to the barest minimum occasions of violent clashes and revolutions. Underlying this harmony was an economic system which guaranteed means of livelihood for all. The system was based on a common ownership of land, the most important means of production. Where land is commonly owned, and everyone has a right to a farm sufficient to support his family, there can be no basis for a dependent relationship. Thus, the conclusion is reached that traditional precolonial African societies were mostly just societies. According to some other accounts, however, this description is an exaggeration of the truth. There were some forms of segregation in many African societies. For instance, there was the *Osu* social segregation system among the Igbo of Nigeria. According to this system, some persons are condemned to the gods as sacrifices. They acquired this status as a result of a social system which legitimizes slavery. Slaves may be offered as sacrifice to the gods of the land as need arises—in periods of communal crisis such as war or famine. This category of persons is set aside for this purpose and cannot therefore mix with free, "pure" communal fellows. They may marry from within their own group but may not intermarry across groups. Their status is automatically inherited by their children, and so the cycle continues. There is also the idea of forced initiation into religious sects. This arises, again, from the communal basis of society. It is important that the religious duties of the group be performed. Specific gods of the lineage must be worshipped. There is need for priests and priestesses. The selection of these functionaries is made by approaching the god of divination, *Orunmila,* and whoever is so selected has no choice in the matter. This is cited as another example of the aspects of unjust social relations in traditional societies. There are, perhaps, many other such examples. What they show is that precolonial Nigeria had its own aspects of social injustice, no matter how insignificant these were. Indeed, it was some of these which the Europeans used as a justification for forcing themselves into the social structure of Nigeria.

Foreign intervention first came by way of Christianity—a religion which promises peace and justice of God for all. Christ was shown as the son of peace, the lover of mankind who does not discriminate between communities or races. He condemns human sacrifice. He condemns the practice of getting rid of twin babies who were considered taboo by the tradition. He insists on impartial justice for all as equals before God. At first, this religion was met with stiff opposition in many places. The idea of not revenging wrongs done by other individuals or communities was something strange to many Nigerian communities. How can a person be expected to turn the other cheek to an aggressor! And how can the community be expected to abandon her own gods, the spirits of her ancestors, for the sake of a foreign God whose origin is unknown! All these thoughts led to strong oppositions as vividly illustrated by Chinua Achebe's *Things Fall Apart*.

In spite of opposition, however, Christianity has come to stay. Its success in the struggle for survival in its mission of spreading the gospel was guaranteed by the earthly powers back home. Colonialism came in the wake of Christian pioneering efforts. It promised good government, peace and justice. It was opposed to those traditional practices which are repugnant to its conception of justice. Thus, like its spiritual counterpart, it was opposed to human sacrifice, trial by ordeal, slave labor and all forms of oppression. It would introduce an impartial adjudication of rifts and "civilize" the people in the art of good government.

If the Christian principles of justice and peace were strange to traditional Nigerians, the colonial principles were equally strange. But in addition to this clash of values and conceptions, there can be no doubt that the people were just exchanging one form of injustice for another. If there was injustice in precolonial society, there was more in the colonial system. Colonialism itself was an embodiment of injustice. How else does one describe the forceful imposition of foreign rule on a whole people! The policy of divide and rule did more harm than good. Chiefs and Obas grew in power *vis-à-vis* their subjects to the extent that traditions of selecting and deposing them were in many cases set side. Colonialism introduced an unjust

God, Destiny and Social Injustice: A Critique

economic system. Work situations were changed. Wage-labor was introduced, leading to a different conception of work. The idea of hiring oneself out to another person in return for money payment was strange. But more than this, colonialism introduced another dimension of social injustice—exploitative relationships. A different land tenure system was introduced in which right to land is tied, not to membership of lineages, but to the financial ability to acquire ownership. This has led to a wider gap between the rich and poor. The correlation between poverty and education cannot be overexaggerated in the case of African countries. So whatever leads to an expansion of the rich-poor gap, will eventually contribute to unequal relations between persons in the society. Colonialism succeeded in promoting this aspect of inequality and injustice.

Political independence came after a fierce struggle and it appeared that the people had won the fight for justice. It seemed that they could now determine their lives themselves. There is no need to recall their political freedom before colonialism. They are now on a "higher plane," having gone through the bitter school of foreign rule. So they can now organize their social life in a way that should belie the theoretical assumption of the colonial master. Justice will prevail. Exploitation will be a thing of the past. We can now operate a just economic system. We can tap our resources and mobilize them for a self-reliant nation. By this time many Nigerians had accepted the sovereignty of the Christian God. He was directly implored to help us build a nation in which no man is oppressed. Dreams were dreamed, hopes were high, there was faith in God. But none of these was coupled with action and genuine struggle.

It was not long before the truth started to unfold that our political independence is a sham. We have merely moved from an unjust social system promoted by colonialism to one promoted by indigenous rule. Oppression started to rear its ugly head. We operated a political system which perpetrated all sorts of evil. Political power was freely used to destroy opponents. Heavy taxation in the form of assessment was an effective weapon to convert opponents to one's side. Deliberate planting of criminal objects (e.g., marijuana) in the farms of opponents was an effective method of getting them into trouble and suppressing them. The ordinary man could not meet his obligations because of the battered economy. All aspects of human social life were politicized and it became almost impossible to live a normal human life without fear of arrest. The rigging of elections in 1964 and 1965 was the straw that broke the camel's back.

Pandemonium was let loose. Innocents suffered terrible damages to life and property, as many victims and their properties were burnt to ashes!

Then the army struck in January 1966. A sigh of relief was heaved by almost all Nigerians. These people have not been tried before. They should be given time and support. They promise to reshape things for the better. They promise to unite the country and eradicate the forces of injustice and poverty with military precision. Then they began to act. But the problem of ethnicity for which they did not bargain crept in and plunged us into a devastating civil war. Again, there was monumental suffering, mostly by the innocent. Children died in thousands. Adults were maimed. There was hunger and disease in the land. But while many were suffering, some were building for themselves an economic empire out of the misfortune of war. While human beings were dying of starvation in the bush, and others were silenced by bullets, some became millionaires, through contracts for the supply of all sorts of things, including ammunitions! It is the irony of life, probably the height of injustice, that the misfortune of some is the foundation of the prosperity of others.

The war lasted thirty months. Unity was achieved and reconstruction and reconciliation began. The slogan was "no victor no vanquished." But as usual, power began to corrupt. Those wartime millionaires were becoming too powerful to be controlled. They were milking the nation at the expense of the common man. It soon became clear that the entire leadership had to go. Indeed, when the charge of corruption was leveled against one of them, rather than deny it, he only boasted that no one could remove him from office because he had the secrets of all the others in his pocket. Suddenly, at the height of disenchantment, it seemed a messiah had come as a bloodless coup ushered in another military administration led by General Murtala Mohammed. He started to reshape things. He was a man of action, bent on introducing sanity and probity into the social system. But he dared too much, and was mowed down by the agents of injustice before he could accomplish much. From that point it was no longer easy. The work of reconstruction continued, but so did injustice. It soon became clear that the ideals of fairness, equality and justice could not be achieved under the system. The army thought it was overstaying its term. Thirteen years is enough to effect reasonably just changes. The army gave up.

The second republic of civil admininstration was ushered in with

God, Destiny and Social Injustice: A Critique

fanfare. The political parties had promised paradise on earth. They were to stop injustice in all its forms. They were to make life meaningful for the downtrodden masses. They were to revolutionize agriculture so as to provide food for the populace. They were to bridge the gap between the rich and the poor by a sound economic policy. But the truth soon dawned on the masses that this was another treachery. Life had never been worse for the ordinary person. Hunger was seen in the faces of some people, while others were swimming in ill-gotten wealth. It was the era of "contractocracy"—government of contractors for contractors by contractors. Contracts were inflated to siphon money into private pockets. Promises were freely broken. There was a conspiracy against the poor. Innocent citizens were victimized by a combination of forces, represented sometimes by the police (supposedly paid to protect), and sometimes by armed robbers. If the latter can be understood, the former hardly can. Police harrassment (killing, maiming) of innocent citizens for political reasons is the height of injustice.

These general remarks about the dimensions of social injustice in Nigerian social history are not exhaustive. Indeed, they are only meant to highlight the reality of the problem. But this may not have been effectively accomplished in the above narrative. I would, therefore, like to end by taking up some specific cases of social injustice in the life of the last civilian administration in Nigeria. First is the Bakolori massacre of 1980. Bakolori is a small community in northern Nigeria. The people thrive on subsistence farming and fishing. They were direct victims of a government agricultural policy, aimed at acquiring land for its river basin agricultural programs. The reluctance of the people to leave their land earned them a mass massacre, the most atrocious in the recent history of Nigeria. No one was prosecuted for the crime. Again, in Kano in 1982, there was a politically motivated riot against the state administration, which was not in the same political camp with the federal administration. The rioters had a freehand as the police, supposedly responsible for maintenance of life and property, appeared helpless. This led to loss of lives, including that of a friend of the common man and fighter for social justice, Bala Mohammed. Nothing came out of the enquiry. Finally, during the general elections of 1983 there were several murders of political opponents with the connivance of the police. These occurred in Ile-Ife, Ondo, Okeho, Yola, to mention a few places. The manipulations of elections to impose an unpopular administration at the center, in spite of the yearning of the masses for change, was the last straw. All this explains and justifies the excitement that welcomed the December 31, 1983 political drama.

Reflections on these dimensions of injustice—which may definitely not be as acute as those experienced elsewhere—should naturally move a person to the point of raising the question of God anew. Is there a God? Is he to blame for the persistence of social injustice? Is faith in God necessary to eliminate injustice? These are pertinent questions of our time; and there may be as many answers as there are cultures and individuals. I will approach these questions from the perspective of the traditional belief of the Yoruba. Then I will raise some problems with this point of view.

The Yoruba Concept of God

For the average Yoruba, especially the devotee of the traditional Ifa religion, God exists to promote goodness and deliver judgment on the wicked and unjust. In addition to this God who controls the affairs of the world, there are also a number of divinities (*orisa*) who assist the Supreme God in the work of creation and governance of the world. The Yoruba concept of God portrays him as the Supreme Being with a status and attributes which underscore his relationship to human beings and his role in their social world.[1]

The Yoruba name for God is *Olodumare*. This signifies fullness, abundance, supremacy and ultimacy. Etymologically *Olodumare* has two stems: *olodu* and *mare*. The first, *olodu* includes a prefix *ol-* the full rendering of which is *oni* meaning "the owner of." Thus *olodu* means *oni odu* or "the owner of *Odu*." *Odu* has more than one meaning depending on how it is pronounced or written. Among its meanings are "large container" (òdù), heading or chapter (odù), and large (odu).[2] It will be noticed that all these meanings are related and have in common the fact that they signify fullness, or largeness. *Olodu* may then be taken to be "the owner of fullness, largeness or greatness," or simply "the full one," or "the great one." *Mare*, on the other hand, appears to be a combination of two words: *ma re* which means "do not go" or "that does not go." Bringing the two together, we have *Olodumare* which now means "the great (full etc.) one that does not go anywhere," or "the great (full etc..) one beyond which nothing goes." In other words, *Olodumare* signifies God as the Supreme Being and Ultimate Reality.

In the Yoruba (Ifa) system, *Olodumare*, as his name suggests, has

God, Destiny and Social Injustice: A Critique

certain attributes which confirm his supremacy and ultimacy. He is, among other things, the most powerful, the wisest, and the kindest in heaven and on earth. With regard to power, the conception is that he has no superior, and is thought of as the one who can do his wish without seeking anybody's approval. Furthermore, he is the only one behind any successful endeavor of human beings in the sense that he approved and sealed such efforts at creation. Whatever has not been so approved cannot come to fruition. *Olodumare,* on this view, is *alewilese* (he who can not only say but can also do.) His power is disclosed in the creation of the world and of man. It is his life-breath that brings life to the moulded body of man. Thus, even though *Olodumare* is assisted by the archdivinity *Orisanla* in the moulding of the physical body of man, the final and most important aspect of creation is done by the Supreme Being himself.[3]

Beside his creative power, *Olodumare* also has governing powers over the entire world—natural and social. Thus, he controls events in nature. Rain, sun, moon, bountiful harvests all occur at his pleasure, and the divinities, who seem to be closer to human beings, are ultimately responsible to him. What he does not permit cannot be accomplished even by his deputies. The fact that the Yoruba mostly worship the *orisa* (divinities) directly does not mean that they have no conception of *Olodumare* (Supreme Being) and his powers. They combine polytheism with belief in a God who is the ultimate power and source of being. There is no good reason to think otherwise.

Omnipotence is not the only attribute of *Olodumare*. He is also thought of as wise and good. His wisdom, as his power, is unparalleled. He has knowledge of all human secrets and can see into man's inward nature. It is part of this power that he gives to *Orunmila,* the god of divination, so that the latter may help human beings discover unknown secrets about their future. But this does not make *Orunmila* an equal of *Olodumare*; and Ifa priests, perhaps more than anyone else, know that ultimate wisdom is God's.

Olodumare is also conceived as a kind Deity. He loves all human beings alike and does not discriminate. He makes the rain fall on everyone's farm, no matter what the individual's social status. Even the wicked are not punished by withdrawing rain. But of course, *Olodumare* is also an impartial judge who has his own way of punishing evil. His judgment may not come when men expect; but it is sure to come.

Olusegun Gbadegesin

Why Social Injustice?

Given this conception of God, the question remains as to how we should make sense of the phenomenon of social injustice, which as has been seen, stares the average Yoruba in the face, either through direct experience of partiality, nepotism and corruption, or through other subtle methods of exploitation and oppression. We are not concerned here with the problem of suffering caused by natural calamities such as earthquakes, hurricanes and fire, but rather with sufferings which are caused by human inhumanity. What then is the role of God in accounting for this kind of human-made evil?

If we follow Yoruba theology, God, is good by nature. He cannot, therefore, be the cause of injustice and unnecessary suffering. Of course, he does what he likes and no mortal has a right to question the actions of *Olodumare* and the *orisas*. However, it is part of the belief that the Deity is good and wants to maximize good rather than perpetrate evil. His purpose in creating the universe is to promote the good.[4] He, therefore, rewards those who conscientiously contribute to the fulfillment of this purpose, while reserving the right to punish those whose conduct detracts from promotion of the good. Such punishment starts on this earth and this explains certain human sufferings as punishment for evils. We may then put the issue this way: since God has a right to punish evildoers, he may choose to use other human beings (rather than natural calamities) as a means of exercising his right. Thus, what looks like social injustice, may really be God's way of maintaining justice. From this perspective, the relevance of God for the promotion of justice (through the means of rewarding good and evil) seems quite obvious. Rather than cause injustice, *Olodumare* is the ultimate dispenser of justice.[5]

This form of theology obviously cannot solve the whole problem of social injustice. Let us assume that it is adequate when applied to deserved cases of suffering. But how about undeserved cases? One can understand, for instance, that the god of vengeance has rightly intervened when an armed robber, after grabbing his loot and killing his victim, met his own violent death in a motor accident caused by a drunken driver of another vehicle. But one cannot understand the untimely and undeserved death of the victim of the armed robbery. In other words, two questions arise with regard to this theology. Is it just for some human beings to suffer as innocent victims of injustice in order that God's method of justice

God, Destiny and Social Injustice: A Critique

may be revealed? Is it just to make human beings misbehave in order that they may thereafter be punished? These are pertinent questions which any theodicy must resolve. They are faced by virtually every practical person involved in the business of living and fighting against injustice. Kurunmi, the great Ijaiye hero of the nineteenth century, had to ask *Ogun,* the god of iron and acclaimed supporter of all those fighting for just causes: *Ogun,* what have I done wrong? Kurunmi vowed to fight against the unjust imposition of a king over Oyo and Ijaiye.[6] In 1858, Alaafin Atiba sensed death approaching and did not want the throne to be given to another family. He therefore demanded the promise of his chiefs to crown his son as the next Alaafin. But it was against tradition which required the son to die along with his father since he had enjoyed power with him during his reign. Also, the oracle should be consulted to determine who the next king should be. This was ignored. Kurunmi vowed to fight against what he perceived as injustice. But he lost the battle. His own sons were killed and the corpses brought to him. In desperation, Kurunmi had to query *Ogun* and *Olodumare.* He voluntarily gave up his own life. To say that Kurunmi's end must have been a deserved result of his own evils is to ignore the reality of social injustice. It is to declare, perhaps unconsciously, that all forms of human social suffering are punishment for past misdeeds. This is a dangerous position, and it hardly excuses the gods, for then the question may be raised: Why should a person be created bad for the ultimate purpose of punishing him?

Destiny

The phenomenon of social injustice may be further explored by appeal to the Yoruba belief in predestination. The justification for this is that the belief plays a predominant role in the explanation of major events in individual and social life. Indeed, it is one important way by which *Olodumare* is excused from indictment for human suffering in Yoruba Ifa theology. To have an adequate understanding of this belief, we need to examine the conception of the human being from the Yoruba perspective.

The human being is made up of body and spirit. The body (*ara*), which is a combination of flesh, blood and bones, is the handiwork of the arch-divinity (*Orisa-nla*). The being of man is made possible by the breathing-spirit or life-breath (*emi*), an immaterial element given by the deity himself to the body. It is part of the divine breath that gives and maintains life. It is life-force. With its presence and adequate functioning, the being of man is guaranteed. With its cessation, man's being collapses and he is dead. Thus, when a person dies, the Yoruba say his *emi* is gone, meaning he has ceased breathing or he no longer has the breathing-spirit in him. The body does not breath; it is the *emi* that breathes, and the being of man ceases when it disappears.[7]

This being—a combination of body and breath—is just one aspect of the human person. Again, this being of man refers only to his existence as a breathing thing. Surely this is recognized as of great importance. As long as one has breath, there is hope of success in life. The breathing-spirit makes it possible for anyone in whom it resides to be hopeful of better modes of existence, and without it, there is nothing to hope for.

However, when we are concerned with the Yoruba concept of human personality, we must realize that it embraces more than a combination of body and breath. There is a third element called *ori*. This is the spiritual personality component of the human being, symbolized by the physical head. In Yoruba thought, *ori* is used to refer to two related things. It refers to the unconscious self, which makes a free choice of one's life-course before *Olodumare,* and it refers to that which is chosen—the individual destiny or portion. As the former, *ori* is the personal spirit or guardian ancestor of an individual. It is believed to determine one's success or failure in life. It is *ori* that determines one's personality, and it is from his *ori* that a person finds out what sort of thing he or she has been destined to do or achieve in life. This is done by consulting *Orunmila,* the god of divination. This is because the individual's *ori* made a choice of his destiny before *Olodumar* and in the presence of *Orunmila* before setting out for the journey to earth. The choice made by *ori* (the personality spirit) is, however, unknown to the (now conscious) person after he has come into the world. Thus, it is possible for a person to embark on a project not chosen by his *ori;* that is, for which he is not predestined. Failure is the result of such efforts. Hence the need to consult one's *ori* to determine the nature of its choice and whether or not one is following the right path. The significance of this for the meaning of human existence should not escape us. *Ori* is the indicator of one's purpose in life. It has the secret of the deity's plan for one. It is like a forerunner, the pathfinder in the earthly bush. Barry Hallen says it well when he observes that for the Yoruba, "*Ori* is, in a sense, my meaning—what

God, Destiny and Social Injustice: A Critique

I shall become while I am in the world this time. It limits my possibilities and provides me with a course to follow."[8]

As a personal spirit, *ori* is also considered a divinity in its own right. Indeed, it is regarded as more important than some other divinities. As an intermediary between the individual and the *orisa*, *ori* is closer to the individual. Besides, it alone knows what one has chosen, and one needs to consult it to act correctly. Even when a divinity (*orisa*) approves one's plan, if *ori* disapproves it one would be foolish to attempt to carry it out. For "no *orisa* blesses a man without the consent of his *ori*."[9]

The combination of body (*ara*) breathing spirits (*emi*) and personality spirit (*ori*) constitutes the human person in Yoruba thought. The three elements are both important in their own way and are complementary. The breathing spirit has to be embodied to exist in the world of man; without it the body is a lifeless figure which cannot make its earthly journey. The Yoruba are dualists in their metaphysical account of man. *Ori*, however, introduces a third aspect, perhaps unfamiliar to the West, and seems the most important of the trio as far as the meaning of human existence is concerned. It determines what sort of life a person will lead; and the ultimate meaning of concrete events in an individual's life are to be understood in terms of the *ori's* choice.

Ori (destiny) is thus a fundamental concept of Yoruba thought. It provides the Yoruba a means of resolving some of the significant puzzles of the human condition. It renders events meaningful, so that human life itself acquires sense. But the concept creates its own problems, and lest one is carried away by the idea of a power that cannot be stopped, it should also be noted that the idea of an unchangeable destiny is held, albeit inconsistently, along with the ideas of blame, freedom and responsibility. It is believed that what cannot *ordinarily* be changed, may in certain respects be amenable to change, given the right approach.

An individual's destiny or portion may be changed for good or bad. For instance, one not only consults the god of divination (*Orunmila*) to find out what one's *ori* has chosen, one also consults him to alter an unfavorable destiny. This seems inconsistent with the belief that a destiny that is affirmed and sealed by *Olodumare* cannot be changed. But belief in *Orunmila's* power is explicable by appeal to his significant presence at the scene of the original choice. If he were there, then he should have influence on the deity to accept a favorable change. But there are limits to this influence, and in the end it may well be that even after the intervention of *Orunmila,* a bad destiny cannot be effectively averted. Then the *ori,* and not the divinity, is to blame for the original wrong choice. Again, this supports the view that *ori* is the meaning of life, in terms of which almost all important puzzles are ultimately resolved.

Other agents of possible change include wicked people and one's own character. The wicked, including, e.g., witches and sorcerers, may through their machinations disrupt the normal path of a good destiny. Though the *ori* makes the choice which is sealed by the deity, it is possible for evildoers to thwart human beings in the process of carrying out their destiny. These may be too powerful for the human agent who therefore needs the continued support of his spiritual personality component. It is believed that once its support is guaranteed, no force can succeed in changing one's good destiny. Again, the idea is that, though others are powerful and wicked, as long as one's *ori* is on one's side, there should be no problem. But one can lose the support of one's *ori* because of one's character.

Character is believed to be the most important of one's earthly possessions, and an otherwise good destiny may be spoiled by a person's bad character. An impatient person will run faster than his *ori,* thereby alienating it and losing its support. In an attempt to acquire the good things of life hastily, one may adopt a short route against what has been one's chosen portion. The Yoruba warn against inordinate ambition, the kind that leads to destruction. It would seem, all things considered, that this is a philosophy of resignation. It appears to allow for idleness in the name of destiny, since what has been chosen can hardly be changed, and because in most cases, an unfavorable destiny has to be borne throughout life. For those who give up easily, destiny provides the necessary facility for early resignation. The issue now is this: proponents of the doctrine of predestination in Yoruba philosophy are aware of the various secular influences on a person's fortune or misery in life. Character, industry or lack of it, mischief by others, etc., as has been seen, are some of these earthly influences on humans. If these are properly handled, the significance of predestination as an explantory model should be considerably diminished. Consider the following example. Eda is an industrious, pleasant young man. Everyone speaks well of him. He cares not only for himself but for others. No one would think of harming him. He succeeds so well that everyone in the village thanks *Olodumare* on his behalf. To

God, Destiny and Social Injustice: A Critique

account for his success, the traditional believer appeals to Eda's *ori* and pre-appointed destiny. This is the first explanation that occurs to him or her. Thereafter, one may add the fact of Eda's character and hardwork as contributory factors. But why are these just contributory factors? If Eda is industrious, loved by all, and has a pleasant character, why do we need to make reference to a pre-appointed destiny to account for his success? To this question, the traditional philospher has a ready answer which may be put as a rhetorical question: Is Eda the only man in his village who happens to be industrious, loved by all, and with pleasant character? Why are others in the same category not as successful?

The same type of explanation is readily available in case Eda should fail in spite of all his efforts and good qualities. If he fails, it is because he has not chosen to succeed in life, and there is nothing anyone can do about it. *Ayanmo ko nii tase,* which means "A pre-appointed lot will never miss," is the appropriate cultural response to such a situation. Indeed, it is especially in pathetic situations, where a person cannot be blamed or held responsible for his or her misfortune, that the Yoruba mind is resigned to explanation in terms of destiny: What is the case has to be the case necessarily because it has been predestined to be so.

Predestination and Social Injustice

We are now in a position to raise the question what is the relevance of *ori* to the explanation and elimination of social injustice? If, as the Yoruba believe, *ori* is the meaning of life, if it renders all events in individual and social life meaningful, then it should also explain the phenomenon of social injustice and render it meaningful. *Ori* indicates the choice made by the unconscious self. To each choice so made—whatever its content—*Olodumare* gives his endorsement. He does not reject a given choice for reason of its being unfair, unjust, or wicked. The prospective wicked person goes before God to declare his mission on earth, as does the prospective victim of his wickedness. *Olodumare* seals up each person's choice or *ori*—one to impose suffering on others, the other to be an innocent victim of the wickedness of others—and allows them to proceed into the world, armed with their respective destinies. And as has been seen, what is so chosen is difficult, if not impossible, to alter on earth. Hence the possibility of innocent suffering and prevalent injustice. The individual would have forgotten his or her choice, but the God in the presence of whom it was made does not forget. God should therefore be excused. After all, he merely listens and seals a choice of *ori*. *Ori*, not *Olodumare*, is to blame for suffering and injustice. As should be obvious, this is a bad defense and hardly serves the purpose of excusing God. It presents the picture of a God, indifferent to the conditions of his creation, and is incompatible with the idea of a universe created for the production of good. If God has endorsed the choice of a wicked *ori*, what justification has he to punish the wickedness of its bearer?

The idea of destiny as an explanation of injustice thus seems to be conceptually mistaken. It cannot adequately accomplish that task. It leaves too many questions unanswered. Why should a wicked destiny be endorsed by *Olodumare*? Why should the bearer of an evil destiny be punished? Why should a person be made to suffer because of a choice made by his unconscious self? If some destinies can be changed, why not those which promote injustice? All these are pertinent questions for which answers are desperately needed. Even though adequate answers are hard to come by, *Olodumare* is never blamed in the system. Rather, to make up for the apparent indifference of *Olodumare*, the belief is that *Orunmila*, the god of divination, has been sent down to the world to divine for human beings in order to counteract the powers of the malevolent spirits (*ajogun*) and wicked persons.[10] A radical reaction to the system might be that either the malevolent spirits are too powerful for *Orunmila* to combat, or he is as indifferent to man's suffering as *Olodumare* appears to be. For social injustice and human suffering continues unabated in spite of the divining power of *Orunmila*.

Though the concept of destiny cannot adequately explain injustice, it has an important role to play in the social life of the Yoruba. Destiny may be seen as an ideology of the ruling class. Its function is to present the phenomena of injustice as transcendentally arranged. Some are predestined to be rich, others to be poor. There is a story of a gentleman whose poverty is beyond description in spite of strenuous efforts to make ends meet. He went to *Orunmila* for help, but to his astonishment and utter dismay, none was forthcoming. The answer is that there is no wealth, only poverty in the man's *ori*.

That the idea of destiny cannot adequately explain the phenomenon of social injustice is not the real issue though. Indeed, it may be argued that the average Yoruba does not, in practice, normally appeal to destiny to justify or explain glaring injustice and

God, Destiny and Social Injustice: A Critique

open misdemeanor. Thus, armed robbers are punished and idlers are censured. But, at the same time, the wealth of a successful exploiter is attributed to his destiny, while the poverty of a zealous worker is also laid at the doors of destiny. What appears to be the case is that those aspects of individual and social life which are, by and large, products of unjust social relations, are easily explained by appeal to the idea of predestination. But as I have mentioned, the real issue is not that of explanation. It is rather that the belief in destiny constitutes a strong intellectual impediment to the idea of struggle for social justice, providing theologico-philosophical strength for the exploiter while further weakening the despairing soul of the exploited.

If some people are predestined to rule and exploit the weakness of others, who are therefore predestined to be exploited, and this is a heavenly arranged affair, then talk about the evils of injustice will make no sense and the idea of struggle becomes incoherent. This works best for the ruling class. The *ori* of the president is to rule, even when it is obvious that his election has been heavily rigged. The *talakawa* (peasants) are indoctrinated into the belief in destiny and, therefore, consider their position as the choice of their *ori*. This is especially the case with those who have made persistent efforts to survive economically. They soon become willing victims of the ideology of predestination. They cannot see their position as probably resulting from a particular organization of their social life rather than from an unconsciously chosen portion. Since they do not see it as such, they cannot engage in any meaningful struggle for just changes.

The idea of destiny seems incompatible with struggle. After all, if you are predestined to be poor, no matter what you do, what use is there for struggle? To this extent, belief in destiny is a basis for legitimizing injustice. It takes the source of injustice away from this empirical world and the flesh and blood humans who perpetrate evil, to a world beyond where different portions are chosen and sealed. Rather than justify *Olodumare,* it really presents him as an uncaring and indifferent creator, instead of a benevolent one. Injustice cannot be adequately accounted for by appeal to destiny. To blame man's inhumanity to man on destiny is to legitimize despair. Human beings are the source of injustice and therefore should be the focus of attention for any meaningful change. For such a change, struggle is legitimate. But struggle does not eliminate God. He is not rendered irrelevant by consistent struggle by people to create a just society. After all, his original purpose is supposed to be to create a world for the promotion of good. Struggle plus faith in such a God must ensure victory in the long run. An important requirement for the relevance of God is the belief that he supports just causes. But this is what belief in destiny appears to eliminate. By appealing to a pre-appointed destiny for human beings, it denies the relevance of struggle and the readiness of God to support just causes. With this denial the notion of destiny seems to legitimize injustice and suffering. Thus, if injustice is an evil to be eradicated, and there is need to struggle to create a just society, then the belief in destiny has to be jettisoned.

= NOTES =

1. E. Bolaji Idowu, *Olodumare God in Yoruba Belief* (London: Longmans, 1962); Wande Abimbola, *Ifa An Exposition of Ifa Literary Corpus* (Ibadan: Oxford University Press, 1976); B. C. Ray, *African Religions: Symbol, Ritual and Community* (New Jersey: Prentice Hall, 1976).
2. Idowu, 30–37.
3. See Wande Abimbola, "The Yoruba Concept of Human Personality" in *"La Notion de Personne en Afrique Noire," Colloques Internationaux du Centre National de la Recherche Scientifique,* No. 554, (1971) 73–89.
4. I explore this theme further in my "Destiny, Personality and the Ultimate Meaning of Human Existence—A Yoruba Perspective" in *Ultimate Reality and Meaning: Interdisciplinary Studies in the Philosophy of Understanding,* Vol. 7, No. 3, (1984).
5. Idowu, 39–47.
6. Ola Rotimi, *Kutunmi* (Ibadan, Oxford University Press, 1971).
7. Idowu, Chapter 13.
8. Barry Hallen, "Phenomenology and the Exposition of African Traditional Thought," *Second Order: An African Journal of Philosophy,* 5(2) (1976), 60.
9. Abimbola, "The Yoruba Concept of Human Personality," (1971), 81.
10. Ibid.

5
Faith, Justice and Violence In Latin American Liberation Theology
GENE G. JAMES

The question 'Is faith in God necessary for the creation of a just society?' is based on assumptions deeply rooted in Western culture. It is immediately intelligible to anyone from a Jewish, Christian or Islamic background. How one answers the question determines to a considerable extent the degree to which one's worldview is religious or secular. However, the distinction between the religious and the secular is also a Western distinction. It presupposes acceptance or rejection of a God who created man and the universe. Since it presupposes this conception of God, the question whether faith in God is necessary to create a just society is much less intelligible to someone from a Hindu or Buddhist background where this idea may be lacking. Someone from these traditions might answer the question by saying that because it is not obvious that Western societies have been more just than Eastern, faith in God is not necessary for a just society. This reply might be met in turn by a denial that any society has ever been just, and the claim that a just society remains to be created. This dissatisfaction with the status quo and emphasis on the need to create a just society is again characteristic of the Western tradition, presupposing a view of human beings as active agents whose goal should be to transform their circumstances for their own benefit. The question 'Is faith in God necessary for the creation of a just society?' also seems to presuppose faith as antecedently given. The assumption appears to be that one should first decide whether God exists, and then having decided that God does exist, ask whether commitment to this belief is required in order for a just society to be brought about.

This paper is a discussion of a challenge to the foregoing ways of conceiving faith and justice. The challenge is not one posed by the nonbeliever who denies that God exists, but one from within the Christian tradition. It is a challenge by Latin American liberation theologians. The dominant conception of faith in the Western world, they argue, has been that faith is a type of belief. The primary concern of the faithful, therefore, has been with right belief or arriving at truths of faith. Truth has in turn been conceived as correspondence with a transcendent realm. The task of theology has been to systematize the truths of faith and to apply them to the world. Sometimes these truths have been said to be found in the Bible alone, sometimes in individual reflection inspired by the Bible, and at other times in infallible pronouncements by the church. In every case, however, the problem of faith has been primarily one of right belief, with right action seen as a derivative issue.

Liberation theologians maintain that this way of conceiving faith is essentially Greek in nature. Christian thought from an early period began to enter into dialogue with Greek philosophy, being first influenced by Platonism and Neoplatonism, and then from the time of Thomas Aquinas by Aristotelianism. In accepting the Platonic conception of truth as correspondence with a transcendent order, early Christians also accepted a dualistic ontology which divided reality into two radically different realms. This was the basis for Augustine's division of the universe into the City of Man and the City of God. It was also the foundation for a conception of the spiritual life as one focused on the eternal realm, removed from the concerns of everyday life. Although the rediscovery of Aristotelianism in the Renaissance led to increased emphasis on worldly life, the underlying conception of truth as correspondence with a transcendent order was not weakened but strengthened. The most fundamental task of theology became the reconciliation of the truths of faith with reason. Liberation theologians believe that this has remained the dominant concern of most theologians down to the present. Thus, like Thomas Aquinas, modern theologians address themselves primarily to nonbelievers. The major problems have been demonstrating that God exists and interpreting the Bible in such a way as to avoid conflict with science.[1]

Liberation theologians also believe that acceptance of a dualistic ontology has led to salvation being interpreted as an individualistic, private affair. Traditional Catholic doctrine, according to Juan Luis Segundo, emphasized merit as a condition for salvation. However, merit was interpreted in a purely intentional rather than a consequential fashion.

[I]n the Catholic view the merit of a human action had no direct relationship to its historical effectiveness. Neither successful . . . nor unsuccessful endeavors are meritorious *as such*. . . . What really counts is the effort expended and a God-directed intention.[2]

Segundo illustrates this thesis by using the example of action by physicians. "What gains merit for the doctor is the effort he makes to cure the patient and the intention to do that for the glory of God rather than for the sake of fame or the life of the patient. The latter merely serves as the occasion for merit."[3] Given this view of the relation of merit to salvation, the religious value of an action has nothing to do with its social or historical value.

For society, for the human and historical plane, the value of a doctor is in direct proportion to the historical results he obtains. For God, for the plane of eternal values, those historical results not only do not count but are actually dangerous. They are dangerous insofar as they are historical *values*, real satisfactions that can compete with the effort and intention that count for eternity.[4]

Traditional Catholic doctrine, then, says Segundo, interpreted human existence as lived out on two different planes. "The *supernatural* plane is the plane of eternal values; the *natural* plane is the plane of temporal values."[5] Since it profits a person nothing to gain the whole world but lose their soul, the mission of the church in announcing the gospel to humans is to constantly call attention to the supernatural plane where salvation is obtained. This means that although the church may criticize political movements and regimes, it can never commit itself to any definite political program. This point of view was modified to some extent by Vatican II, but in Segundo's opinion it did not make a clean break with the past and therefore adopted an inconsistent position. Although Vatican II represents a major attempt by the Catholic Church to address the problems of the modern world, one can also "look to it for support . . . in defending the older view of faith as an autonomous value."[6] Consider, he says, the following statements from *Gaudium et spes*, no. 42. "Christ, to be sure, gave His Church no proper mission in the political, economic, or social order. The purpose which He set before her is a religious one."[7]

Protestant theology, Segundo believes, severed the connection between religious and social values even more than Catholicism.

In Catholic theology the only thing that united the plane of human activity in history with the plane of God's "eternal" kingdom was the notion of *merit,* that is, the "eternal" worth of human effort and right intention. But even this tie was cut in the Protestant theology of salvation by faith alone.[8]

Catholic doctrine at least found merit in social and political action even if it did not think that such action had causal efficacy in bringing about salvation. But the doctrine of salvation by faith alone turned faith into a solitary, "essentially passive acceptance of God's fixed plan for human destiny and . . . his eschatological kingdom."[9] Even so-called political theology now popular in Europe, liberation theologians contend, is deficient because it remains at the level of general statements and abstract theory rather than putting forth specific, concrete proposals for the liberation of oppressed people.[10]

The conceptions of truth and faith found in the Bible, liberation theologians argue, are quite different from the Greek notions of truth and faith. Knowledge is not spoken of in the Bible as insight into a transcendent realm but as a type of practical activity. Truth is not correspondence with a transcendent realm, but something that must be verified in one's life. Furthermore, verification is not merely an intellectual act; it requires adoption of a way of life. Faith is conceived of the same way.

> Faith is always a concrete obedience which relies on God's promise and is vindicated in the act of obedience: Abraham offering his only son, Moses stepping into the Red Sea. . . . [T]he faith of Israel is consistently portrayed, not as a *gnosis,* but as a *way,* a particular way of acting.[11]

The biblical view, liberation theologians claim, is that to know God is to do his will. But God's will is progressively identified in the Bible with acting justly. This theme first appears in the Prophets. The Book of Amos contains one of the best known statements. God says to the Israelites:

> I hate, I despise your feasts, and I take no delight in your solemn assemblies. . . . Take away from me the noise of your songs; to the melody of your harps I will not listen. But let justice roll down like waters, and righteousness like a mighty stream.
>
> (Amos 5:21, 23–24)

Similarly in the Book of Isaiah God says:

> Is not this what I require of you as a fast: to loose the fetters of injustice, to untie the knots of the yoke, to snap every yoke and set free those who have been crushed? Is it not sharing your food with the hungry,

taking the homeless poor into your home, clothing the naked when you meet them and never evading a duty to your kinfolk?

(Isa. 58:6–7)

Liberation theologians interpret the new covenant, which Jeremiah and Ezekiel record God making with the Israelites, in light of the foregoing passages.[12] Henceforth, to know God will not be a matter of keeping the letter of the law or of performing the proper ceremonies. Nor will it be merely a matter of cultivating a state of internal piety. To know God will be to do justice (Jer. 22:13–16).

Just action as understood by liberation theologians requires much more than the negative duty of simply refraining from harming others. It requires that one take positive action on behalf of the poor and oppressed. God is not impartial, treating all people alike. He takes sides with the poor and oppressed. This can be seen in the Exodus story, which liberation theologians take as a paradigm of the relations between God and humans. The Israelites were enslaved in Egypt but God heard their complaint and took their side against Pharaoh. He appointed Moses as their leader and helped them gain liberation from the Egyptians. God still takes sides with the poor and oppressed today. He is against modern Pharaohs such as capitalists and military oligarchs who exploit the people of the third world.

Salvation in the Old Testament, liberation theologians claim, meant first of all liberation from foreign domination. It meant the liberation of the Israelites from slavery in Egypt or from the captivity in Babylon so that they could return to their former ways of life and worship. Salvation was, therefore, simultaneously a political and a religious event. It was the salvation of a people rather than of isolated individuals. It was an historical event in the life of the people, not a purely spiritual, inward occurrence in which God revealed himself to an individual. The latter way of conceiving salvation is a corruption of the biblical notion and comes from Greek dualism. Salvation required the cooperation of the people, their commitment and dedication to the way of the Lord. It was liberation from sin, from a life-style contrary to God's commands.

The concept of sin in the Old Testament, like that of salvation, liberation theologians maintain, cannot be interpreted as an individual phenomenon. Because of the influence of Greek dualism on our interpretation of the Bible:

We have lost our knowledge of what sin is. . . . We must get beyond the partial notion of sin as a merely individual violation of some law. We must recover the social dimension of sin as the annulment of God's presence among human beings and domination of evil which prohibits the freedom of God's children.[13]

Although it is true that sin is rooted in individual attitudes, these are expressed in social practices. Insofar as social practices and institutions are unjust, sin is embedded in society. Furthermore, to the extent that one fails to act to change unjust social structures, one is in a state of sin. Just as doing justice is required to know God, failing to act justly is alienation from God. "When justice does not exist, God is not known; he is absent."[14] We love God only by loving our neighbor. If we do not love our neighbor then we do not love God. But love for one's neighbor is not an inward or purely "spiritual" state. It is working to bring about a just society. Sin, on the other hand, is a hardening of the heart against the just complaints of the oppressed. It is being content and complacent in the face of injustice.

To be free from sin is to have a change of heart and be converted from one's former way of life. Conversion, then, as understood by liberation theologians, is not "an inward-looking private attitude, but a process which occurs in the socio-economic, political and cultural medium in which life goes on, and which is to be transformed."[15] To conceive of conversion as involving only the receipt of supernatural grace, is, in their opinion, to falsify the Bible. "To be converted is to commit oneself to the process of the liberation of the poor and oppressed, to commit oneself lucidly, realistically, and concretely."[16] Conversion requires that one undertake effective action to change the structures of unjust societies. "Without a change in these structures there is no authentic conversion."[17]

Only the individual who has undergone conversion can be said to live a spiritual life. Although the spiritual life includes prayer and reflection it is not one of withdrawal into a private, inner, realm. To live a spiritual life is to live in "a concrete manner, inspired by the Spirit, of living the Gospel; it is a definite way of living 'before the Lord,' in solidarity with all men. . . ."[18] Living in solidarity with others must not be thought of as merely a means of knowing God. "The neighbor is not an occasion, an instrument for becoming closer to God. We are dealing with a real love of man for his own sake and not 'for the love of God,'. . . . This is the only way to have a true encounter with him."[19]

Faith, Justice and Violence in Latin American Liberation Theology

Liberation theologians believe that human being's most profound encounter with God is to be found in the life of Christ. In his life, love of humanity and love of God came together in inseparable unity. The Gospel of Luke, they point out, records that the very first act of Jesus' ministry was to identify his mission with the new covenant proclaimed in Isaiah by reading the following passage in the synagogue.

The Spirit of the Lord is upon me, because he has anointed me to preach good news to the poor. He has sent me to proclaim release to the captives, and recovering of sight to the blind, to set at liberty those who are oppressed, to proclaim the acceptable year of the Lord
(Luke 4:16–21, Isaiah 61:1–2)

Since the year of the Lord was a period during which all debts were canceled, liberation theologians argue that the good news announced here was first of all a promise of economic liberation. The sight promised the blind, and the liberty proclaimed for the oppressed, were also physical sight and political freedom, not spiritual insight and so-called inner freedom. Jesus' mission, they maintain, has been distorted by being "overly spiritualized."[20] He displayed equal concern, they insist, for man's physical and spiritual needs. Any distinction between spiritual and temporal salvation, therefore, rests on a dualism of spirit and matter which is foreign to the Bible. The people Christ addressed lived in one world, not two. Neither they nor Christ distinguished profane from spiritual history. There is only one history, the history into which Christ was born.[21] The central message of Christianity is that God has been made flesh. Christian salvation is, thus, not something to be obtained in an afterlife, but in history. It is not a consequence of believing in certain abstractions, of words alone—but of an encounter with the word made man. To be a Christian, then, is not primarily to accept certain doctrines, but to follow the way of Christ.

Christian faith, liberation theologians believe, should be thought of as a journey into the unknown undertaken with confidence in God.

This is what was demanded of the one Paul calls the father of faith: "Yahweh said to Abraham, 'Leave your country, your family and your father's house, for the land I will show you'" (Gen. 12:1). Faith is entry into a new world, one in a way unforeseeable. It is making a journey without knowing beforehand the route we shall be following (John 21:18).[22]

Faith, like salvation, liberation theologians insist, is not a private matter. To the contrary it is "the very negation of retreat into oneself."[23] It requires a life of witness in which the deed is more important than the word. In support of this doctrine they cite the statement in James (2:14–26) that faith without good deeds is dead. They also quote Matthew: "It is not those who say to me, 'Lord, Lord,' who will enter the kingdom of heaven, but the person who does the will of my Father in heaven" (Matt. 7:21). Faith is for them above all love for one's fellow human being. "Anyone who says 'I love God,' and hates his brother, is a liar, since a man who does not love the brother whom he has seen, it cannot be that he loves God whom he has not seen" (John 4:20). However, as noted earlier, liberation theologians do not think that love for one's fellow man can be reduced to merely having good will towards others, or even to engaging in charitable acts on behalf of the unfortunate. It requires one to take positive action to change the status quo.

Christian love, liberation theologians argue, is fundamentally *subversive*. Love demands that one act on the behalf of the poor and oppressed. But to act in favor of the poor and oppressed is to act against the interests of the rich and powerful. It is to participate in class struggle.

The Gospel announces the love of God for all people and calls us to love as he loves. But to accept class struggle means to decide for some people and against others. . . . To love all men does not mean avoiding confrontations. . . . Universal love is that which in solidarity with the oppressed seeks also to liberate the oppressors from their . . . power, from their ambition, and from their selfishness. . . . One loves the oppressors by liberating them from their inhuman condition as oppressors. . . . But this cannot be achieved except by resolutely opting for the oppressed, that is, by combating the oppressive class.[24]

The thesis that Christian love must be subversive of the status quo is the most controversial doctrine of liberation theology. For many, if not most Christians, the doctrine that in order to express universal love one must engage in class struggle seems both contradictory and contrary to the gospel. Thus, critics respond that Jesus did not teach violence and revolution; he taught men to love their enemies and to turn the other cheek. Nor did he come to liberate men from economic and social injustice, but to bring them eternal salvation.

Liberation theologians reply to this criticism by arguing that this interpretation of Jesus' teaching puts undue emphasis on isolated passages of the gospel. It is true, they concede, that Jesus was not a Zealot calling for violent overthrow of the Roman empire. But he also did not preach that salvation was a purely private affair. Had he done so he would never have been condemned to death by the religious and political leaders of the day. Jesus was crucified because the rich and powerful correctly saw him as a threat to the status quo. The social and political dimensions of Jesus' teaching and actions have been obscured because the New Testament has been interpreted in terms of Greek dualism. A more historical reading shows that Christ's attitude toward violence is much more complicated than traditionally believed.[25]

Liberation theologians argue that there are three possible attitudes which Christians may take toward violence.[26] They may, like Charles de Foucauld and the Little Brothers of the Gospel, attempt to mitigate the effects of violence by living with and aiding its victims, but without fighting on their behalf. They may, as Martin Luther King Jr. did, adopt a strategy of nonviolent action intended to provoke people of good will into helping change the situation of the oppressed. Or, finally, they may follow the path of Camilo Torres who concluded that in the situation in which he found himself violent revolution was the only way he could effectively express his love for the oppressed. According to these liberation theologians, Jesus seems to have adopted the first position, but his teachings do not rule out the other two. Although one should only engage in violence as a last resort there are situations in which it is justifiable. Self-defense and the just war are examples. What Christians cannot do is remain silent and inactive when confronted with oppression.

Liberation theologians believe that European and North American theologians who denounce the use of violence by Latin Americans to overthrow oppressive regimes, but who do not protest United States economic and military assistance which keeps those regimes in power, are acting hypocritically. Revolutionary violence in Latin America, liberation theologians maintain, is a justifiable response to institutional violence—to regimes which stay in power by the use of torture and terror. In denouncing the former but not the latter, European and North American theologians exhibit ideological captivity. They identify themselves with the Pharaohs of the world rather than with the poor and the oppressed. In the opinion of the liberation theologians only Christians who have adopted absolute pacifism and are actively working to change United States foreign policy in Latin America can justifiably criticize the use of revolutionary violence. But, whether revolutionary violence in a given situation is justifiable from a Christian perspective cannot be decided by appeal to abstract principles. It can only be decided by a conscientious examination of the facts of the situation in light of a total commitment to the poor and oppressed.

European and North American theologians influenced by the Western philosophical tradition, liberation theologians claim, seem to conceive of theology as a kind of abstract, neutral discipline. Liberation theologians believe to the contrary:

All genuine theology has its point of departure in the life of faith. Faith is after all what leads us to become disciples of Christ, and theology is about discipleship. Discipleship is not simply listening to a teaching. Before all else discipleship is the following of Christ.[27]

Theology is, therefore, said by liberation theologians to be the "second act," grounded on an initial act of faith.[28] Since faith is primarly a matter of deeds rather than words, it follows that:

Theological reasoning is an effort on the part of concrete persons to form and think out their faith in determinant circumstances, to plan activities and make interpretations that play a role in the real-life occurrences and confrontations of a given society.[29]

Theology as conceived by liberation theologians is thus primarily concerned with *orthopraxis* rather than *orthodoxy*.[30] They are less interested in inculcating Christian beliefs than in finding allies in the struggle against poverty and oppression. To reiterate an earlier theme, they do not believe that it is those who say "Lord," "Lord," but rather those who do his work who are the faithful.

Liberation theologians are ready to borrow doctrines from any source which will help them work out an orthopraxis of faith. Since they have frequently appropriated Marxist social analysis, this has led to the charge that they are Marxists. Although most of them believe that revolution is necessary to redistribute economic resources in Latin America, they deny that they are Marxists in the sense in which that term denotes a philosophical system. They reject, for example, the doctrines of atheism, deterministic materialism, and the thesis that religion is always an opiate of the people which are characteristic of Marxism.[31]

Critics charge that liberation theologians reduce the gospel to ideology. Although they admit that this is a danger, liberation theologians do not think they are in a unique position with regard to this danger. They point out that criticism of their position is usually made by people who consider themselves impartial, objective observers. In fact, however, the critics are people who benefit from the present system. For them to claim neutrality is to adopt an ideology in favor of the status quo. Furthermore, one cannot be neutral and claim to be a Christian. Christian faith demands that one take a stance in favor of the poor and oppressed. When one reads the Bible from this perspective, Jose Miguez Bonino claims, so-called "'scientific,' 'historical,' or 'objective' exegesis reveals itself as full of ideological presuppositions."[32] One comes to realize that:

The ideological appropriation of the Christian doctrine of reconciliation by the liberal capitalist system in order to conceal the brutal fact of class and imperialist exploitation and conflict is one—if not *the*—major heresy of our time.[33]

I think that it is evident from the foregoing that liberation theology is not only an attempt by Latin American theologians to think through their faith in their particular circumstances, but is also a major challenge to current conceptions of faith and theology in Europe and North America. My goal in this article has been to present a systematic interpretation which makes these challenges explicit. Although I believe that a number of legitimate criticisms may be brought against liberation theology, simplistic responses, such as Michael Novak's labeling it a "theological fad," or charges such as those that it glorifies violence and reduces the gospel to ideology, are not adequate ways of meeting these challenges. Only a reexamination of the teachings of Christ regarding the social and political order, a more sophisticated hermeneutics, a clarification of the roles belief and action play in Christian faith, and a more profound analysis of the nature and moral status of violence can meet the challenges liberation theology poses. Above all, however, liberation theology challenges us to reevaluate and change the consequences which our life-styles have for the "wretched of the earth."

NOTES

1. For a discussion by liberation theologians of traditional conceptions of faith and theology see especially; Gustavo Gutierrez, *A Theology of Liberation* (Maryknoll, NY: Orbis Books, 1973), Chapters One and Four. See also Jose Miguez Bonino, *Doing Theology in a Revolutionary Situation* (Philadelphia: Fortress Press, 1975), Chapter Five.
2. Juan Louis Segundo, *The Liberation of Theology* (Maryknoll, NY: Orbis Books, 1976), 139.
3. Ibid.
4. Ibid., 139–40.
5. Ibid., 140.
6. Ibid., 134.
7. Ibid.
8. Ibid., 142.
9. Ibid., 143.
10. For discussion of political theology by liberation theologians see Gutierrez, Chapter Eleven; Segundo, Chapter Five; and Bonino, Chapter Seven; see also Hugo Assman, *Theology For a Nomad Church* (Maryknoll, NY: Orbis Books, 1976).
11. Bonino, 89.
12. See especially Gustavo Gutierrez, *The Power of the Poor in History*, (Maryknoll, NY: Orbis Books, 1982), Chapter One.
13. Ignacio Ellacuria, *Freedom Made Flesh* (Maryknoll, NY: Orbis Books, 1976), 151.
14. Guiterrez, *A Theology of Liberation*, 195.
15. Gutierrez in *The Mystical and Political Dimension of the Christian Faith*, edited by Claude Geffre and Gustavo Gutierrez (New York: Herder and Herder, 1974), 66.
16. Gutierrez, *A Theology of Liberation*, 205.
17. Ibid.
18. Ibid., 204.
19. Ibid., 202.
20. See especially Ellacuria, op. cit., 120 ff.
21. See in particular Enrique Dussel, *History and the Theology of Liberation* (Maryknoll, NY: Orbis Books, 1976).
22. Gutierrez, *The Power of the Poor in History*, 20.
23. Ibid., 67.
24. Gutierrez, *A Theology of Liberation*, 275–76.
25. For a discussion by liberation theologians on Christ's attitude toward violence see especially Ellacuria, Chapters 1–4, and Jose P. Miranda, *Marx and the Bible* (Maryknoll, NY Orbis Books, 1974).

Faith, Justice and Violence in Latin American Liberation Theology

26. Although most liberation theologians believe that there are situations in which violence is justified, some adopt positions similar to that of Martin Luther King, Jr. The most notable of these is Dom Helder Camara. See especially his book *Spiral of Violence* (Denville, NJ: Dimensions Books, 1971).

27. Gutierrez, *The Power of the Poor in History*, 90.

28. See Gutierrez, *A Theology of Liberation*, Chapter One.

29. Gutierrez, *The Power of the Poor in History*, 212.

30. See Gutierrez, *A Theology of Liberation*, Chapter One; and Bonino, 168–73.

31. See, for example, Bonino, Chapter Six.

32. Ibid., 102.

33. Ibid., 121.

6
Is Faith in God Necessary for a Just Society? Insights from Liberation Theology
WILLIAM R. JONES

I have selected liberation theology as the perspective from which to discuss whether faith in God is necessary for a just society. To avoid repetition, I shall refer to this as the QUESTION. There are several compelling reasons to seat liberation theology as a participant in this debate. It is one of the major movements today where the QUESTION is addressed not only theoretically but existentially in the daily life and death choices of millions. Moreover, because the goal of a just society is explicit in its announced purpose to eradicate economic, social and political oppression (hereafter esp),[1] we can examine how it links esp goals and theological norms as one of the concrete answers to the QUESTION. Equally important is the fact that liberation theology has conducted a broad, though not exhaustive, audit of theological systems to assess which concepts of God are foundations for oppression, as well as which must be affirmed to correct the unjust community. In all of this, we find a wealth of case studies that help us to confirm or disconfirm various answers to the QUESTION.

However, certain preliminary matters must be treated. Any response to a question, especially the type we are considering here, should be approached as a response to two distinct but related questions. First, there is the logically prior issue: what is the meaning or sense of the stated question; or, for our purpose, the QUESTION? This issue commands our attention because a question is seldom, if ever, self-interpreting; nor is its meaning self-evident. We invariably imprison the question in a specific context as well as a particular universe of discourse. Additionally, unstated and question-begging presuppositions, even a hidden agenda, may be camouflaged and packed into the question. Thus, if we bypass this initial determination of the "real" question, not only are we apt to respond to a question that was not asked, but we are also likely to give certain answers a validity they have not yet earned. For these reasons, it is doubly important to isolate the multiple senses of the quesiton. Given this understanding of what is at stake, let me identify the questions that I detect within the QUESTION.

Questions Within the Question

The QUESTION can be reduced to the following questions or issues, although they are, obviously, not exhaustive.

(1) *What are the prerequisites for a moral system?* More precisely, what are the necessary and/or sufficient conditions for a viable moral code? If we accent this dimension of the QUESTION, the focus of the debate is whether theism is necessary and/or sufficient for morality. If the answer is affirmative, several other questions must be addressed: Which *variety* of theism? And the related issue, which *features* of theism? Is it the transcendent dimension, an ontological ground, a supra-human absolute, etc.?

An analysis of the commonly established connection between immortality and immorality identifies the drift that the argument would take if this sense of the QUESTION is honored. Luther, and more recently, Francis Schaeffer[2] among others, argued that immorality increases as belief in immortality decreases. Humans, it is concluded, adopt an "eat, drink, and be merry" morality if they think that there is nothing beyond the grave, especially no eternal punishment for ungodly acts committed in this life. The heart of this understanding is some belief about God as judge and punisher of the evildoer as a prerequisite for a moral code. In sum, the QUESTION forces us to identify the specific roles or attributes of God that the just society requires.

(2) Focusing the debate on the issue of prerequisites also forces us to consider a *logically prior* issue that the QUESTION appears to ignore: the *refutation* of moral nihilism. Since moral nihilism claims that morality is an illusion, that there are no moral facts or truths, in short, that morality is impossible, it constitutes the unavoidable threshold issue for any moral system. Given these claims, no code of morality is justifiable a priori. If we want to ground our just society on a foundation that is not question-begging, we must rebut the claims of moral nihilism. The QUESTION, unfortunately, states the issue as if moral nihilism had been disproved. In launching the debate at this point, where it is allowed that a moral system and the just society are both possible, the only unresolved issue is the

content of the moral system. In this, there are unmistakable signs of begging the question.

What is at stake is the logical and theological maneuverability available to construct a moral code. Also at stake is whether the initial "taking a position" that the threshold issue of nihilism compels, establishes some of the parameters within which we must respond to the QUESTION. If we, for instance, are forced to invoke a subjective principal to rebut nihilism, internal consistency and coherence command us to construct our moral system within these restraints.

My only concern here is to highlight three things; that a refutation is necessary, that we identify the norms used in the refutation and that these norms must be part of the formula for constructing the moral system. Otherwise, the refutation of nihilism is a sham, and we are back at square one, the original threshold issue.

(3) Another dimension of the question, which requires illumination, is the connection between faith in God and legitimating the blueprint for the just society. Given that the just society must be legitimated if it is to survive, the QUESTION yields the following meanings: Is (a) a *theistic*[3] legitimation or (b) a *specific*[4] form of theism necessary? A third meaning requires a more detailed discussion: (c) Is *God* or *faith* in God the foundation for the just society? It is important to decide whether God (i.e., a transcendent being) or whether belief in God, transcendent or not, is the minimal requirment. As in the case of Santa Claus, whether there is an objective reality corresponding to the content of our belief is not important. Or, as in the case of the Wizard of Oz, belief in the Wizard's power was efficacious though the Wizard actually lacked the powers ascribed to him.

(4) The final unpacking of the QUESTION must tease out the meaning of the just society since we lack a consensus about its essentials. One need only examine Hitler's model of the just society, or South Africa, or the slave period in American to recognize that gross inequalities are characteristically basic structures of the just society. Indeed, one is hard-pressed to isolate some form of dehumanization that has not been religiously sanctioned as part of the just or good society. Moreover, when one considers that the authority and name of God are commonly borrowed to support both the just and unjust society, it becomes clear that our reply to the QUESTION must accommodate a response to this query: Is faith in God necessary for the *unjust* society? Indeed, if we extract from

Is Faith in God Necessary for a Just Society?

liberation theology's method, we would have to conclude that we cannot adequately answer the QUESTION until the connection between God and the unjust society has been explored.

With the foregoing analysis as background, let me indicate the focus of this paper. My response to (1) is that theism or faith in God is neither sufficient nor necessary for the just society. This is discussed only tangentially. With regard to (2), I find Pascal's and Camus's[5] refutation of nihilism persuasive. Nihilism, they demonstrate, is ultimately inconsistent, affirming some value that cannot be defended by the nihilist's own claims. Moreover, because the inner logic of nihilism is self-negating, it leads, if consistently practiced, to its advocate's demise.

This way of rebutting nihilism requires that we adopt at least two norms: a method of internal criticism and the common distinction between what is practiced and what is preached. If the negation of nihilism is to stick, I suggest that these norms must become part of one's own theological apparatus. This is not consistently practiced by most thinkers, thus raising the issue of a question-begging element in their system.

The focus of this paper will be questions (3) and (4).

ESP Oppression: A Preliminary Analysis

Liberation theology addresses the QUESTION from several angles, two of which are germane to our discussion: those concepts of the divine that must be rejected because faith in them maintains the unjust society, and those that must be affirmed if the unjust society is to be reformed. It is important to appreciate the radical difference between these pictures of the divine. This demands, however, that we grasp liberation theology's view of the nature and operation of oppression, for it is through this that liberation theology defines the just society and determines which concepts of God are compatible or antithetical.

It is also important to note that liberation theology approaches the QUESTION from a specific context that establishes the framework for its method. It is a context in which oppression is firmly entrenched and undergirded by a specific belief and value system. This means that liberation theology approaches the QUESTION from the perspective of theological *deconstruction,* isolating and exorcising the ideological roots of oppression. Consequently, liberation theology approves those images of the divine that must serve as the antitoxin for the conceptual toxin of oppression. For this reason it is more accurate to speak of those theological categories that support the unjust society and those that counteract that support. The latter is not necessarily the preferred picture of the divine that would emerge if one approached the QUESTION from a context in which oppression is not present.

Oppression, for liberation theology, is a defining element of the unjust society, and its advocates assert that any authentic definition of sin in the Judeo-Christian tradition must include esp oppression as a necessary ingredient. Speaking in general terms, oppression structures the society to maintain a specific human group at the top of the esp ladder, while chaining another to the bottom. The oppressor, accordingly manufactures fundamental esp inequalities that endure from generation to generation.

These trans-generational inequalities[6]—and this is the crucial feature for our discussion—are justified on the grounds that they have an ontological foundation. This point must be highlighted if we want to avoid the common misunderstanding that liberation theology is radically egalitarian, condemning all hierarchical arrangements. Speaking more accurately, liberation theology mistrusts hierarchical inequalities that are trans-generational and ontologically legitimated, because these two features conspire to maintain the unjust society. Inequalities that result from human exploitation—that are not the product of nature or the supernatural—are easily misinterpreted as ontologically based if the trans-generational factor is prominent. A creature from Mars would be hard-pressed to determine if the lower GRE scores of blacks, for instance, indicate genetic inferiority or trans-generational oppression.

If we move from a general to a more detailed description of oppression, the following should be accented:

(1) Oppression can be analyzed from two different perspectives, both of which are critical for assessing the connection between God and the unjust society. On one hand, oppression can be reduced to *institutional structures:* this is its esp or *objective* dimension. On the other, we can condense oppression to the *belief* and *value* system that is its anchoring principle. This, for our purposes, comprises its *subjective* factor.

If this point is understood, it should not be surprising that the most cursory historical analysis will show that gross inequalities, indeed identical ones, are characteristic of both the unjust and the just society. God has and can be invoked to support and attack the

Is Faith in God Necessary for a Just Society?

same inequalities. Liberation theology draws several critical conclusions from this. It is on this basis that a distinction is drawn between the pre- and post-enlightened oppressed. The latter interprets the objective inequalities as negative, as hostile to her/his highest good; whereas the pre-enlightened do not. Wherein lies the difference? Not, as many believe, in a marked difference in the *objective* situation of each, but in the dissimilar theological grids used to assess these inequalities.

(2) The inner logic of oppression divides the human family into at least two distinct groups, hierarchically arranged along lines of superiority and inferiority. In-group, out-group; human, sub-human; male, female; black, white; rich, poor; Christian, Jew; Aryan, non-Aryan; master, slave are familiar examples.

(3) The hierarchical division is correlated with a gross imbalance of *power,* as well as unequal access to life-sustaining and life-enhancing *resources* and *privileges*. The alleged superior group will possess the unobscure *surplus* and the alleged inferior group, a grossly disproportionate *deficit*. To make the same point in different terms, the alleged superior groups will have the *most* of whatever the society defines as the *best* and the *least* of the *worst*. In stark contrast, the alleged inferior group will have the *least* of the *best* and the *most* of the *worst*.

(4) The hierarchical division may be a necessary condition for oppression, but it is never sufficient. For oppression (i.e., the unjust society) to be born, the hierarchical division must be coupled with a gross imbalance of power enabling the alleged superior group—and here we come to the next controlling feature of oppression—to *institutionalize* its esp rank order.

To avoid a fatal misunderstanding, it is necessary to explore in more detail the importance of the institutional factor. Examining the distinction between racism and racialism provides the nuances needed for an accurate interpretation. Racialism is a belief system that affirms both the reality of superior and inferior groups, and that ontological factors, natural or supernatural, are the ultimate foundations for this hierarchical division.

Racism, however, is not the inevitable product of racialism. Though racialism may be prominent in a group, racism does not always develop. And though reprehensible, its consequences are not as deadly. For racialism to blossom into racism, the racialist must amass power that places the organization and control of society in her/his hands. The Nation of Islam (the so-called Black Muslims), under the leadership of Elijah Muhammed, is a case in point. Tracing the genesis of whites to the machinations of a Frankenstein-type scientist, Elijah Muhammed affirmed the superiority of blacks and the inferiority of whites; hence, the explicit racialism. But the Nation of Islam never accumulated the power to institutionalize its racialism as the esp environment where white America had to live.

Given this understanding, a critical factor differentiating the unjust from the just society is the distribution of esp power. Accordingly, liberation theology concludes that an adequate response to the QUESTION must address the connection between faith in God and the esp institutionalization of power.

Oppression, Quietism and the Divine Authority

This controlling feature of oppression brings us to the heart of our discussion. The hierarchical division, with the accompanying inequalities of power and resources institutionally installed, all of this is alleged to be grounded in ultimate reality, God or nature.

This feature pinpoints the mechanism that oppression uses to maintain itself. To perpetuate the unjust society, the oppressor must persuade the oppressed to accept their lot at the bottom of the esp totem pole, and to embrace these inequalities as good and/or inevitable. It is here, as Benjamin Mays instructs us, that the linkage between one's concept of God and the unjust society is most evident.

The Negro's social philosophy and his idea of God go hand in hand. Certain theological ideas enable Negros to endure hardship, suffer pain, and withstand maladjustment, but . . . do not necessarily motivate them to strive to eliminate the source of the evils they suffer. . . . The idea has persisted that hard times are indicative of the fact that the Negro is God's chosen vessel and that God is disciplining him for the express purpose of bringing him out victoriously and triumphantly in the end. The idea has also persisted that "the harder the cross, the brighter the crown." Believing this about God, the Negro . . . has stood back and suffered much without trying aggressively to realize to the full his needs in the world.[7]

What Mays is calling attention to here is the connection between quietism and our understanding of God's nature and operation in history. Whether the wretched of the earth embrace or take any means necessary to eradicate their maldistributed suffering depends upon the kind of God in which their faith resides. A review of a classic novel, written more than a century ago, reveals the same insight.

> Altogether *Jane Eyre* . . . is preeminently an anti-Christian proposition. There is throughout it a murmuring against the comforts of the rich and against the privations of the poor, which as far as each individual is concerned is a murmuring against God's appointment.[8]

To make clearer the connection that liberation theology sees between our God concept and the unjust society, it is necessary to look briefly at the inner logic of quietism and its kith and kin relations to oppression. Quietism, in the lexicon of liberation theology, is a refusal to reform the status quo, especially where traditional institutions and values are involved. Concession, accommodation, and acquiescence are its distinguishing marks.

Quietism becomes our operating principle if we believe that esp correction is (a) *unnecessary,* (b) *impossible,* or (c) *inappropriate.* Corrective action is unnecessary, for instance, if we believe that some agent other than ourselves will handle it. Another quietist tendency is found in the familiar adage: "If it ain't broke, don't fix it." This bespeaks the attitude that correction is gratuitous if the ideal is already present, in the process of being realized, or if changing things will make them worse. We are also pushed to quietism if remedial action is impossible. We reach this conclusion when we encounter an invincible force or when the item to be corrected is a structure of ultimate reality.

With this analysis as background, we can now describe the mechanism of oppression more adequately. The unjust society maintains itself by claiming that its fundamental institutions and its hierachy of roles and status are the product of or in conformity with reality itself. By invoking the supernatural/divine order—one could just as well appeal to nature, the created order—as its foundation, we accomplish several things that the maintenance of oppression requires. On one hand, we establish a supra-human foundation that, by virtue of its superior power, compels our conformity and obedience. Human power can never win against divine omnipotence; "Our arms too short to box with God." On the other, we guarantee the goodness and moral superiority of the existing social order.

As the review of *Jane Eyre* shows us, rearranging the social hierarchy is unthinkable if the esp order expresses the will of God. Whatever status we have is just: it is the station that God intends for us; what is, is what ought to be. Given this understanding, esp remodeling would be sinful rebellion against God. Even if we had the necessary power to readjust things, esp remodeling would be blasphemous and therefore inappropriate. A similar conclusion would follow if we interpret esp suffering and inequalities as divine punishment.

The aforementioned mechanism of oppression should be examined from another perspective: its strategy to remove human choice, power and authority as causally involved in society's superstructures. To use Peter Berger's distinction[9], oppression locates traditional norms and institutions in *objective reality*—that which is external to the human mind and not created by our hands—not *objectivated reality*, i.e., that which is external to the human mind that we did create. Oppression, thus, reduces the conflict between the haves and have-nots to a cosmic skirmish between the human and the supra-human. The theological paradigm in liberation theology, as we will see, relocates the fray, making it a struggle between human combatants.

Theocentric Theism and the Logic of Injustice

Selecting a viable foundation for the just society is no simple matter. If the point of departure is the reality of an unjust society, as it is for liberation theology, a functional concept of God must serve two masters. It must counteract the extant God-consciousness already enlisted by the oppressor to guard her/his "sacred order," and it must also provide a sturdy foundation for the "new sacred order." These dual concerns must be executed in a manner compatible with the inner logic of each. Further, it must accommodate a legitimating authority that does not replicate the original theology of injustice. At the same time, however, it must provide the minimal sanctity that any institution requires for its longevity. Getting a handle on this is simplified if we interpret it from the background of our discussion of oppression/quietism. Using this approach, we can grasp which pictures of the divine have merit and which are useless in light of the foregoing criteria.

To draw up liberation theology's "most eligible list" of God candidates requires that we treat two opposing images of the divine, which I term *theocentric theism* and *humanocentric theism*. The former identifies the God concept that is most commonly associated with the unjust society, the latter with the just community. The distinc-

Is Faith in God Necessary for a Just Society?

tion between these competing pictures of the divine is clarified if we analyze how each specifies: (a) God's role and manner of operation in human history, and (b) the status and value of human freedom relative to divine freedom.

Taken to its logical extremes, theocentric theism affirms God's controlling and overruling sovereignty in history; whether the same claim is advanced for the natural order is unimportant for our discussion. To borrow the metaphor of the theater: God is the playwright, director, producer, star, agent, and critic. The inner logic of this way of thinking, as the following citation shows, relegates the human to the role of spectator or cheerleader for the "perfect play."

> There is only one almighty being whom we call God. He is eternal, infinite, invisible, perfectly wise and just. He created all things. . . . Everything was made in accordance with his plan and is dictated by his will. Everything has a cause and purpose, and nothing happens by chance or by luck. Man exists for God and not God for man, but men should pray to God who will consider their prayers in the enactment of his will.

> Cannot we believe that God so overrules man's actions that no matter how when or where he dies, he does not die a moment before God meant him to. . . . With the solitary exception of the act of sinful will, nothing is done in the world of which God is not the doer. . . . Suppose A willfully murders B. The act of sinful will on A's part is his free act and A alone is responsible. But he could not have murdered B unless God had willed it. He could have had no power at all against him except it had been given him from above.[10]

The import of this understanding of the divine for the unjust society is obvious: quietism is the outcome. Given this view of God's causal linkage to history, the eradication of oppression is aborted at the outset. The preconditions for esp correction are the beliefs that what is, is not what ought to be; that what is could be otherwise—even the opposite—and that what is not yet is what ought to be.

The inner logic of theocentric theism affirms the opposite sentiment, and we are back where Jane Eyre's reviewer left us. Whatever our station, we are where we ought to be; and we cannot dare, nor should we hope, to tear down what God has carefully planned and constructed.

William R. Jones

Humanocentric Theism: Antidote to Quietism

Given the inner logic of oppression, especially its maintenance code, its opponents must endorse theological constructs that are antithetical to theocentric theism. Room must be made for the exercise of human freedom and authority with regard to at least the substructures of history. Such is the inner logic of humanocentric theism. It affirms the radical freedom of the human, but within a *theistic* framework—hence its difference from humanism that assigns a similar freedom to the human.

Humanocentric theism, as the adjective suggests, elevates human freedom relative to the sphere of history; the human is given the status of co-determining power with God, at least up to the eschaton. It also affirms a view of divine sovereignty that extends human freedom to other areas that once were under the direct sway of the divine, thus refuting the hypothesis: "If God exists, man is nothing; if man exists...."[11] To avoid collapsing humanocentric theism into humanism, it is important to note that the human has the exalted status of co-determining power by virtue of God's gracious endowment. Moreover, the ground for this endowment is the self-limitation of God's overruling authority in human history.

One can easily cull examples of this picture of the divine from the liberation theologians. For my illustrations here, however, I prefer to draw upon theologians not identified as liberationists. In this way, I can correct some common misconceptions. One inaccurate interpretation restricts the scope and popularity of this position to those concerned only with a self-serving esp agenda. A second misunderstanding collapses humanocentric theism into humanism because human freedom is accented in both. The following descriptions from William D. Cobb and Eliezer Berkovits correct both misconceptions.

Arguing for "man as moral creator," Cobb opts for a "moral universe in the making." For Cobb, the Judeo-Christian affirmation of man as created in "in the image of God" means:

Man was not intented to be simply another natural being but to be an active participant in and creator of the moral orders of the Universe.... If he allows [the external moral (and natural) orders] to rule him completely, then he is living "heteronomously" and ... in direct contravention of the will of God for his creation. The will of God ... does not consist of specific rules and goals for human beings to conform to and seek, but of an *intention* that men and women exercise their creative moral powers to construct a *human* universe of *moral* order confluent with yet transcendent of the *natural* universe of *physical* order.... Indeed we might say that God created man with the intention that man should "make what *God* did not make" and what is more, that man should "make what God did not *think* to make" as a consequence of God's gracious self-limitation of his own power in the act of creating man ... [God has limited his own power] for the sake of giving man "space" in which to be more than a "robot" or a "puppet" in a "stage play."[12]

Eliezer Berkovits advances a similar view as a central motif of Judeo-biblical faith.

Man alone can create value; God is value. But if man alone is the creator of values ... then he must have freedom of choice and freedom of decision. And his freedom must be respected by God himself. God cannot as a rule intervene whenever man's use of freedom displeases him.... If there is to be man, he must be allowed to make his choices in freedom.[13]

With these descriptions as background we can now summarize the value of humanocentric theism as an antidote for quietism and oppression. (1) It cuts off the theological and moral escape route commonly used by the oppressor. The oppressor can no longer point to anything but the human being as the sustaining force behind the unjust society. (2) Central to humanocentric theism is the belief that "God has no hands but our hands," that "all is in our hands." Until the oppressed accept this belief and, accordingly, see themselves as centers of power and their communities as collective sources of transforming power, it is doubtful that they will become active agents for their own liberation. Nor are they likely to assume responsibility for eradicating their oppression as long as they believe that God will miraculously intervene and release them from the oppressor's clutches. (3) Further, it effectively de-legitimates those unjust structures, already in place, that carry the "divine" stamp of approval. This de-sanctification, as we have noted, is a sine qua non for esp change.

Humanocentric Theism: Problems and Implications

The concern of this paper has been to show how a particular theological perspective would address the QUESTION. However, even if we grant absolute merit and accuracy to liberation theology's analysis, which I do not, a number of unresolved issues and nagging problems remain. I consider the following to be the most important for our discussion:

(1) If our purpose is to reform the unjust society *where nature and supernatural, i.e., ontological absolutes, have been its legitimating foundation*, we face an immediate dilemma that Peter Berger's[14] formula helps us define. Given that what humans have created, other humans can change, societies are loath to ground morality on human authority. The need to protect the moral code from whim and caprice recommends the strategy of the divine logo. However, as we have seen, this carries within it the germ of quietism and its potential for oppression. Thus, the esp reformer must deabsolutize the extant esp order to make place for the new, the just social system. This de-sanctification of the divine bulwarks is almost always advanced in the name of the divine. The result of this is pregnant with implications for the QUESTION.

(2) The clash of absolute and counter-absolute, of God's commandment to conform and to transform, diminishes the authority of absolutes per se. Absolutes are seen as devices of legitimation and not solely as divine revelation. This relocates the issue so that the issue becomes the *authority* by which to legitimate the legitmating apparatus. The legitimator must be legitimated, and here we appear to be plunged into an infinite regress where ultimately the human being, as the measure, must function as moral creator; in sum, the position of humanocentric theism.

But this is not without its improbable consequences for the just society. Does the "God has no hands but our hands" philosophy, or the elevation of the human to co-determining power, mean that everything is permitted? The problem of nihilism confronts us here again. (I would add in passing that my analysis of the most dehumanizing instances in human history have as their explicit legitimation the logo of the absolute—nature or supernatural—not the principle of human freedom and authority that informs humanocentric theism.)

(3) Given the insights of humanocentric theism, we are also pushed to ask what it means to advance God, the transcendent, as the grounds for the just society? Does it mean more than the claim that the transcendent is both the ground for human freedom/autonomy to operate as moral creator and foundation of the world in which this freedom is exercised? Or does it mean that ultimate reality sponsors, and thus guarantees, the ultimate triumph of spe-

Is Faith in God Necessary for a Just Society?

cific activities in human history? That is, once humanity is given the staus of moral creator, does *ontological priority*—that is, the transcendent—still establish *moral priority*? It seems clear that the species of human freedom endorsed by humanocentric theism precludes, at the very least, any immediate movement from ontology to ethics, from the "is" to the "ought," without the intermediate operation of human evaluation.

(4) Humanocentric theism is not without its quietist dimension. This potential becomes visible when we note that history here becomes open-ended and multi-valued, capable of supporting either the just or the unjust society. Does not the inner logic of humanocentric theism remove God from anyone's side? If this is so, then an oppressed group, that is both powerless and a numerical minority, is susceptible to defeatism. David is reluctant to challenge Goliath unless he or she believes that God will tip the scales in her/his favor.

(5) The previous comment points to an unsettled question in humanocentric theism that bears upon its attractiveness as a counterstrategy to oppression. It also raises a larger issue, also unsettled, that bears upon its value as the foundation for the just society. Having argued for the self-limitation of the divine freedom to counter the unjust society, are we forced to the conclusion that marked an early stage of Howard Burkle's theological evolution? "God," he argued, "cannot guarantee the ultimate triumph of the good.... The good may be forever blocked.... The creature retains a veto even though he had nothing to do with the determination that gave him birth."[15]

If this is so, does the just society have an *ontological* base or warrant that is superior to its rival? Are both equally "right" as far as reality is structured? If not, how is the rank order to be determined? If so, why make the supreme sacrifice to usher in the just society if its day in the sun is in doubt?

NOTES

1. This is the shorthand expression for economic, social, and political.
2. *The Christian Manifesto* and *Whatever Happened to the Human Race?* Both works are in *The Complete Works of Francis A. Schaeffer: A Christian Worldview* Vol. 5 (Westchester, Illinois: Crossway Books, 1982).

3. Humanism, for instance, would be excluded if this is answered affirmatively.
4. Cf. Schaeffer's analysis, for instance in *Whatever Happened to the Human Race?*, that only specific forms of theism, i.e., his interpretation of Reformed Christianity can be the foundation for the just society.
5. See the *Pensees* and *The Myth of Sisyphus*.
6. The transgenerational feature differentiates oppression from catastrophe, which can also be enormous. Since, however, the catastrophic event does not visit the same group generation after generation, the factor of maldistribution is less acute.
7. Benjamin Mays, *The Negro's God: As Reflected in His Literature* (New York: Atheneum, 1969), 155.
8. M. A. Stoddard, "Review of *Vanity Fair* and *Jane Eyre*," in the *Quarterly Review* 84 (Dec. 1848), 173–174.
9. Peter Berger, *The Sacred Canopy* (New York: Doubleday, 1969), 11–12.
10. Robert P. Green argued this in 1700 in *The Problem of Evil, Being an Attempt to Show that the Existence of Sin and Pain in the World is not Inconsistent with the Goodness and Power of God*.
11. Jean-Paul Sartre, *The Devil and the Good Lord* (New York: Vintage, 1962), 141.
12. William D. Cobb, "Morality in the Making: A New Look at Some Old Foundations," *The Christian Century*, 1–8 January 1975.
13. Eliezer Berkovits, *Faith After the Holocaust* (New York: KTAV Publishing House, 1973), 105.
14. "The historically crucial part of religion in the process of legitimation is explicable in terms of the unique capacity of religion to 'locate' human phenomena within a cosmic frame of reference. . . . The efficacy of religious legitimation can be brought home by asking a recipe question. . . . If one imagines oneself as a fully aware founder of a society . . . how can the feature of the institutional order be best ensured . . . ?Let the institutional order be so interpreted as to hide, as much as possible, its constructed character. Let the people forget that this order was established by men and continues to be dependent upon the consent of men. Let them believe that in acting out the institutional programs that have been imposed upon them, they are but realizing the deepest aspirations of their own being and putting themselves in harmony with the fundamental order of the universe." *The Sacred Canopy*, 33.
15. Howard Burkle, *The Non-Existence of God* (New York: Herder & Herder, 1969), 212.

7
The Creation of Just Social Order in Islam
ABDULAZIZ A. SACHEDINA

O You who believe! establish the justice, being witnesses for God. . . . (The Qur'an, 4:135)

The notion of God's kingdom on earth is shared by all major religions of the world. Christians, Jews, and Zoroastrians, who, at different times, were subjected to the rule of those who did not share their religious heritage, cherished their traditions concerning an expected deliverer, who will come and humble or destroy the forces of wickedness and establish the rule of justice and equity on earth—His kingdom. Such an expectation concerning the establishment of justice through a Messiah or Saoshyant of a divinely chosen line to end the suffering of the faithful and the rule of enemies of God is closely connected with the notion of ultimate salvation of the believers in each of those traditions. Although the notion of God's kingdom on earth has a specifically Judeo-Christian ring and the terms 'messiah' and 'messianic' imply a whole series of Jewish-Christian doctrines, it is, nevertheless, perfectly permissible to employ the terms in an Islamic context, bearing in mind the differences in which these traditions conceive the idea of establishment of justice on earth. As a simple matter of fact, the Christian, Jewish and Islamic traditions differ in the way the formula of an expected deliverer is employed in order to attain the final salvation.

The Christians think of a Second Coming, the Jews of one who is yet to come, while the Muslims conceive of a person who will "appear" or "rise against" existing intolerable secular authority. The term 'messianism' in the Islamic context, is frequently used to translate the notion of the creation of just social order by an eschatological figure, the Mahdi, who as the foreordained leader, "will rise" to launch a great social transformation to restore and adjust all things under devine guidance. The Islamic messiah, the Mahdi, thus, embodies the aspirations of his followers in the restoration of the ideals of Islam which will bring true and uncorrupted guidance to all mankind, creating a just social order and a world free from oppression in which the Islamic revelation will be the norm for all nations.

Although the similarity of Islamic messianism to Judeo-Christian ideas of the Messiah has been noted, the idea of the Mahdi held by Muslims has a distinctively Islamic coloring. As noted above, the idea of the establishment of justice is related to Islamic soteriology. The Islamic doctrine of salvation does not conceive of man as a sinner who must be saved through spiritual regeneration. Rather, it holds that since man is not dead in sin, he does not need spiritual rebirth. Nor does the doctrine conceive of salvation in nationalistic or ethnic terms, with the assurance of the realization of the kingdom of God in a promised land for a unique, autonomous community. The basic emphasis of Islamic salvation lies instead, in the historical responsibility of its followers, namely, the establishment of the ideal religio-political order with a worldwide membership of all those who believe in God and his relevation through Muhammad.

This responsibility carried within itself the obligation of Muslims to help one another build a new order of social life on the scale of divine justice which their faith had more and more obviously demanded. Furthermore, such an obligation implied the revolutionary challenge of Islam to any inimical order which might hamper its realization. The seeds of this responsibility, which were to bear fruits of rebellion throughout Islamic history in the persistent aspirations of its followers for a more just future, were sown by the Qur'anic requirement to establish a viable social order on earth that will be just and ethically based. The Prophet Muhammad was not only the founder of a new religion, but also the guardian of a new social order. His message was the natural outgrowth and context of the Qur'anic requirement; and, as such, it provided tremendous spiritual as well as moral impetus for the creation of a cosmopolitan just society. Consequently, in the years following the Prophet's death, a group of Muslims emerged who, dissatisfied with the state of affairs under the successors of Muhammad, looked backward to the early period of Islam, which was dominated by the brilliant figure of Muhammad, the Prophet and the statesman; a period which came to be regarded as the ideal epoch in Islamic history, unadulterated by the corrupt and worldly rulers of the expanding Islamic empire. This idealization of the Prophet himself gave rise to the notion of his being something more than an ordinary man; he must have been divinely chosen and, hence, the true leader who would guide his people to salvation.

This was the basis for Islamic messianism. Among certain Meccan tribes there existed messianic expectation even at the time Muhammad emerged as a prophet. These Arabs, who accepted neither Judaism or Christianity, were instead looking for a new revealed guidance, so that they might be even better guided than the two older communities. There were also some among the People of the Book (the Jews and Christians), according to the Qur'an, who had accepted the message delivered by Muhammad, seeing in his mission their messianic hopes fulfilled.[1] In a subsequent period, when the Islamic polity was established in Madina, the messianic expectations toward Muhammad became even more pronounced. Owing to the feeling of the special status of the Prophet, some of his followers began to look forward to the rule of an individual from among his descendants "whose name will be also Muhammad, whose patronymic, will also be like that of the Apostle of God, and who will fill the earth with equity and justice, as it has been filled with injustice, oppression and tyranny."[2] As a result, although the concept of Islamic salvation as taught by the Qur'an had not envisaged the appearance of a messianic leader to guide the community of the believers towards the establishment of the just social order, it was, in all probability, the personal devotion of the faithful to the Prophet that made them await the advent of a divinely guided Mahdi from his family.

The growth of such a hope among the pious Muslims, who could not come to grips with political circumstances and relations as they unfolded after the Prophet's death, and who had been wronged and oppressed by the ruling authority, was the inevitable outgrowth of the Islamic revelation which required the realization of the just society under divine guidance. The Muslims aspired, like others before them, for the restoration of an ideal order. With the establishment of various Muslim dynasties which failed to promote this ideal, the need for a deliverer became imperative. Those who desired the appearance of the messianic savior were generally people who sympathized with the claims of the descendants of the Prophet as being heirs to the Prophetic mission. These were the early Shi'ites. The most important factor in the development of Shi'ism in Islam was the idea of the messianic leader (Imam) who promised the end of corruption and wickedness. Thus, the belief in the appearance of the Islamic messiah became a salient feature of Shi'ite Islam, especially Imami Shi'ism, in which the conviction of the advent of the Mahdi, the twelfth Imam to establish the rule of justice, continues to be expressed in the most repeated Shi'i prayer: "May God hasten release from suffering through his (the Mahdi's) rise."[3]

If the Islamic doctrine of salvation, discussed above, was conceived in the formation of an ideal religio-political community living under a fitting legal and social system of Islam on earth, then such an ideal was dependent on the leadership which would assure its realization. If not immediately following the death of the Prophet, as the Shi'ites assert, at least in subsequent decades the question of Islamic leadership became interwoven with the creation of a just order and formed the crucial issue which divided the Muslims into various factions. The doctrine of salvation was bound to require divine guidance through the appointed mediation of the Prophet, who was responsible for delivering the revelation to human beings.

The early years of Islam were characterized by a constant succession of victories of the Muslim army under the Caliphate, but not by the establishment of justice. Accordingly, the debate began regarding who should be responsible to lead the community toward salvation after the Prophet's death. By the end of this early period, when the civil wars broke out after the murder of Muhammad's third successor in A.D. 656, the Muslims were confronted with an unfulfilled idea of a just order, which made even more imperative the necessity of finding qualified leaders to assume the Imamate of the community. It was concluded that the establishment of a true Islamic order depended on such leadership. Most of these early discussions about leadership were at first sight political, but eventually the debate encompassed the religious implications of salvation. This is true of all Islamic concepts, since Islam as a religious phenomenon was subsequent to Islam as a political reality. The rise of several individuals from among the Prophet's descendants as the Imams, and the sympathetic and even enthusiastic following that they mustered, clearly show an attempt to visualize the manner in which Muslim society must be ordered to fulfill its historical responsibility: the formation of a just society, including its political organization.

The creation of a just society, thus, has become the focal point of the Islamic belief system or cosmology, in which the Prophet and his successors are visualized as representing the transcendental, active God on earth. Accordingly, it is this basic religious focus on the creation of a just order and the leadership that can create it, that orients the authoritative perspective or worldview of the faithful in Islam. It is, therefore, important to discuss this worldview in light of the conception of justice in Islam, both in its political as well as its religious manifestations. In order to achieve this end we will discuss the notion of justice in Islamic revelation and its implications for political justice.

The Qur'anic Notion of Justice and its Political Implications

O You who believe! establish justice (al-qist), being witnesses for God—even if the evidence goes against yourselves or against your parents or kingsmen; and irrespective of whether the witness is rich or poor, under all circumstances God has priority for you [over your relatives]. (4:135)

There is little doubt that a primary aim of the Islamic revelation is to establish a viable social order on earth that will be just and ethically based. However, since the Qur'an was revealed against the background of the tribal society of Arabia, moral exhortations such as to "establish justice" in the above passage have to be understood the way the Arabs conventionally understood them. The exhortation to establish justice (4:135) refers to the notion of 'justice' as an objective and universal moral truth on the basis of which one can maintain it to be a universal and natural guidance to which humankind is called upon to respond. In other words, justice is a moral prescription which follows from a common human nature, and is regarded as independent of particular spiritual beliefs, even though all practical guidance regulating interpersonal human relations springs from the same source, namely, from God. This observation regarding the objective nature of justice is important to bear in mind because the notion is not intelligible without reference to an objective state of affairs.

The concept of justice is an essentially relative concept. Whenever an individual asserts what he considers a just claim, in order for his claim to be valid, it must be relevant to an established public order under which a certain scale of justice is acknowledged. Scales of justice vary considerably from culture to culture, and each scale is defined and ultimately determined by a particular society in accordance with the public order of that society. Yet, no matter how scales differ one from another, they all appear to have certain elements in common, which we have called the universally objective nature of moral virtue.

Broadly speaking, there are two major ways the scales of justice in public order are conceived. There are societies which believe that men are capable of determining their individual or collective interests so that they may have knowledge of that to which they aspire. They, therefore, believe that they have been endowed with an innate capacity, individually or collectively, to establish a social order under which certain scales of justice are likely to evolve by tacit concurrence or formal agreement. This kind of justice, which is a result of the interactions between individuals, or between social expectations and existing socio-moral conditions, may be called positive justice. Being positive it lays no claim to being perfect; consequently there is continuous effort on the part of that society to refine and improve it. Ideal justice is a mirage, and real justice develops by improvisation from generation to generation.[4]

The other trend presupposes that man is essentially weak and, therefore, incapable of rising above personal failings. The idea that fallible human beings can determine their collective interests, and lay down an impartial standard of justice, is not accepted. In such a society, divine guidance is invoked to provide either the sources, or the basic norms and principles, of the social organizations under which a divinely sanctioned standard of justice is established. The kind of justice that flows from such a source, and which is exercised by a representative of the divine authority on earth such as an inspired prophet commands respect and can have a lasting impact on the administration of justice in that society. Moreover, the justice which flows from such a high divine source is regarded as universally applicable to all humankind.

The Islamic notion of justice, as we shall see below, although essentially falling into the second category, recognizes elements of positive justice as a valid standard for public order. In the final analysis, the source of both categories of justice, according to the Qur'an, is divine "guidance," either in the form of "innate disposition" or "infallible inspiration" from God. To understand the religious and ethical implications of the notion of justice in Islam, it is important to first understand divine guidance in the Qur'an, since it is constitutive of God's purpose in creating human beings.

The most important aspect of divine guidance, according to the

The Creation of Just Social Order in Islam

Qur'an, is to make human beings attain the purpose for which they are created, namely, to attain "prosperity."

> By the soul; and That which shaped it and inspired it to [know the difference between] lewdness and godfearing! Prosperous is he who purifies it, and failed has he who seduces it. (91:7–8)

Thus, God, according to this passage, has endowed human beings with the necessary cognition and volition to further their comprehension of the purpose for which they were created, and to realize that purpose by using their knowledge. Moreover, the verse also makes it plain that the distinction between "lewdness" (evil) and "godfearing" (good) is ingrained in the soul in the form of inspiration, a form of guidance with which God has favored human beings. It is through this guidance that human beings are expected to develop the ability to judge their actions and to choose those which would lead them to "prosperity" (i.e., justice). But this is not an easy task to achieve. It involves spiritual and moral development; something that is most challenging in the light of the basic human weaknesses indicated by the Qur'an (70:19–20).

This weakness reveals a basic tension that must be resolved by further acts of guidance by God. It is at this point that God sends the prophets and "Books" (revealed messages), to show human beings how to change their character and bring it in conformity with the divine plan for human conduct (2:2, 5). The guidance from God signifies the "direction" he provides to procure the desirable human society: first by creating in the soul a disposition that can guard against spiritual and moral peril, if a person hearkens to its warnings; and then, by further strengthening this natural guidance through the Book and the Prophet. "Guidance," in the signification of "showing the path," is a fundamental feature of the Qur'an and is reiterated throughout to emphasize that this form of guidance is not only part of normative human nature, but is also "universal," i.e., available to all who aspire to become "godfearing" and "prosperous."

Human beings can reject this guidance, although they cannot produce any valid excuse for the rejection. Nevertheless, rejection pertains to the "procuring" or "appropriating" of that which is desirable, and not the act of first apprehending what is desirable. Thus, when God denies guidance to those who do not believe in his signs (16:104), the denial pertains to the procurement of the desirable end, and *not* to the initial guidance that is originally engraved upon the hearts of all human beings, to guide them to prosperity. The verse 4:70: "And We guide them to a straight path" points to "guidance" which signifies the procurement of the good end—the creation of the Islamic order. It implies that this guidance is available to an individual after that person has consented to lead a life of uprightness (*taqwa*).

It becomes evident, then, that the Qur'an is speaking about two forms of guidance. The first form is the one by means of which an individual becomes "godfearing" (*muttaqi*); while the second is the one which God bestows *after* the attainment of "piety" or "moral consciousness." This latter guidance helps the individual remain unshakeable when encountering those who challenge this conviction in the matter of divine planning. *Taqwa*, which means "keen, [spiritual and] moral perception and motivation,"[5] is a comprehensive attribute that touches all aspects of faith, when faith is put into practice, i.e., when the social order based on justice is created.

Given these observations about the notion of guidance, it would be accurate to visualize people who possess *taqwa* as situated between "universal" and "prophetic guidance." In other words, being equipped with the necessary cognition and volition, they are ready to follow the commands of God to attain the social dimension of *taqwa*, namely, "prosperity."

Since the question of guidance is related to the source of knowledge of ethical values such as justice, in classical as well as modern works of Qur'anic exegesis, we have taken some care to explicate the various forms of guidance in the Qur'an. Significantly, it is at this point that theological differences among Muslim scholars become explicitly marked. These differences are rooted in two conflicting conceptions of human responsibility in the procurement of divine justice. The discussion of the Qur'anic material in this connection has been dominated by the proponents of the two major schools of Muslim dialectical theology: the Mu'tazilite and the Ash'arite.

The basic Mu'tazilite thesis is that human beings, as free agents, are responsible before a just God. Furthermore, good and evil are rational categories which can be known through reason, independent of revelation. God created man's intellect in such a way that it is capable of perceiving good and evil objectively. This is the corollary of their main thesis, that God's justice depends on the objective knowledge of good and evil, as determined by reason, whether the Lawgiver pronounces it so or not. In other words, the

The Creation of Just Social Order in Islam

Mu'tazilites asserted the efficacy of natural reason as a source of spiritual and ethical knowledge, maintaining a form of rationalist objectivism.[6]

The Mu'tazilite standpoint was bound to be challenged. The Ash'arites rejected the idea of natural reason as an autonomous source of ethical knowledge. They maintained that good and evil are as God decrees them, and it is presumptuous to judge God on the basis of categories that God has provided for directing human life. For the Ash'arites there is no way, within the bounds of ordinary logic, to explain the relation of God's power to human actions. It is more realistic just to maintain that everything that happens is the result of his will, without explanation or justification. However, it is important to distinguish between the actions of a responsible human being and the motions attributed to natural laws. Human responsibility is not the result of free choice, a function which, according to the Mu'tazilites, determines the way an action is produced. Rather, God alone creates all actions directly, but in some actions a special quality of "voluntary acquisition" is superadded by God's will in order to make the individual a voluntary and responsible agent. Consequently, human responsibility is the result of the divine will known through revealed guidance. Values have no foundation except the will of God that imposes them. This attitude of the Ash'arites to ethical knowledge is known as theistic subjectivism. This means that all ethical values are dependent upon the determinations of the Will of God expressed in the form of revelation, which is both eternal and immutable.[7]

Both these theological standpoints are based on the interpretation of Qur'anic passages, which undoubtedly contain a complex view of the task of human responsibility in procuring the divine will on earth. On the one hand, it contains passages that would support the Mu'tazilite position which emphasizes the complete responsibility of human beings in responding to the call of both natural guidance as well as guidance through revelation. On the other, it has passages that could support the Ash'arite viewpoint that upholds the omnipotence of God, and, hence, denies man any role in responding to the divine guidance. However, the Qur'an allows for both decision and divine omnipotence in the matter of guidance.[8]

Actually, the concept of universal or natural guidance has wider implications than merely demonstrating the existence of volitional capacity in the human soul (91:7), and proving human responsibility with regard to the development of a keen sense of spiritual and moral perception and motivation that will lead to the establishment of justice on earth. It appears that the Qur'an regards humanity as one nation in reference to "universal guidance," before "particular guidance" through the prophets is sent, and consequently holds humanity collectively responsible to procure divine planning in human affairs, namely, to establish justice:

> The people were one nation; then God sent forth Prophets, good tidings to bear and warning, and He sent down with them the Book with the truth, that He might decide between the people touching their differences. (2:213)

Universal guidance treats all human beings as equal, and as potentially believers in God, before they become distinguished through more particular guidance as believers, unbelievers, hypocrites, and so on. So construed, religious differences cannot diminish the responsibility for the establishment of justice on earth, because that obligation is derived from the natural guidance "ingrained in the human soul."

On the basis of the notion of 'universal guidance,' it is possible to speak of natural-moral grounds of human conduct in the Qur'an which parallels, for instance, St. Paul's presupposition in Romans 2:14–15 and 3:19. These passages refer to an objective and universal moral nature on the basis of which all human beings are to be treated equally and held equally accountable to God. In other words, certain moral prescriptions follow from a common human nature, and are regarded as independent of particular spiritual beliefs, even though all practical guidance ultimately springs from the same source, namely, from God. It is, therefore, important to emphasize in the context of the Qur'an, that the notion of theistic justice logically appeals to universally objective justice "ingrained in the human soul," in order to become relevant to an established public order. In an extremely important passage, the Qur'an recognizes the universal and objective nature of justice (equated with "good works" or moral virtues which transcend different religious communities), and admonishes humankind to be "forward in good works."

> To every one of you [religious communities] We have appointed law and a way [of conduct]. If God had willed, He would have made you all one nation [on the basis of that law and that way]; but [He did not do so] that He may try you in what has come to you; therefore, be you forward [i.e., compete with one another] in good works. Unto God

shall you return all together; and He will tell you [the Truth] about what you have been disputing. (5:48)

There is a clear assumption in this passage that all human beings have to strive towards the establishment of a certain scale of justice, objectively acknowledged, regardless of differences in religious beliefs. Interestingly enough, the ideal human being is conceived of as combining this moral virtue with complete religious surrender:

Nay, but whosoever submits his will to God, while being a good-doer, his wage is with his Lord, and no fear shall be on them, neither shall they sorrow. (2:112)

Undoubtedly, we have here a clear basis for distinction between theistic and objective justice in the Qur'an, where objective justice is further strengthened by the religious act of "submission" to the sacred authority. It is indeed in the realm of universal objective justice that human beings are treated equally, and held equally responsible for responding to universal guidance. Furthermore, it is this fundamental moral responsibility of all human beings at the level of universal guidance that makes it plausible to maintain that the Qur'an does manifest something akin to the Western notion of natural law, which is the source of positive justice in societies founded on tacit agreement or formal action. Since the Qur'anic notion recognizes both objective and theistic justice, it is possible to call it 'natural justice' in the sense meant by Aristotle, who regarded natural justice as a product not of social but of natural forces.[9]

Following Aristotle, scholars often equated divine justice with natural justice; but, unlike the natural-law scholars who were concerned with the relation of justice to society, Muslim scholars of Islamic jurisprudence focused their primary concern on the concept of justice in relation to God's will, and related it to the destiny of humanity. These scholars maintained that divine justice is the ultimate objective of Islamic revelation, expressed in its early form in the sacred laws of Islam. This sacred law was known as the Shari'a.

The Concept of Justice as Embodied in the Shari'a

In Islam, Shari'a law is closely interwined with religion and morality which are regarded as expressions of God's will and justice. But, whereas the aim of religion and morality is to define and determine goals and provide practical guidance to achieve salvation, the function of the Shari'a is to teach men the "way" to achieve their salvation (the term 'shari'a' bears this signification) by virtue of which God's justice and other goals are realized. Thus the Qur'an commands Muslims to arbitrate with justice, to give true evidence, to fulfill one's contracts and, more importantly, to return a trust or deposit to its owner. All these commands have one purpose, namely, to create a new society on a religious and moral basis, in order to supersede Arabian tribal society. Again, the Qur'anic prohibition of gambling, of drinking wine and of charging interest are directed against ancient Arabian standards of behavior, with the purpose of creating an essentially ethically based society. It is possible to discern an underlying concern of Qur'anic legislation, namely, to enunciate ethical principles in the form of moral exhortations which ought to be followed in the administration of justice in the Shari'a.

The Shari'a preserves this concern of the Qur'an when the purely legal attitude, which is the result of an examination of a relevant act and its legal consequences, is often superseded by the concern to require adherence to ethical standards enunciated by the Qur'an. The aim of Islamic revelation was, thus, to provide an impetus to structure the Islamic public order on the basis of the administrative and legislative functions of the Prophet embodied in the Qur'an. Accordingly, the Qur'an, in addition to stating the Prophet's personal elaboration and practice, determines the ultimate course or direction the community ought to follow in establishing public order. The Prophet's elaboration in communicating the revelation and his practice formed the "model pattern of behavior"—the Sunna—for his community and, in the subsequent period, was promulgated in the Shari'a as an authoritative source for practical life. It was as a consequence of the promulgation of the Sunna as a normative prophetic tradition that Islamic revelation became composed of two authoritative sources—the Qur'an and the Sunna, both of which were declared the embodiment of God's will and justice.

These two sources provided the raw material on the basis of which later Muslim jurists, through use of a third derivative source based on human reasoning called *ijtihad,* laid down the law of Shari'a. The foundation of Islamic social order was firmly laid on the fundamental principles of the Shari'a, and the elucidations of the succeeding generations of Muslim jurists, which came to be regarded as the system sanctioned by God. The ultimate adherence to

The Creation of Just Social Order in Islam

the Islamic system, which has provided the Islamic standard of life, was achieved through the concurrence (*ijma'*) of the Muslim jurists who concerned themselves with the transformation of local administrative law into a unified religious law of Islam. As a result, their concurrence became another source of deriving decisions in points of Shari'a. Through their concern with the preservation of the Islamic way of life, they came to be acknowledged as a group of pious persons, specializing in points of law and morality, who could advise the community about correct Islamic behavior. Furthermore, it was this group of pious specialists who became the defenders of Islamic ideal of a social political order against corrupt behavior of the ruling class, whether the caliph or his governors, which was regarded as detrimental to the creation of justice and inequity.

The Nature of Islamic Public Order

Since the scale of justice in any given society must be related to its public order, a few words about the nature of Islamic public order is relevant at this stage. In the Islamic theory of public order, God is the sovereign of the community of the believers. He is its ultimate ruler and lawgiver. The revelation and the prophets' personality were the primary sources of the Islamic order, presuming to fulfill the responsibility that was collectively laid upon the community. The principles and maxims of justice, derived from these two primary sources, were regarded as infallible and immutable, designed for all time and characterized by universal application to all those who accepted the faith. In principle, the Shari'a laid down by the divine lawgiver is an ideal system. But, the public order, based on the Shari'a, as well as state acts and the rulings and legal opinions of the jurists on matters arrived at through independent judgement of human reason, was subject to adaptation and refinement to meet changing conditions and developing exigencies in the community.

Although the Shari'a may be God-given, it is a human being who must apply the laws. It is for this purpose that God appointed among humankind those who are delegated to exercise his authority, being instructed to rule with justice by applying the laws of the Shari'a. This delegation of authority was the logical consequence of the strict monotheistic doctrine in Islam, which did not consider it possible for God to exercise direct rule over believers. Thus, a ruler who represents God on earth was deemed necessary to implement the Shari'a in order to achieve justice.[10] This form of government, often called theocracy, is obviously not based on the principle that authority is exercised directly by God (whether as a Pharaoh or a Caesar); it is based instead on the principle of a representative who derives his authority not from God but from God-given Shari'a. The basis of all the decisions and actions of an Islamic state is the Shari'a, which is but one of the several manifestations of the divine wisdom, regulating all phenomena in the universe, material or spiritual, natural or social. By characterizing the normative character of God's wisdom as *mizan* (scale), *gist* and *'adl* (justice), the Qur'an has tried to impress the significance of the Shari'a on the minds of the faithful. Upholding the Shari'a as the embodiment of divine justice, Islam affirms the necessity of government on the basis of norms and well-dated guidelines, provided by the two authoritative sources of the Qur'an and the Sunna.[11]

Thus, the Qur'an and the Sunna of the Prophet formed the constitutional instruments, the proximate source of authority, rather than personal preferences of different groups within the Islamic polity. These sources, although regarded as the original divine proposition for Islamic public order, were inevitably at human disposition for implementation, which included an extensive field of intellectual activity and decision. It was the strength of this intellectual activity, which engaged the energies of Muslim scholars in the correct interpretations of the Qur'an and Sunna, that settled the question of the legitimacy of a government in power. All leaders claiming authority had to appeal to Shari'a norms and principles determined by reason, revelation, or both, to assert the legitimacy of other claims. Hence, it is accurate to maintain that the legitimacy of any Islamic government based on constitutional principles provided by the divine guidance was dependent upon the interpretations of this guidance by the jurists, who sought to legitimize one claim against another by diverse arguments—theological, juridical and others—on the grounds of justice. Although the scholars agreed on the divine nature of justice, they disagreed on how it should be realized on earth.

It was the realization of the divine justice on earth that held the religious implications for the Islamic doctrine of salvation, discussed above. It has been pointed out that the rise of several individuals in the early days of Islamic history was a response to the Qur'anic challenge of creating a just society. These different types of attempts to fulfill this historical responsibility, would, at a later time, charac-

The Creation of Just Social Order in Islam

terize the main groups with their sectarian epithets: the Sunnites and the Shi'ites.

The Sunnites, or as their Islamic title goes, *ahl al-sunna wa al-jama'a* (people of the custom and community), looked upon salvation as possible only through the allegiance and loyalty of all believers in the community. As long as the community continued to be fully committed to the promulgation and observance of the Shari's, its salvation was guaranteed regardless of the qualities or, as it was later held, descent of the leaders who headed the community. "Justice," declared al-Shafi'i, "means acting in obedience to God [i.e., in conformity to his law]."[12] After all, the leader, as conceived by later Sunni theorists, was merely a protector of the Shari'a, and this function was vested in him through the process of allegiance paid by the members of the community. The solution offered by the Sunnites was, in fact, a simple expression of recognition of a historical reality, namely, that the leadership of the Muslims after that early period of the "rightly guided" caliphs (A.D. 632–660), which was idealized by them as the golden age of Islam, depended not on the individual on whom it was conferred, rather, it was subject to the commitment and loyalty granted by the community to that leader. Thus, in the final analysis, it was acceptance of the tradition by the community and its membership (*al-sunna wa al-jama'a*) that guaranteed salvation: the formation of a just society.

The Shi'ites, on the other hand, did not find community allegiance (the *jama'a* principle), as maintained by their opponents, capable of ensuring the salvation that Islam had envisaged. From the early days of the civil war which followed the murder of Muhammad's third successor in A.D. 656, Muslims not only thought about the question of leadership in socio-political terms, but also laid religious emphasis on it. To begin with, they maintained that Muhammad himself was a charismatic leader who embodied the religio-political character of Islamic salvation. As such, his prophetic authority included the power to interpret the message of the Qur'an in order to realize the just order without corrupting revelation. After his death, Islam, in order to continue its function of directing the faithful toward justice, needed a leader who could authoritatively perform the Prophet's spiritual and temporal roles. In other words, only another charismatic leader could succeed the Prophet and accomplish the creation of an ideal Islamic society. Who could be better qualified for such a crucial task than his own family members, who would have inherited his charisma? The national exaltation of the Prophet and his rightful successor, along with the hope of the ill-treated mentioned earlier, gave rise to the concept of messianic leadership among the descendants of the Prophet—the Imam who could save the believers. Faith was conceived in terms of personal devotion to this Imam and what he symbolized with regard to Islamic justice. Salvation was impossible if a person failed to acknowledge the true Imam of his time, to whom devotion and obedience was incumbent, since he alone could bring a true Islamic rule of justice and equity into the world, the main function attributed to the Islamic messiah, al-Mahdi.

The Shi'ite conception of salvation was bound to meet with much resistance, since it not only demanded recognition of the rightful Imam with a messianic role, but more importantly, because it also challenged the right of the existing regime to rule. This right of the ruling dynasties to exercise their authority, had in part depended upon the scholars to legitimize their rule on the basis of the Shari'a. It was the messianic role of the Imams that became a rallying point for all those who thought they had been discriminated against or maltreated by the ruling house. Hence, we can see the debate concerning justice began from the outset on the political level, with loaded religious implications. Legitimacy and justice were often used interchangeably by political leaders and scholars, in an attempt to rationalize the legitimacy of rival claimants to authority. They provided one scale of justice or another, drawn from the emerging public order, which was a simple expression of recognition of a historical reality. I have attempted, however, to briefly state the underlying standards of justice of two main schools of thought, namely, the Sunni and the Shi'ite.

But, even within these two major schools, once the debate on justice started it never really ended. It led to further schism in the body politic and the rise of rival groups and factions, each seeking to rationalize its standard of political justice on one religious ground or another. From the political level the debate gradually shifted to other levels—theological, juridical, etc.,—although ulterior political motivation continued to reassert itself in one form or another. As Islamic public order advanced, the debate moved to higher levels of sophistication, and scholars in fields other than theology and law—philosophers and other men of learning—were soon drawn into it. For no serious thinker, whether in the Islamic, or any other community, could possibly remain indifferent to a debate on a subject so engaging and central as justice.

Conclusion

The Prophet Muhammad grew up in a society in which he found widespread inequity and oppression; consequently, he was deeply concerned about justice as the Qur'anic passages bear out in their central aim of establishing a just and ethically based social order. Indeed, this central aim of his message became the core of the soteriology expounded above. Islamic salvation meant to establish order and harmony within which the divine standard of justice, objectively and universally comprehended, would, through "universal" guidance, be acknowledged.

As a prophet, who had received divine revelation, Muhammad naturally stressed religious values. But, he was also a social reformer, and his decisions provided precedents on the basis of which the issues that were to rise in future were resolved. We have identified this aspect of his guidance as "particular" (the Book and the Sunna), as contrasted with "universal" guidance. However, both these forms of guidance are embedded in the same divine source. The idea of justice was of particular interest to the Prophet, and he dealt with the problems of his day with "uprightness," "balance," and "fairness."[13] The Qur'an stands as the testimony for his incessant demand for justice, expressed either in qualitiative or quantitative terms. The absence of coherent social order and political unity in the tribal society of Arabia necessarily subordinated the scale of justice to the requirements of survival. Consequently, the appeal of justice took the negative form of retribution, such as retaliation and payment of blood-wit, rather than the positive forms of fairness, balance and temperance.

The Prophet, while conceding the value of courage and other virtues, felt the need to assert religious and moral values to temper cruelty and harshness. For this reason, the Qur'an and the Sunna often warned believers against bigotry and oppression. Believers were also admonished that in the fulfilling of their religious obligations they must above all be just. Since the Prophet dealt essentially with practical questions affecting the scale of justice, the actual formulation of the theories of justice was left to posterity. However, neither in the Qur'an nor in the Sunna, can one discover the constituent elements of justice or the manner in which justice can be established on earth. It was mainly for this reason that Muslims, distrustful of the capacity of their leaders who had so far failed to promote the Islamic ideal, began to look forward to the rule of an individual from among the Prophet's descendants "whose name will be also Muhammad, whose patronymic, will also be like that of the Apostle of God, and who will fill the earth with equity and justice, as it has been filled with injustice, oppression and tyranny." Ibn Khaldun has summarized the Muslim expectation for the creation of just social order in the following terms:

It has been well known [and generally accepted] by all Muslims in every epoch, that at the end of time a man from the family [of the Prophet] will without fail make his appearance, one who will strengthen Islam and make justice triumph. Muslims will follow him, and he will gain domination over the Muslim realm. He will be called the Mahdi.[14]

NOTES

1. Fazlur Rahman, *Major Themes of the Qur'an* (Chicago: Bibliotheca, 1980), 136–137.
2. For this and other traditions on the messianic leader of the Muslims, see: A. J. Wemsinck, *A Handbook of Early Muhammadan Traditions* (Leiden, 1927), under *MAHDI*, 139.
3. The idea has been fully dealt with by the present author in *Islamic Messianism: The Idea of Madhi in Twelve Shi'ism* (Albany, New York: State University of New York Press, 1981).
4. Although one can trace a variety of notions of justice existing in such a society, most of them, however, seem to be revolving around two major schools of thought, namely the utilitarian and the social contract. For recent critique of the theories of justice, see: John Rawls, *Theory of Justice* (Cambridge, Massachussetts: Harvard University Press, 1971).
5. I have preferred this translation of *taqwa,* with slight variation, which Fazlur Rahman gives in his *Major Themes,* 56. In fact, he has offered different though similar definitions of the concept *taqwa* in several places (14, 28, 29, 56).
6. G. F. Hourani, *Islamic Rationalism: The Ethics of "Abd al-Jabbar* (Oxford, 1971), 3.
7. Ibid.
8. Even the Ash'ari exegete al-Razi, who maintains complete subordination of human will to the Divine Will recognizes two forms of "guidance": first, guidance by means of demonstration (*dalil*) and proof or evidence (*hujja*), both

The Creation of Just Social Order in Islam

activities of the human rational faculty, which he considers limited; and second, guidance through inner purification of the soul and ascetic practices. He does not speak of revelation as a separate form of guidance; rather, as an Ash'ari, he considers the revelation (i.e., the will of God) to superimpose all forms of guidance. See his *Tafsir* (Cairo, 1938), 1, 9ff.

9. Aristotle, *Nichomachean Ethics*, 1134B, 18.
10. Thus the Qur'an says in connection with David's appointment by God:

    O David! We have appointed thee as a viceroy (khalifa) in the earth; therefore judge upright between mankind, and follow not desire . . . that it beguile thee from the way of God. (38:26)

11. For this reason some authors maintain that a proper Islamic state should be called a nomocracy, or more accurately, divine nomocracy, because, after all, it is only the Shari'a-law that is binding in Islam and not law in general. See: Majid Khadduri, *War and Peace in the Law of Islam* (Baltimore, 1955), 14–18.
12. Shafi'i, al-, al-Risala, 25; *Islamic Jurisprudence,* being the translation of the *Risala* by Majid Khadduri, 70.
13. All these are the meanings of the word '*adl* in Arabic. '*Adl* is an abstract noun, derived from the verb '*adl,* which means: first, 'to straighten' or 'to sit straight', 'to amend' or 'modify'; second, 'to run away', 'depart' or 'defect' from one (wrong) path to the other (right) one; third, 'to be equal' or 'equivalent', 'to be equal or match', or 'to equalize'; fourth, 'to balance', or 'counterbalance', 'to weigh' or 'to be in a state of equilibrium'. Ibn Manzur, *Lisan al-Arab* (13, 457) defines '*adl* as, "a thing that is established in the mind as being straightforward." Anything that is not upright or in order is regarded as *jawr,* meaning 'unfair'. See also: E. W. Lane, *Arabic-English Lexicon,* Book I. Part 5, 1972–75.
14. Ibn Khaldun, *The Muqaddima,* trans. Franz Rosenthal, 2d. ed. (Princeton: Princeton University Press, 1967), 2, 156.

8
A Buddhist View of Creating a Just Society
ILHAN GÜNGÖREN

Is faith in God necessary for the creation of a just society? This question brings with it several other questions. First and foremost, the following issue has to be clarified: What is meant by 'a just society'? If a just society is one which gives freedom, happiness, and opportunities for the development of the physical and mental health of its members, and also provides conditions in which each person can develop their potential to a maximum degree, and receive a share proportional to their contribution to the welfare of that society—well, then to this day such a society has never existed. All through history, among the civilizations in which a strong faith in God has prevailed, not a single instance of a society that fits our description can be cited. Another question also arises in our minds: What kind of "faith in God"? Faith in a god with whom we can converse and settle our accounts? A god who protects us and rewards us when he is satisfied with our deeds, and punishes us when he is not? Or, perhaps, a universal supremacy totally unconcerned with the destiny of human beings, which does nothing but set up laws and regulations with which individuals can or cannot keep in step? In short, is this a faith in a living and anthropomorphic god? Or an impersonal god whom we might identify with the laws of nature?

According to Buddhist thought, which I share, the most fundamental law is the law of causality (karma). Undoubtedly, the one and only absolute thing in the universe, is the unerring certainty of causality, which cannot, or will not, be altered even by God himself. As is written in the scripture, just "as the wheel of the cart follows the beast that draws the cart,"[1] causes and actions drag behind themselves their effects and reactions. Buddha, thus, assigned the task of gods to the law of causality. According to the Buddhist view, even the entirety of existence is a result of the law of causality; and

A Buddhist View of Creating a Just Society

nonexistence caught in the spokes of the wheel of karma, is transformed into existence.

Since the future of humanity is shaped by effects that are born by causes, the likelihood that a man can escape from the law of causality is unimaginable. Even God cannot, or will not, interfere with the workings of this law. Belief in divine intervention on behalf of some particular person, or in some particular situation, means believing in the possibility of God's power disconnecting the ties binding cause to effect. Such a belief is not compatible with the concept of an orderly universe governed by the laws of nature. Such a belief is not consistent with the universe we observe scientifically. God is not able to cancel or temporarily stop the workings of karma for the sake of any individual. Hence, the futility of hoping for help from God, and of praying, vowing and making sacrifices to God, becomes clearly evident.

Since neither God nor any other power is able to save us from the consequences of our actions, there remains no other option for us but that of accepting responsibility for our actions. It would be only a childish sentiment, if we expected from God the same sort of love and kindness we have received from our parents. If we wish to prevent the evil consequences of our actions, and be able to do things which will bear good results, we should, prior to everything else, understand all aspects of the law of causality. Here is a point we have to understand primarily: all events are products of the law of causality, and this phenomenon cannot be interrupted for a moment, not even by God himself. Every so often, we might not be able to see the subtle web of causality, and, again, some events might seem to us as if they were products of sheer coincidence, but this can in no way be taken as a proof of the possibility of occurrence of any event beyond the influence of causal inevitabilities.

How does karma weave its invisible web inside and outside of our beings, tying up our hands and feet, enslaving and turning us into puppets? *Dhammapada,* one of the most important books of the Pali Canon, begins with these words: "What we are today comes from our thoughts of yesterday, and our present thoughts build our life of tomorrow. Our life is the creation of our mind."[2] But here a question arises: from where and how do these thoughts come? Well, thoughts come from previous thoughts, previous decisions and actions. Thoughts rooted in ignorance turn into decisions, shape our actions, and eventually our actions shape our thoughts and decisions. Every thought limits and determines our successive thoughts. Let us suppose that just for once we have thought of something in complete freedom; then our next thought will not be as free as that one. The scope of freedom will shrink more and more; our subsequent thoughts will follow the grooves dug by our previous thoughts.

Every thought, every action bears lasting, indelible results. It certainly is impossible to eradicate an event or a word that has already happened or been uttered. Can we find a way of freeing ourselves from this enslaving, entrapping network? Buddha claims we can find such a way, and he shows the way: the only way which will free us from this trap is being aware of the reasons which cause us to think and behave as we do; that is, in the words of Buddhists, awakening and freeing ourselves from ignorance rooted in desires and passions. According to the Buddhist view, ignorance is not to see one's own true nature and the world around us as they really are; not to see the objective world in its suchness (*tathata*), and not to perceive things in their reality (*yathabhutam*), and to draw an alienating line between one's self and the world.

In that case, what is the true nature of self? In Buddhist thinking, the true nature of self is nothingness, emptiness or *sunyata*. We may compare *sunyata* to mud in the hands of a sculptor or the paint an artist uses. Like the actions of a sculptor or an artist, causal consequences are moulding and shaping the self continuously. Self is nothing but a product of causal circumstances. We don't have any permanent and unchangeable entity which we can call "self" or "soul." As we know, Buddha rejected the idea of an eternal and unchangeable self, along with the existence of a soul as an extension of self. Buddha said: "Neither self nor aught belonging to self can be accepted. Consequently, the view which declares 'I shall continue to be in the future, permanent, immutable, eternal, of a nature that knows no change' must be recognized as simply and entirely a doctrine of fools" (*Majjhima*, I: 138).

At first glance, Buddha's views on the subject of self and soul, and his acceptance of *samsara* (the round of birth and death) might seem inconsistent. But if we consider them profoundly we shall see nothing inconsistent in them. According to Buddha, it is not a self or soul that reincarnates, but causal consequences that pass from one life to another. We are nothing else but inheritors of past karmas. Buddha expressed his views in the following sentences: "This, o bikkhus, is not your body, nor the body of anyone else, rather you can consider it as a product of past karmas, which took shape and materialized by the will and became palpable" (*Samyutta Nikaya*, Vol. II).[4] And again: "I am the inheritor of past karmas. I was born from the past karmas; but I also am the father and mother of all actions. I am doing all actions, good and evil; and also I am inheriting them" (*Majjhima Nikaya*, I: 390).[5]

We find that in the earlier periods of Buddhism, the doctrine of karma was viewed from the standpoint of individual salvation. The social implications of this doctrine were overlooked. Buddhist negation of self had brought with it the concept of the futility of any attempts at individual salvation. However, in later Buddhism, this contradiction has been settled by an extremely rationalistic explanation.

According to the new understanding that has emerged from Mahayana Buddhism, all human beings, all sentient beings, the whole of existence, are transient manifestations of one and the same reality. Life and existence are one indivisible whole. This whole is such a state of indivisibility, such a oneness, such a net of intertwinement, that not even the tiniest fragment could ever be broken away from it.

In the *Vajracchedika Sutra*, this oneness, this indivisible aspect of life and existence has been expressed in the following words which are ascribed to Buddha: "All Bodhisattvas should cultivate their minds to think: all sentient beings of whatever class are caused by me to attain the boundless liberation of Nirvana. Yet when vast innumerable, and immeasurable numbers of beings have thus been liberated, in truth no being has been liberated! Why is this Subhuti? It is because no Bodhisattva who is truly a Bodhisattva holds to the idea of an ego, a personality, a being or a separate individual."[6] We can also quote the *Avatamsaka Sutra:* "For as much as there is the will that all sentient beings should be altogether made free, I will not forsake my fellow creatures."[7]

This conception brings a different dimension, a different vista to the doctrine of karma. From this point we see that all existence shares a common karma, all actions have a meaningful part in the construction of the whole. Here we find a priority placed ahead of egoistic desires of saving the self: that priority or goal is the salvation of all humanity, of all the family of sentient beings, and even of all existence. Since I am nothing but a tiny and insignificant phenomenon of the whole, a transient ripple on the surface of a gigantic ocean, how can I expect individual salvation? There remains nothing for us to do but undertake responsibility for total existence. My seemingly self-advantageous actions will in the end harm me, if those actions are harmful to society, because I am a part of society. This can clearly be seen in the example of the man who pollutes the environment for his selfish goals. Inevitably, in the end he will also have to bear the injurious effects of a polluted environment.

In the later periods of Buddhism, especially in Mahayana philosophy, the idea of the oneness of all living beings, the indivisible wholeness of all existence, has been widely accepted and explicitly expressed. Adhering to this view, we see that there is really no need for a mediator like self or soul, or anything of that sort, in the transferring of karma from one life to another. When we thoroughly realize this truth, we see that each newly born baby is like a virgin field ready to be tilled and cultivated—a field that embodies all past lives, and in which all kinds of seeds of greed, craving and hatred will take root. This way of understanding adds a new dimension and a wider perspective to the doctrine of karma. It inspires us to interpret once more the social implications of this doctrine.

A good deed performed by one individual, will benefit several other persons. A well done deed will initiate a chain of right and useful deeds. We all are in the same boat—we, along with all of existence, share the same karma. Each act of mine will create either beneficial or harmful effects for other human beings, sentient beings, and the whole of existence. And these harmful or beneficial effects continue influencing, shaping and conditioning future generations. As S. Kurada put it: "Our present life is the reflection of past actions. Men consider these reflections as their real selves, their eyes, noses, ears, tongues and bodies—as well as their gardens, woods, farms, residences, servants, and maids—men imagine to be their own possessions; but in fact they are only results endlessly produced by innumerable actions. In tracing back to the ultimate limit of the past we cannot find a beginning. Again when seeking ultimate limit of the future we cannot find the end."[8]

When we look at the matter this way, we realize that the nonexistence of a self or a soul which could be rewarded or punished, or again the nonexistence of a concept of a rewarding or punishing God, does not relieve human beings of their responsibilities. To the contrary, it immensely increases our responsibility. As an example, we can mention the responsibility of a ruler or a political leader. A ruler's decisions, initiating a series of events, will either increase the

A Buddhist View of Creating a Just Society

welfare and progress of the citizens, or bring disaster and peril upon them, either facilitating their lives or making them miserable. These effects will further influence future generations, either positively or negatively. Again, a political leader's right decisions may bring happiness, freedom, prosperity and opportunities for development to the members of the society or, in the opposite case, wrong decisions may cause disaster, captivity and unhappiness. For this reason, a ruler or a political leader has responsibilities far beyond his or her selfish interests and desires.

Likewise, the person in the street also has responsibilities towards other people and fellow creatures. Each person's actions, starts a chain of reactions that will have either beneficial or detrimental effects on others. Even a trifling thought, just passing through the mind, will shape subsequent thoughts and give rise to actions born of that very thought. Thus insignificant thought has the potential of creating the future, because the future is made of the actions transpiring from thoughts. The role played by a single person in shaping the future, might seem like a tiny droplet in the immensity of an ocean. However, the great ocean of the future is nothing but those tiny drops accumulated.

Whether we realize this truth or not, we, each and all, are architects of the future. Just as we are products of past generations, so future generations will be our product. Today, you and I and everybody else, are shaping, conditioning and creating the future through our thoughts and actions. Thus, our responsibility should be towards humanity, towards life, towards the future and even towards the whole of existence, rather than towards a meager individual salvation.

Expecting God's help for our selfish interests such as personal prosperity and salvation, and wishing him to grant us our selfish desires, is an injustice to God's greatness. For God's exalted status is well above that of a universal ruler. We need not mention that, even a minor chieftain knows how to stay out of the ordinary pursuits and involvements of his subjects.

To create a just society, we need a greater number of people to relinquish their attachments to narcissistic goals, and, instead, accept their responsibility towards total existence. Humanity can reach such a height only by acquiring a compassionate heart (*karuna*)— and the way to this kind of heart is through enlightenment!

NOTES

1. *The Dhammapada,* trans. Juan Mascaro (Harmondsworth: Penguin Books, 1973), 35.
2. Ibid.
3. Quoted in Sidney Spencer, *Mysticism In World Religion* (Harmondsworth: Penguin Books, 1963), 70.
4. Quoted in H. Oldenberg, *Le Bouddha* (Paris: Librairie Félix Alcan, 1934), 259.
5. Quoted in Ananda K. Coomaraswamy, *Hindouisme et Bouddhisme* (Paris: Gallimard, 1949), 167.
6. Quoted in Alan Watts, *The Way of Zen* (Harmondsworth: Penguin Books, 1957), 81.
7. Quoted in Ananda K. Coomaraswamy, *Buddha and the Gospel of Buddhism* (New York: Harper and Row, 1964), 230.
8. Ibid., 233.

9
A Just Society is Possible Only When the People are Just
DOBOOM TULKU

Introduction

There will be no dispute regarding the assertion that if virtuous ideas and deeds prevail among the citizens, creation of a just society is guaranteed, for a society is constituted by its members, and a just society is possible only when people themselves are just, whether or not they have faith in God. In this paper, I present some basic Buddhist ideas that bear on this theme.

In Buddhism, rather than relying on God as the dispenser of justice, one is taught to become more aware of what is to be followed and what is to be avoided (positive and negative karma). Man-made laws and regulations may be best described as aids for bringing about justice in a society, but the ultimate factor is the *mind*. Actual justice in a society depends upon whether or not a sense of fairness exists in the society, especially among key persons. One is also encouraged to take responsibility not only for one's own destiny but also for bringing about a just society.

Buddha's Teachings

Tathagata Buddha said in the *Chandrapradip Sutra:*

Though I have preached the noble teachings, if you having heard do not put them into practice, just as a patient carrying a bag full of medicines without taking them, my teachings do not serve the purpose.

The implication is that deliverance from suffering and the well-being of this individual depend entirely upon practicing Dharma; that is, following the correct path. This also implies that in Buddhism the ultimate safeguard is Dharma. Among the Triple Gem, the Buddhist Trinity, the Buddha is never regarded as an authority on law or rule. Nor he is regarded as creator of the animate and inanimate world. Buddha is simply regarded as a guide to states of liberation and omniscience. In another sutra, Buddha asked his followers not to take his teachings merely out of respect but to first analyze and investigate each, as a goldsmith does with gold, and to accept only after one is convinced of its validity and applicability to oneself. This shows Buddha wanted his followers to take this rational and scientific way of approach towards his teaching. Buddha is also compared to a medical doctor whose duty is to diagnose and prescribe proper medicine to his patients. But responsibility lies with the patient himself; the relief one obtains from sickness depends on how one follows the doctor's advice. While traversing the spiritual path, living examples of practioners are necessary. Therefore, there is need of the Sangha or spiritual community. Thus, the Budddhist Trinity is justified.

In the following, I shall compare the similarity and/or inter-applicability of the qualities attributed to Buddha in Buddhism with those of God in theistic faiths. The principal qualities of Buddha as a savior of sentient beings from cyclic existence and miserable states of birth can be grouped into three categories:

Infinite wisdom
Immeasurable compassion
Peerless strength

We shall discuss the first two together.

Buddha as Omniscient and Omnipresent

In all Buddhist scriptures irrespective of Sravakayana, Bodhisattvayana or Mantrayana, omniscience is attributed to Buddha as one of the main qualifications to be savior of the world. But within the different tenets, emphasis seems to differ slightly on the explanation of "All Knowing." Abhidharma texts seem to suggest that wherever the Buddha applies his mind, all objects appear to his mind as clearly as any object lying in front of him, thus fulfilling the requirement of a guide to salvation.

Acharya Dharmakirti in his *Pramanavartikakarika* while explaining his definition of the validity of Buddha wrote:

Whoever sees the nature of what is to be followed and what is to be avoided, along with their methods, he is to be regarded as valid here. Whether he sees far distance or not, who sees the object of aspiration (of seekers) is valid.

A Just Society is Possible Only When the People are Just

He also said:

He may or may not be knowing the number of insects under the earth. This question does not apply to our need.

In Madhyamaka literatures, seeing the two truths simultaneously and directly is attributed to a special quality of Buddha. It is said that while traversing Bodhisattva Bhumis, one alternates between direct seeing of the two truths. In the meditational state, only the ultimate truth is directly perceived; during the interval of meditations only conventional truth is directly seen.

Generally, most proponents of later Buddhist tend to assert that the Buddha sees every knowable thing, that is, whatever he sees is without obstacles or barriers of time and space. This theory is backed by the reasoning that Buddha has removed all the obstacles of knowledge through immeasurable efforts and accumulation of merits over countless aeons.

The second quality, compassion, is one of the main factors of the production of Buddha's attainment. As stated in Chandrakirti's *Madhyamakavatara*, compassion is important in the beginning, in the middle, and at the end. Compassion is likened to the seed, water and ripening of crops in the stages of agricultural cultivation. It is compassion that urges one to enter Buddha's path in the beginning and that safeguards the adherent from falling into pitfalls of the state of self-peace in the middle. Finally, it is due to compassion that Buddha always engages in the activities for the well-being of sentient beings.

Except in the case of a few commentaries on Tantra, not many Buddhist literatures are found in which omnipresence is attributed to the Buddha. The arguments or reasons for the theory of the Buddha as omnipresent are, according to Tantrayana, that the subtle body and the subtle mind are inseparable entities. Since Buddha's mind, *Sarvagyan,* or "All Knowing" reaches to all existing objects, so it is inevitable that his body is also all-pervasive.

Is Buddha Omnipotent?

The controversial concept of a super-mundane creator of this world is inevitably involved in the question of Buddha's omnipotence. But it is also appropriate to explore this question along with the third quality of Buddha, namely peerless strength or energy. Here

ten strengths (*Bhalas* in Sanskrit) are attributed to the Buddha. These strengths or *Bhalas* are as follows:
Strength of knowledge of what is possible and impossible,
of the consequences of actions,
of the different dispositions of sentient beings,
of the different elements,
of the higher or lower mental power of sentient beings,
of the progress that leads everywhere,
of all which concerns the origin of miseries of every kind and which will lead to equanimity, mystic meditations, complete emancipation and *dhayana*,
of remembering afterwards former abodes,
of birth and death, and
of destruction of afflictions.

The connotation of the word 'omnipotent' is being able to do anything one wishes, and none of the above mentioned strengths suggest that Buddha is able to do everything. Dialectical arguments may also be advanced that if Buddha has the power of doing everything he wishes, then, he would have delivered all sentient beings to the state of Nirvana and there would be no miserable beings in the world. Thus, it is clear that there is no place in Buddhism for the concept of a supernatural being as creator of the world.

What is the Creator?

The previous assertions do not imply that the world comes into being without any prime factor. A verse from the *Madhyamakavatara* of Acharya Chandrakirti should be quoted here:

The mind itself creates various animate and inanimate worlds; all living beings are produced by the Karma, and without mind, there can be no Karma.

Here we should not forget that the main problem giving rise to the concept of a creator in Buddhism is whether individual sentient beings remain in cyclic existence or are delivered to the state of cessation of suffering. The major point is that both the tamed and untamed mind bring about happiness and misery. So the mind that is harmonious with positive qualities is the basis of not only the ultimate and highest goal (Nirvana or Buddhahood) but also the basis of day to day well-being.

Disciplines

The Lord Buddha prescribed cultivation of ten virtues. They are to refrain from:

(Three bodily disciplines) Killing
Talking what is not owned
Adultery

(Four verbal disciplines) Lying
Slanderous speech
Hard and abusive language
Frivolous talk

(Three mental disciplines) Greediness
Desire to harm others
Wrong views

Beside these informal disciplines, there are formal vows of restraint which include: Pratimoksha discipline *(Hinayana)*, Bodhisattva discipline *(Mahayana)*, and Mantra discipline *(Vajrayana)*. The essence of the first of these is to avoid harming others; the essence of the second is to avoid the thought of self-interest; and the essence of the third is to cut off ordinary perception of the world. In Pratimoksha disciplines the main effort is to control the body and speech against fallacious actions. For example, all 253 vows of a fully ordained monk are concerned with eliminating faults of body and speech. On the other hand, the Bodhisattva and Vajrayana disciplines are mainly concerned with controlling the mind from fallacious activity. Here an inner resolve is made and inner negative conditions guarded against.

The Pratimoksha disciplines deal with controlling gross external faults as a means of paving the way for controlling subtle inner faults through Bodhisattva and Vajrayana disciplines. Therefore, those interested in accomplishing the path should take one form of Pratimoksha ordination in accordance with one's personal capacity as a basis for the higher training of the Bodhisattva and Mantra paths. Buddha himself, although born as a prince, abandoned his kingdom and adopted higher disciplines. As a result of this, he achieved higher *samadhi,* and dependent on higher *samadhi,* he attained higher wisdom and eventually the state of full enlightenment.

Bodhisattva Thoughts and Deeds

Without bothering to go into the specific vows of the Bodhisattva, we shall briefly outline the idea and activities of such a being. A person who is eligible to be called a Bodhisattva is one who has generated a determined aspiration for Buddhahood, not for the individual's sake but for the sake of all sentient beings. The activities or deeds of a Bodhisattva are summed up in six perfections (*paramita* in Sanskrit). It is interesting to note that each of these *paramitas* is presented in a threefold way as follows:

1. Perfection of generosity
   (a) Giving spiritual teaching or imparting any useful knowledge is generosity in terms of Dharma.
   (b) Giving any materials ranging from food and water to one's entire body is generosity in terms of material.
   (c) Giving protection to those who are threatened by any kind of fear is generosity in terms of protection.

2. Perfection of morality
   (a) Learning and following the Bodhisattva path is the morality of accumulating merits.
   (b) Keeping one's vows with great care is the morality of safeguarding oneself from non-virtuous forces.
   (c) Serving all sentient beings without discrimination is the morality of serving others.

3. Perfection of tolerance
   (a) Bearing hardships such as hunger, thirst and unfavorable weather for the sake of spiritual practice is tolerance against hardships.
   (b) Checking anger towards those who cause harm to oneself is tolerance against intentional harm.
   (c) Appreciating profound teachings such as those of emptiness *(shunyata)* and selflessness *(niratma)* and not being shocked by them is tolerance of understanding.

4. Perfection of assiduity
   (a) Keeping the inner resolve of achieving Buddhahood for the sake of all sentient beings is assiduity of armory.
   (b) Never discontinuing learning, thinking and meditation is assiduity of accumulation of merit.
   (c) Guiding sentient beings to virtuous deeds with skillful means is the assiduity of engaging for sentient beings.

5. Perfection of concentration
   (a) Engaging in various states of worldly absorption is concentration leading to happiness in the present life.
   (b) Engaging in various concentrations leading to the achievement of super-mundane qualities of Buddhahood is concentration for high quality.
   (c) Engaging in various activities for the well-being of sentient beings by means of the six clairvoyances is concentration of engaging oneself on the behalf of sentient beings.
6. Perfection of wisdom
   (a) Being well versed in scriptures dealing with the spiritual path is the wisdom of knowing the means by oneself.
   (b) Being well versed in the sciences of healing and the sciences of craft is the wisdom of knowing the means of other's well-being.
   (c) Being well versed in knowledge of logic and grammar is widsom of knowing the means of subduing opposing forces.

Conclusion

There will be no dispute in asserting that if these virtuous ideas and deeds prevail among the citizens, creation of a just society is guaranteed, for a society is constituted by its members and a just society is possible only when the people are just, whether or not they have faith in God. Man-made laws and regulations may be described as aids for bringing about justice in a society, but the ultimate factor is the *mind* which brings about justice or injustice depending on its tamed or untamed state.

10
On the Need of Faith for Justice
JAMES GAFFNEY

The question we have before us is multiply ambiguous inasmuch as all its major terms admit a remarkable variety of conventional understandings. As a result, one may be tempted to respond glibly to the question, 'Is faith in God necessary for the creation of a just society?' that "It all depends on what you mean by 'faith', 'God', 'creation', and 'just society'." It is a daunting response, in that the terms whose meanings have apparently to be determined before we can get on with answering our question are among the most controverted terms in the history of our culture, whole libraries having been filled with disquisitions and disputations, many of them wise, learned, and impassioned, trying to persuade or instruct us about what is, or should, or should not be meant by faith in God or creating a just society, or even to show us that such phrases can mean nothing at all.

Under the circumstances, it seems to me that perhaps the most practical way to proceed is by investigating whether or not our question can be answered affirmatively on any understanding of its terms that is not altogether arbitrary, and that refers to some reality or possibility. It is clear to me, moreover, that my own selection of meanings for these terms cannot pretend to range competently beyond those usages of Western culture that chiefly reflect biblical and classical traditions.

Before dealing with the substantive notions that must chiefly occupy this essay—faith in God and just society—it will be well to pay preliminary attention to the verbal components of our question, the references to necessity and creation. And, as far as creation is concerned, I wish to leave room for both its metaphysical sense, as the uniquely divine power of absolute origination and maintenance of being, and its more popular derivative sense of highly original, distinctively human, practical accomplishment.

Recognizing that the preceding distinction must also be accommodated in what we mean by necessity, let us broach a second clarification by asking how faith in God (whatever that means) might be conceived as necessary for the creation (divinely or humanly) of a just society (whatever that means). One possibility is that faith in God is requisite for sufficiently comprehending what a just society is, to envisage the thing one is trying to create or hoping to get created. In this sense, faith in God would furnish an idea or ideal without which the creative enterprise would have no clear objective to guide it or to measure its success. A second possibility is that faith in God furnishes a kind of power, otherwise unavailable, for attempting to bring a just society into being. Such power might be either psychological or physical, a kind of interior motivation, or a kind of external force. A third possibility is that faith in God is necessary not, or not only, to envisage or to achieve a just society, but actually to participate in one. This last sort of necessity would entail a limitation upon even divine power, in the sense that a just society would be absolutely unrealizable, and indeed unintelligible, except within a society of persons having faith in God. In summary, then, faith in God may be conceived in at least three distinct ways, corresponding to three possible understandings of its necessity for the creation of a just society: first, as a kind of enlightenment, necessary for envisaging a just society; second, as a kind of empowerment, necessary for effecting a just society; and third, as a kind of qualification, necessary for comprising a just society.

Each of these conceptions of how faith might be necessary for the creation of a just society, as a kind of enlightenment, or empowerment, or qualification, thus intimates some particular component of a hypothetical definition or description of faith. Such a hypothesis is testable in the sense that it is or is not conformable with usage.

There can be no doubt that faith has often been represented as a kind of enlightenment, although Christian theological polemics have given rise to an unwarranted exclusive insistence of this understanding of faith, and, by way of reaction, to exaggerated denials of it. Nevertheless, as is commonly conceded in the more ecumenical mood of recent decades, religious thought expressed in and under the influence of the Bible plainly does entertain a conception of faith which includes what may be called enlightenment—as we are reminded by the familiarity of such phrases as "the eyes of faith" and "the light of faith." Enlightenment is, of course, a metaphorical reference to light's function in making vision possible, and faith is accordingly often likened to a kind of vision. The essential idea, enablement to perceive, is expressed by the term 'revelation' which is commonly associated with faith and is related etymologically to the idea of removing a concealing veil. The Greek equivalent term, apocalypse, has identical etymological implications. The term disclosure, favored among some modern philosophers of religion, conveys the same idea of exposure to view. Whether one prefers the symbolism of turning on lights or taking off veils, the essential point is unaltered, that faith entails a gratifying kind of awareness, different in kind from the ordinary discoveries of our perceptive and inferential powers. What makes it different is a sense that awareness comes into touch, however tenuously, not merely with a deeper or higher order of truth or reality, but with the deepest and highest, a sense of ultimacy. Insofar as the import of such awareness can be enunciated declaratively, faith may be reflected in statements of belief. Perhaps the chief importance of such discourse is confessional and credal, furnishing a medium for the communication of faith and the association of those who discover the commonness of their faith. It makes possible also, and to the same effect, a kind of documentation of faith, as in sacred scriptures, which tends to acquire normative status in communities united by faith. Given such status, articulations of faith are employed as principles, whose elaboration engenders theologies which, although ranging far from the fundamental enlightenment or awareness of faith, serve to link that awareness to other areas of thought and behavior. Although a distinction is rightly made between faith and beliefs, and disjunctions often occur between them, it is as natural and advantageous for faith to engender beliefs as for any valued intuition to issue in judgments and reasonings.

No less ordinary than the understanding of faith as a kind of awareness or enlightenment, is the attribution to it of that dynamic character I wished to suggest by the term empowerment. Perhaps the context in which this character is exhibited most prominently is that of conversion, understood as the process (or moment) of transition to faith from faithlessness. Experiences of conversion have many aspects and admit many peculiarities, but they are typically marked by an extraordinary sense of enhanced, integrated, and directed energy. The convert from faithlessness to faith feels inspired, in the literal sense, as if inhaling a new vitality, acquiring a new life, regenerate, being born again—recalling terms that, precisely as cliches, evidence the familiarity of such notions. But faith is not, under this aspect, merely an experience of heightened vigor, for its effects are perceived not as sheerly self-generated, but as responsive to a benign influence that impinges upon and penetrates the self. A sense, not of power, simply, but of empowerment, it essentially involves a recognition of being sustained and carried forward by ultimate power and purpose, and elicits a determination to submit to that power and participate in that purpose. Faith in this sense, no less than in the preceding one, seeks to express itself in appropriate language. Declarations of beliefs, however, are a poor idiom for expressing the implications of entrusting oneself to ultimate power and purpose. It is not cognitive but volitional terms that are in order here, and the language of faith tends accordingly to adopt expressions connoting resignation, conformity, commitment, obedience, as attributes of faith. Correlatively, the object or occasion of faith tends to be referred to in terms that connote summoning, guiding, bidding, and directing. It thus naturally results that moral, ethical, and even legal language is typically brought into the service of faith's vocabulary. Such language is again evoked by social purposes of testimony and teaching, and it serves those purposes by indicating and commending the characteristic direction taken by a life that is animated by faith. What is experienced as inspiration thus comes to be proclaimed as ideal, and actions and attitudes congenial to such inspiration come to be regarded as standards of virtue. While such standards may extensively resemble familiar rules of ethics, they are very often combined with more strictly ascetical norms, and concerned with interior as well as external behavior. Here again, systematic elaboration is, of course, possible, and may, in certain cultural circumstances, go far in the direction of tortuous legalism and scrupulous moralism, familiar exaggerations of human efforts to harmonize the ordinary with the ideal.

The last of my three suggested modalities of faith is what I have designated by the term 'qualification'. That is, faith is commonly thought of as entailing or imparting a new potentiality. In virtue of faith, one is enabled to become something, or to participate in something to which otherwise one would have no access. This idea is closely related to the preceding one; yet sufficiently distinct to require separate attention. As already noted, that aspect of faith which involves an experience of empowerment normally elicits a sense not merely of being activated, but of being activated purposefully, so that, in entrusting oneself to the source of power, one is likewise committing oneself to some destiny towards which that power is oriented. The convert's sense is typically not one of arrival, but rather of embarkation. One who is born again acquires a new life, the maturation of which is directed to a goal. Perhaps, nothing points more directly to this aspect of faith than its typical acknowledgement in ritual, inasmuch as the ceremonial response to faith so commonly assumes the form of some kind of initiation. The profession or demonstration of faith is here regarded as constituting basic eligibility to participate in a community predicated upon faithful ones aspiring to a communion of holy ones. Faith thus normally entails a sense of election, although the history of such usage obliges us to recall that a sense of election is no ground for a judgement of reprobation. As a component of faith, election implies only inclusion; notions of exclusiveness arise from quite different sources.

In the present state of our culture, it appears that talk about faith in God strikes many—and, among the educated, probably even most of our contemporaries—as a recondite, if not actually fantastic exercise in esoteric discourse, whereas talk about a just society elicits the ready interest of down-to-earth realists and people who generally pride themselves on hard-headed practicality and common sense. The former is the business of theologians, notoriously an odd lot employed in a a dubious enterprise, whereas the latter attracts the energies of lawyers, political and behavioral scientists, and philosophers of a healthily un-metaphysical ilk. Although I am myself not a theologian, nor an aspirant to become one, I find this a strange view of things. For it seems to me that although talking about faith in God can get one into deep waters, not to mention murky shallows, the thing itself is not unfamiliar, even now, to ordinary human experience, and is abundantly reflected in all sorts of cultural records, whereas the more one hears and reads about just society the more that appears to be a will-o'-the-wisp, stubbornly misrepresented as a solid prospect. I, at least, know, in a quite downright and empirical way, what I am talking about when I allude to faith in God, and I find that, with only ordinary conversational adaptation, I discover that what lots of other people talk about under the same heading is sufficiently similar to facilitate amicable and constructive discourse. But it is otherwise when I try to think, talk, or apprehend what others are thinking and saying about just society. I have come to suspect that the fundamental reason for this is that, whereas faith in God is something of which a great many people have familiar experience, no one has experienced what is referred to as a just society, and, since those experiences that most nearly suggest such a thing are the last to be consulted for light on the subject, scarcely anyone seems to be much good at imagining one in a fashion satisfactory to anybody else.

Plato, for example, is one of the very few prescribers for a just society who gives a fairly clear account of what he thinks would result from following his prescriptions, but I have yet to meet anyone who would really wish to take up permanent residence in anything approximating Plato's republic. Plato is also one of the few to deal with the relationship between what we mean by justice as a personal attribute and what we mean in predicating it of a state—but, again, I have yet to meet anyone who fully agrees with him about this. Yet it is in the context of that explanation that Plato established what remains central to nearly everybody's notion of justice, classically (and ambiguously) abbreviated *suum cuique* by the Roman Stoics, to each his own. Plato's more ample formulation, "the having and doing of what pertains to oneself and one's household," brings out the two basic aspects, of having and doing one's proper share. While Plato is more interested in the doing, Aristotle tends to emphasize the having, and he elucidates this on the basis of the popular assumption that justice involves equality. He attempts to interpret this equality, compatible with realism about seemingly irreducible disparities among persons, by his concept of proportional equality, which he associates with the idea of merit. That association becomes clear when he proposes that, in the political sphere, each one's share be equally proportioned to his contribution; in that sense one gets what one deserves, and what one deserves is measured by what one contributes. These notions, supplemented by the more obvious one of fair restitution, Aristotle's "corrective justice," established the classic categories that continue to undergird most of our thinking on this subject. The important additional presumption, that justice requires freedom, is also established by Aristotelian theory—sufficiently so to render inconsistent its simultaneous approval of slavery. Thus, in Western secular tradition, a just society has been commonly thought of as one comprising persons who are to some extent free and in some sense equal, doing their share, getting their share, and paying their debts.

However, especially in recent times, 'just society' seems most often to designate a much more comprehensive ideal than such a phrase would have suggested to Aristotle, for whom, after all, justice was only one of the excellences desirable in either an individual or a society. A good person or a good society must, indeed, be just, but must also possess a number of other virtues in order to achieve that well-being which is, for Aristotle, the point of it all. Curiously, it seems to have come about that, on the one hand, we persist in explaining justice in ways traceable to Aristotle, yet insist on attributing to it a sufficiency that would have astonished him.

How this has come about historically is a complex matter. I shall content myself with suggesting that the primary reason is related to the fact that we have inherited our ideas and our words about justice *(iustitia, dikaiosune)* not only from classical sources, but also from biblical ones. Insofar as notice is taken of this fact, an effort is sometimes made to reduce the resulting confusion by differentiating between justice, as classically defined, and righteousness, as biblically understood. But such a verbal distinction was precluded throughout most of our cultural history by the limitations of Latinity (even now it is difficult to achieve in the Romance languages), in which *iustitia* became not only a vehicle for each of two traditions, but an instrument of their attempted synthesis and, consequently, an occasion of their frequent confusion.

Human beings in the Western world have thus been taught by their composite culture to set their hopes on one conception of justice, that of a biblical realm of righteousness, while basing their ethical analyses and moral policies on a much more modest conception of it, that of the classical *suum cuique*. And so we find ourselves confronted, again and again, with well-argued accounts of, or plans for, a just society, experiencing profound disappointment. And we express such disappointment by an insistence that justice means more, promises more, demands more, than such theories and projects encompass.

In our own time, the most usual way of voicing this insistence has been by recourse to terminology transfered from the realm of law to that of ethics, the language of rights, and particularly of natural and human rights. The need for such language is felt as it becomes apparent that, in our schemes of justice predicated on traditional understanding of the *suum cuique,* a great deal of human wretchedness, of a kind that normally evokes moral indignation, remains not only unprevented, but systematically perpetuated. We are, for example, dissatisfied with arrangements for fair distribution based on Aristotle's formula of proportional equality, because we discover it to be a formula that assures not only extreme human

On the Need of Faith for Justice

inequalities, but utter destitution in the case of those who can merit nothing because, for whatever reason, they contribute nothing.

And so, in respect of such cases, we eventually hear an outcry to the effect that the resultant deprivations are not merely unfortunate, but unjust, because the disadvantaged have a positive right to more than the tragic insufficiency allotted to them by proportional equality. But, since proportional equality was conceived from the start as the measure of desert, this is to affirm the paradox of their having a right to more than they deserve! And there our troubles begin practically as well as theoretically, for, having enunciated a positive right, we have to find somebody to incur a correlative obligation. But, since our classical traditions of justice do not effectively identify such obligations, we rely at last upon some civic consensus to support public means of assuring at least minimal provision of "welfare." And usually we must elicit such consensus by appealing to feelings of compassion, because the very poor can be touchingly pathetic, or to fear, because the very poor can be ominously desperate. Unfortunately, on that basis the only measure we have for determining when enough has been done is the receding of such feelings below a threshold of discomfort; a result which can, of course, be brought about in ways having little or no connection with the relief of poverty. Insofar as we do, occasionally, manage to achieve some kind of public, formal consensus about human rights, the rights agreed upon turn out to be mostly negative and, if positive, extremely general and detached from specified assignments of obligation.

The most discussed theory of justice in recent times relies, like Aristotle, on a presumption of equality, identified practically with fairness. Fairness, however, is not interpreted as proportional equality, but as equal participation in an arrangement of responsibilities and rewards constituted with a view to best satisfying the occupants of all roles in society. The conception of such an arrangement is ingeniously introduced by supposing it to issue from the reasonable planning of persons who knew they would be part of it, but who did not know what roles would fall to their lot. In such an arrangement, it is plausibly argued, inequalities are to be expected and may be welcomed, but only insofar as they result in compensating benefits for all, and especially for society's least advantaged members. Such a theory of justice may appear to be one of the rare instances in which something very like the Golden Rule (usually applied to transactions between individuals) is effectively transposed into a context of comprehensive social relationships. For, in formulating arrangements for justice as fairness in the manner described, one is indeed arranging to treat others as one would have others treat oneself. But, one is doing so in a fancied ingorance of who one is, where one stands, and who everybody else is and where they stand. Within the limits of that fancy, adopting the Golden Rule is sober prudence, making no demand on altruism and posing no threats to egoism. One will make up all the accommodations as nicely as possible, because one never knows which of them may turn out to be one's permanent abode. But, supposing it to be revealed by some mischievous divination where one's own accommodations and those of one's friends will be located, familiar practices of discrimination may be expected to ensue. In social planning, loving one's neighbor as oneself is neither strenuous nor problematic as long as one cannot tell one's neighbor from oneself. But we can tell. And so it is strenuous and problematic.

It is strenuous, because making the necessary adjustments is more or less painful to many, whose spontaneous resistance must be overcome by either uncommon virtue or uncommon coercion. It is problematic in all sorts of ways, of which perhaps the most basic is the notorious difficulty of making fair interpersonal comparisons in the distribution of goods. Are they, for instance, to be based merely on equalizing satisfactions, despite normal convictions that many persons' satisfactions are themselves deplorable? (Mill's contrast of Socratic with porcine pleasures is not a problem for utilitarians alone.) Or are they to be based on a supposedly enlightened assessment of human values which when reduced to policy, draws accusations of elitist paternalism and increases the strenuousness by bringing in educational tasks that, if successfully discharged, add to it still further by raising thresholds of satisfaction?

In the light of such considerations it has to be asked whether or not a just society is even imaginable, much less attainable, among persons who differ widely and deeply in their fundamental assumptions concerning human values and the order of priorities among them. As far as I can see, the nearest we come to prescribing just arrangements for societies of such radical pluralism is represented by the liberal formulae currently favored in our own societies, which strive to reduce the initial inequalities of persons and groups of persons conceived essentially as competitors, leaving the rest to competiton itself, apart from emergency care for the graver casualties.

I wish to suggest, therefore, that our aspirations to a just society, being, as they plainly are, enormously more ambitious than any supportable by classical conceptions of justice, are in fact strictly unachievable by a collectivity that comprises extreme differences in the assessment of fundamental values. Augustine is right; societies, at least in his pre-Weberian usage which does not contrast them with communities, are fashioned by human beings insofar as they agree about what it is they love. The justice of a society, in the demanding sense of that phrase which we seem to have adopted without exploring its origins or its implications, is achievable only through cooperation in the furtherance of what is unanimously loved. "Two loves built two cities," and any number of loves build any number of cities; but cities built on incompatible loves have little basis for any justice beyond that of insuring fair play among contestants. And on that basis, in the last analysis, the justice of a just society differs only in degree from the justice of a just war.

All this seems clearer to most of us when we are talking about little societies than when we are talking about big ones. Thus, we should hold out little hope of lasting justice for a married couple or family which was unable or unwilling to agree about what the members loved, to establish fundamental common values and an order of priorities respecting them. We are saddened but scarcely surprised at what we perceive in families that neglect this condition of justice. The idea of organizing a family upon principles of fair competition strikes us as bizarre, and efforts to do so strike us as either pitiful or contemptible. We know what Tolstoy meant when he wrote that marvelous opening sentence, "All happy families resemble one another, but each unhappy family is unhappy in its own peculiar way." But, even though we often transfer familial terminology to larger societies, the moral analogy is not much attended to.

In this connection, religious movements like that of the Unification Church offer a salutary perspective by their primacy of attention to family goodness or holiness. And it is notorious how often, in social movements that aspire to more than conventional justice, the terminology of parental, filial, and sibling relationships spontaneously commends itself. One recalls how naturally in early Christianity, brothers and sisters became the ordinary designations of community members, and how regularly afterwards that usage was mimicked by religious communities, who came together in agreement about what it was they loved and how they would cooperate in its furtherance. Even in the effort to establish just society on strictly secular premises, the same tendency appears when the ideals of liberty and equality are significantly supplemented by that of fraternity. The very term 'comrade', originally denoting a roommate, is not entirely out of touch with the domestic paradigm of social goodness.

That is, I submit, the paradigm that still most nearly captures, as an experienced reality, the persistent ideal called just society, which is never satisfied for long, even theoretically, with anything philosophers can offer based on a classical understanding of justice. We do not want or expect domestic sharing to be controlled by measures of proportional equality. We take for granted, in that context, that needs will be provided for by standards not of merit but of generosity, regardless of discriminate obligations. We expect cooperation, not competition, to be the basis of familial sharing. We require, in short, that quality of social behavior which expresses awareness of and esteem for kinship and which is, for that reason, known as kindness. We talk a language of rights and deserts, but the very ways we stretch and strain that language to encompass our real desires make clear that we are, all the while, thinking thoughts and glimpsing visions of righteousness and grace. The exasperated resisters of every social reform are, after all, correct: if you give them an inch they will want a yard. Never will they be satisfied with any society that is unequivocally and literally just. Getting what we deserve is not, after all, a prospect many of us can contemplate with tranquility. What is wanted, and bit by bit demanded, is not an arena of equal opportunity, but something a good deal more like a peaceful household—a Beth shalom, a Dar-es-Salaam, a Domus Pacis.

And that, I propose is a sign to us, from wherever we suppose such signs are given, that what we really seek, incompetently but incessantly, as a just society, is not a conclusion from reasonings upon justice. Rather is it a prospect about which faith enlightens us, towards which faith empowers us, and for which faith qualifies us. Throughout our endlessly revised schemings and strivings for a just society, we look forward and press on towards "a city that is to come," one where we shall all find ourselves at home, as good children are at home with one another in their good parents' house.

On the Need of Faith for Justice

"Faith," we are told, "is the substance of things hoped for, the evidence of things unseen." And, being such, it is, in our human societies, the source of that abiding restlessness, that divine discontent, which keeps requiring better arrangements, and even manages from time to time to make better arrangements, knowing them to be better by applying the standard not of rational calculation but of a visionary ideal. "Ah, but a man's reach should exceed his grasp, or what's a heaven for?" Progress in social goodness is indispensably quixotic, inseparable from the dreaming of impossible dreams and the fighting of invincible foes. And, as the familial analogy suggests, it is progress towards a condition that depends on having not only sound policies, but sound people. For a just society comprising unjust people is ultimately as silly an idea as that of a good family made up of bad relatives. The sort of vision and the sort of motivation necessary for achieving social improvement remains necessary for preserving it. And in that sense, the faith that reveals and empowers is likewise the faith that qualifies; it is socially creative as God is creative, not merely as initial impetus, but as continuing sustenance. "The righteous person lives by faith." And the righteous society lives by the faith of its members, or it does not live very long or very consistently.

Is, then, faith in God necessary for the creation of a just society? If my phenomenology of faith in God is not altogether wrong, and if I am at all right about what ordinary people really mean by their never-satisfied demand for a social betterment they call justice, then it seems to me believable that, for the creation of a just society, faith in God is necessary. That, even though it be necessary, it is decidedly not sufficient, may seem demonstrated by history and experience. But that is, anyway, inseparable from the idea itself. For what the necessity of faith implies is not its own sufficiency, but rather the necessity of its object or ground. "Unless the Lord builds the house, those who build it labor in vain."

To become persuaded, as indicated here, of the necessity *and* sufficiency of faith *and* God for the creation of a just society, is to occupy, at least intellectually, a religious position. It is a kind of religious position whose theological implications have already a certain definiteness, to which certain of the world's existing religions and spiritualities appear, at least immediately, more congenial than others. But those are matters lying beyond the scope and above the plane of this essay, which it would be this essay's chief merit merely to introduce.

11
Just Society: God's Shadow or Man's Work?
SHIVESH C. THAKUR

The question I shall answer is: 'Is faith in God necessary for the creation of a just society?' My intuition—for whatever it's worth—seems to dictate a negative response. For one thing, I can recognize or imagine a just society in the creation of which faith in God has played no noticeable part. Equally, I can envisage an individual or a group which, in certain obvious respects, may even be "God-intoxicated," but which nonetheless might create a highly unjust society. It certainly does not seem to be all that difficult to find instances of this phenomenon in history. My intuitive judgement appears to me also to receive vindication from logic. There would seem to be no analytic connection between 'faith in God' on the one hand and either 'just society' or 'the creation of a just society', on the other. The necessity, if any, then, cannot be of the strong, logical variety: there seems to be no obvious nonsense or self-contradiction involved, at least on the face of it, in asserting that a just society can be created—if it can be created at all!—without faith in God.

However, showing that there is an absence of logical necessity does not by itself show that there may not be a weaker form of necessity obtaining here, such as the causal variety. I will, for the moment, ignore the Humean dictum to the contrary, and allow that the necessity obtaining in a causal relationship is more than merely an habitual predisposition to think and speak in certain ways. If such a non-logical, 'physical necessity' (it will be seen that I am allowing—contrary to a well-known piece of philosophical wisdom—that the term 'physical necessity' is not incoherent) obtained between 'faith in God' and a 'just society' or 'the creation of a just society', then, at the very least, one would expect to see invariable concomitance between the two. But, as I hinted earlier, I find no such concomitance historically, and cannot see how anyone could establish a case for it without using 'justice' in peculiar senses.

Just Society: God's Shadow or Man's Work?

If my argument so far is sound, and there is in fact no relationship of necessity here, then the question I must ask now is why anyone should have thought that there was, or might be, one. I could, of course, ascribe the thought to naiveté or intellectual confusion, and leave it there. But this requires a degree of arrogance which I do not believe I have. Besides, this device seems to me to be methodologically barren, and perhaps dangerous. So I must honestly look for grounds on which it might be thought that faith in God is necessary for the creation of a just society. Here are some possibilities:

(a) 'Justice' may be understood and/or defined in theocentric ways, so that it could then be possible to show that there is, or was, an analytic connection, after all, between faith and the creation of a just society. For example, if justice consists in or presupposes sinlessness on the part of members of a society, and sin itself is understood as trangression of God's will and laws, then it should be fairly easy to demonstrate the analyticity that I failed to find above, especially if it is stipulated additionally, that only God's grace could lead to sinlessness. Such a view would imply that other conceptions of a just society are either wrong, misguided or narrow.

(b) Alternatively, 'justice' may be defined, at least broadly understood, in secular terms such as the liberal, utilitarian, or Marxist sense, but it may be held that such conceptions of a just society require divine inspiration and action for their actual fulfillment. Finite as they are, human beings will, as a matter of fact, be unable to put their precepts into practice, however well they understand what a just society ought to be like. Neither human intention nor intellect may here be suspect, but simply the power, without divine aid, to deliver the goods.

(c) On the other hand, the authenticity of human intention may itself be disputed. A just society, it may be argued, is impossible of achievement unless all, or most, members of the society are righteous, unselfish and caring about the rights and welfare of all others. But even a casual look at human nature, the argument might run, reveals that they are selfish, greedy and frequently brutal in the pursuit of their own ends; and, therefore, any profession of commitment to justice for all is no more than mere "crocodile tears." For this argument to succeed, it may not be necessary to impute a vile character to every human being: a warranted attribution to most of them will do. Given this awesome, and awful, fact, if it is a fact, the creation of a just society will remain a pipe dream, unless God intervenes to transform and transfuse our characters in appropriate ways, and in appropriate degrees.

(d) Finally (and I do not mean that there are no other ways left, but merely that this is the last which I intend to consider), proponents of a relationship of necessity may concede that there may be no way of demonstrating the logical dependence of a just society on faith in God, nor of any strong physical or empirical inevitability. But, it may still be held that this failure to demonstrate this necessity, need not entail that such a relationship does not after all exist, as a matter of fact. Not every fact need be demonstrable; and of those that are, some can only admit a "weak" demonstration. In the context of the issue at hand, such a weak demonstration may, for example, be said to have been given, if it is argued successfully that only societies based on faith have ever been just, or even approximated the ideals of justice. This might serve as a weak, inductive, vindication of the relationship of necessity.

Now, what can one make of the lines of reasoning in (a)–(d), or any other, for that matter, that may be advanced in support of the claim that faith is necessary for the creation of a just society. It seems to me that I have no choice here but to confront a very intimidating and formidable task—that of delineating, in howsoever crude a fashion, the meanings of 'justice' and of a 'just society'. For, unless we have some idea of what these concepts mean, there will be no way of assessing the force and validity of the arguments we need to examine. I intend to tackle the task by, first, making a clear distinction between the 'defining' and 'identifying' properties of the concepts in question. I admit, without any false sense of humility, that it is extremely difficult, if not impossible, to offer a definition of 'justice', such that everyone, or even almost everyone, will assent to it, irrespective of the time, place and larger conceptual framework at or within which the subject is being discussed. To say this is not to enter into the controversy about realism versus relativism in respect to justice: all that is meant is that even if justice has an objective, time-independent content of its own, this content does at least require, and elicit, reinterpretation and refinement from time to time. It is an evolving, not a static concept: it has an "open texture," like all empirical concepts. That is partly why it is so difficult to define. It is easier, however, to specify a cluster of identifying marks or properties, such that if an alleged case of a just society fails to exemplify a reasonable number of them in reasonably adequate

Just Society: God's Shadow or Man's Work?

proportions, we may have no hesitation in rejecting the claim of true instantiation. This will perhaps sound less controversial, and hardly arbitrary, if it is paraphrased by saying that inability to define a concept does not necessarily entail inability to recognize a particular specimen as being a good, bad or indifferent exemplar of the concept. Indeed, unless the truth of this proposition were assumed, it is difficult to see how one would set about the task of defining any empirical concept whatsoever.

What, then, are the identifying marks of a just society? In the first place a just society must be based on the "rule of law": that is, it will not be a society in which anything goes. This itself presupposes the primacy of equality for all citizens, irrespective of any considerations of race, sex, color, and the circumstances of birth and upbringing. Given the context, the equality in question may be equality of being, that of equal treatment under the law or of equality of opportunity, or all these and other forms of equality. For justice has everything to do with the the idea of (human or other), rights, and these rights tend to be largely—though not entirely—about the right to equality of one or another of the kinds mentioned earlier. It is because members of a society are deemed to have the right to equality of citizenship, that it is considered just or fair to take steps to eliminate or minimize the natural or historical disadvantage that some of them might otherwise suffer. Incidentally, it must be instructive here—in the context of a discussion of the necessity of faith for the creation of a just society—that it is supposed also to undo, as far as it can, effects of "natural injustice," some, if not all, of which could, in suitable contexts, be said to owe their origins to divine creation, imposition or oversight.

Primary among the fundamental rights that members of a just society are said to enjoy is the right to three liberties—i.e., freedom of thought, speech and action, limited only by the requirement that such liberties must not infringe the identical rights of other members of the society. For, whatever the origins of this system of rights, once in being, it operates as a social contract between members of the society, where the rights are balanced by relevant obligations. Finally, a just society incorporates some system for equal distribution of primary goods, as far as is possible within specified or specifiable limits. Primary goods are usually thought to include such things as food, housing, medical care, and other "want-satisfying" goods and, arguably, wealth. The differences between the liberal, the utilitarian, and the Marxist, for example, on the question of what constitutes a just society, do not lie in that one accepts equality and the other does not; nor in that one thinks liberty is a good thing and the other does not; nor again in that one advocates and the other rejects the goal of a roughly equal distribution of social wealth, welfare and opportunities. They lie, in fact, in their different ordering of the priorities between these (and other) requirements of justice; in the theories they put forward regarding the principles of justice; and in their views of what count as acceptable (or unacceptable) limits to equality, liberty and welfare, etc. Even this extremely brief account gives us, I think, a reasonably clear—and, I hope, noncontroversial—cluster of the identifying marks of a just society.

It should be evident that this "cluster" is not exhaustive: it merely pinpoints those attributes, the possession of all or most of which might enable us, today, to identify a just society. The advantage of this way of talking is that it should allow us to pick out examples of just societies in a realistic but flexible manner. It allows us to recognize, for example, that some societies can be more just than others; and that some of them put a greater stress on certain features of justice than on some others. It enables us, too, to recognize that at certain times, e.g. during war or a natural catastrophe, some usual rights and benefits may be held in abeyance, without requiring us, for that reason, to call an otherwise just society unjust. But, equally, it leaves us in no doubt that if a society is utterly lacking in all, or even most, of the important attributes, without countervailing reasons to account for this lack, then we can only characterize it as unjust. There could, of course, always be a borderline case where we will be uncertain about what to say. But that would not be peculiar to this method of identification: it would happen with any method we might care to devise.

We now have what I believe to be at least a rule-of-thumb method of understanding what a just society should be like and, therefore, of understanding what (social) justice should be about. Let us now return to the four arguments I formulated earlier as possible supporting grounds for the position that faith in God is necessary for the creation of a just society, and see what can be said by way of assessment of the arguments.

It looks to me that there may be nothing wrong with argument (a), at least not with its structure. There is nothing illogical about explicating the concept of justice in a theocentric way, nor about taking the view that a society is just, only because and only insofar

Just Society: God's Shadow or Man's Work?

as it is good according to certain specified criteria, formulated in theocentric ways. For, as Rawls quite correctly maintains, justice may be the first, but it is only one of the virtues of a society; and a theist is free to argue that an ideal society must not only be just, but also sinless, God-fearing and suffused with *amor dei*. Such a conception of society may well be laudable as an ideal; but the point to note is that if it is to count as a just society, then it will only do so if it shows in its workings all or most of the identifying marks of a just society, I outlined earlier, and in adequate proportions. The fact that this society displays other, "divinely endowed" virtues, while counting as a useful bonus, will only support the conclusion of argument (a) if it can be shown that there is a necessary connection between these other virtues and justice, such that it is impossible to have the latter without the former. While conceding, for the sake of the argument, that this can be done, I cannot see that this is going to be easy.

For a start, the notion of human (or other) *rights* does not exactly fit in with a society in which God's authority is deemed to be supreme. God's grace must militate against the idea of rights. Besides, the goal of eliminating or minimizing natural disadvantage or natural inequalities—one of the hallmarks of a just society—will surely look suspect in a theocratic society; for such a society will have to assume that God must have some purpose in creating these inequalities in the first place. In any case, given that we can have some understanding of what a just society should be like, without presupposing God or faith in God, I do not see how it can be claimed that it is impossible to conceptualize justice from a non-theistic standpoint. Sinlessness, etc., may well be a sufficient condition for the creation of a just society—although I have given reasons above why even this may be arguable—but it does not seem to be a necessary condition. And I still see no analytic connection between 'faith in God' and 'the creation of a just society'. If there is one I should be grateful for a demonstration.

As for argument (b), it seems to me that a demonstration of its unsoundness can be given. What possible point could there be in resting in faith, praying for God's aid in the creation of a just society, when injustices of many kinds can only be seen as God's "gift" or punishment, at least by those who believe in God and have faith in him. I am aware of theological explanations of physical and metaphysical evil, and fully appreciate some of the arguments. But I have to admit that in the face of these natural injustices and evils, and God's singular failure to do anything about them so far, these arguments do not seem to me to amount to more than an apology for God's unwillingness or powerlessness to take corrective action. And, surely, there is something odd about apologizing for God and having faith in him at the same time. God's ways may indeed be mysterious; and it is possible that one day he will surprise us. But in the meantime, to all of us who care about the creation of a just society now, my only advice is to forget about God and get on with the job at hand.

The third of the arguments, (c) above, starts by making a point which is possibly true, i.e., that human beings are selfish, greedy and frequently brutal. But it cannot be deduced from this that they may not be sincere in their profession of commitment to justice, except by ignoring that they are also *rational*. And by 'rational' I here mean nothing more lofty than that they know which states of affairs will best serve their own interests. Clearly, some humans are more rational than others; but, equally, some are less selfish than others. However, the point is that this rationality can itself be said to provide a basis for the creation of a just society. This has indeed been the supposition behind the social contract theory of justice, which has a very distinguished ancestry. I do not wish to suggest that this is the only acceptable theory of its kind, nor that there is no other route to take from the premise of human selfishness, etc. But, as long as at least this one route remains a viable approach—and I believe it is—it would not have been shown that faith in God and his redemptive action is the only route to take from the initial datum of human selfishness. Additionally, and very importantly, it must make more sense, rationally that is, to have faith in the doctrines and persons of those humans who have actually led humanity towards justice, than in a divine being whose conception of justice, if he has one, may be utterly different from our own; and whose commitment to removing injustice seems, on the face of it, to be at least suspect. We might have been justified in coming to the opposite conclusion if we had reason to believe that all modern instigators of a just society had themselves been God-fearing and God-inspired creatures whose conception of and commitment to justice, therefore, owed all or much to faith in God. But that does not seem to be the case: Kant, Hume, Mill and Marx, to mention only a few distinguished names, were singularly unenthusiastic about God. It is possible, of course, that unbeknown to them, God was working through them; and that, except for that invisible hand,

Just Society: God's Shadow or Man's Work?

they might not have succeeded in taking us even as far as they did towards the goal of a just society. But I think rationality demands a preference for grasping firm, visible hands rather than groping for invisible, possibly non-existent, ones!

I now come to the last of the four arguments, argument (d), and wish to consider whether it is possible to provide weak, inductive vindication of the supposition that faith is necessary for the creation of a just society. The evidence, it seems to me, does not look very promising. For a start, in the sense that we wish to understand a just society (outlined earlier through the cluster of identifying marks), there have not been many examples in history of just societies, but there have been quite a few of cruel and unjust ones, all or most of which were religion and/or God-based. Inequalities, injustices and the exploitation of the many by the few, were the rule rather than the exception; and, what's more, these were often said to be justified *because* they constituted God's will and ordinance. Not much to be said for faith in God here. Indeed, the injustices and inequalities of traditional societies can only become excusable, if they do, by arguing that, after all, they did not understand 'justice' in the "full-blown" sense that only we, at our stage of the evolution of this term, properly can.

I here anticipate a possible defense for the need to have faith along the following lines. While God, it may be said, has an interest in us being led to the creation of a just society, he is not in a hurry, as we tend to be. Consequently, he has waited this long in history in order to give us the chance to make the discovery ourselves of what a just society could be like; and since this has only begun to happen relatively recently, perhaps we should be looking at only modern examples of just societies in order to determine if faith is necessary for the creation of such a society. This argument, I must confess, sounds a bit limp already; but since it is not self-evidently invalid, I propose to examine the inductive evidence, briefly of course, relating to the contemporary world. For this purpose, I will divide the world's regimes today into the following classes: (1) Liberal Democratic, (2) Democratic Socialist, (3) Socialist Collectivist, (4) Traditional Feudal, (5) Fundamentalist Theocratic, and (6) Miscellaneous Charismatic. There may well be some reason for adding a seventh class, the "Theatre of the Absurd;" but, for that very reason, it will not be possible to say much about it!

This classification is obviously a bit simplistic, but not altogether arbitrary, nor, I hope, altogether uninstructive for our purposes. For fear of raising avoidable controversies, I will not name regimes as falling into this or that class; and I hope that it is not considered necessary: we can all look around and come to our own conclusions about which belongs where. It is also not my intention to suggest that certain regimes do not share the characteristics of more than one class: they frequently do. Nor do I wish to insinuate that the character of any society is necessarily or entirely reflected in its political regime. To the contrary my classification is merely a convenient way of getting a bird's eye view of the social, economic and political conditions of distinct social groups with a view to seeing what role, if any, faith in God might be said to play in their just character—if any of them are, in fact, just. I suggest that those that are just, are only more or less so, rather than being the utopias in respect to justice they are depicted to be by their citizens or admirers. So much by way of clarification. Although much more clarification is no doubt needed, in providing it we might run the risk of missing the forest for the trees.

Given the cluster of identifying marks outlined earlier, it will come as no surprise that I regard the first three classes (i.e. Liberal Democratic, Democratic Socialist and Socialist Collectivist) as the only ones that, *as classes,* seem to be even attempting to approximate the ideals of a just society; although all of them fall short in some important ways. And it is significant that none of them proclaim faith in God as a prerequisite; in fact the last clearly frowns on this possibility. It may be that this is why they have not come closer to being fully just societies. But that is an unproven and unprovable assumption. Traditional Feudal regimes can hardly be said to make justice the first virtue of society; although specific regimes may be said to display occasional charity. Fundamentalist Theocratic regimes are, by definition, committed to the centrality of faith in all that they might wish to achieve; but they are almost invariably found wanting in their understanding and respect for fundamental human rights, even though some of them have succeeded in improving the economic well-being of their citizens. The sixth, and last of the seriously meant classes, namely, Miscellaneous Charismatic, defies generalizations. Some are just and others repressive and reactionary; and what roles faith in God, or God himself, are supposed to play is hard to determine because they vary from society to society. But clearly there is not much material here that could either conclusively establish or refute the case for the necessity of faith in the creation of a just society. I conclude, then, that the examination of contemporary societies also fails to show that faith in God is necessary for the creation of a just society, although it may be sufficient. I must, however, confess that when it comes to the class of societies I named the "Theatre of the Absurd," if they function at all, then someone, somewhere must have a lot of faith in either God or something closely resembling God!

There are two final points I wish to make briefly. If it is contended that the four arguments I put forward in possible defense of the necessity of faith are only "strawmen," which I put together with the aim of quick demolition, I would, while eschewing the intellectually disreputable motive attributed, honestly affirm my ignorance of any better ones, and beg to be enlightened. The final point is this. I can see faith in God serving as an important and useful tool—*if* it helps make those interested in the creation of a just society more humble, patient and, therefore, less prone to violence whenever the goal of a just society seems to elude quick fulfillment. For, the purpose of justice cannot be served by violence which is itself a prime embodiment of injustice. I do not think that men of faith are necessarily less prone to violence. But nothing much may be lost by entertaining the illusion. Or might it?

12
Is Faith in God Necessary for the Creation of a Just Society? A Process Perspective
GENE REEVES

The question posed for our discussion is whether faith in God is required for the creation of a just society. In this paper I make two separate claims: (1) that in one sense faith in God is necessary for any kind of human existence, and (2) that in another sense faith in God is necessary for an adequate public or social ethics. From these two propositions it follows that faith in God is necessary for creation of a just society.

We must deal however with words. In the proposition 'faith in God is necessary for the creation of a just society' there are at least five key terms: 'faith', 'God', 'necessary', 'creation', and 'just society'. In this paper the terms 'necessary' and 'just society' will remain relatively unexamined. At least in popular English usage 'necessary' has stronger and weaker senses. Here I will use it (and such approximate equivalents as 'essential', 'indispensible', and 'required') in a strong or strict sense; that is, I take it that if A is necessary to B, B cannot exist without A. By 'just society' I will mean whatever anyone might mean by that term; that is, my claim is that whatever a just society might be, faith in God is required for its creation. Naturally I have some notions of what a more just society might be. They are not, however, required for the present discussion.

Faith is another matter. I do not think it is possible to hold a genuinely fruitful discussion of our topic without some clarity about what is meant by 'faith'. In the West, as used in such phrases as 'faith in God', the term has had two quite distinct meanings. On the one hand, it has been identified as fundamentally intellectual assent or belief. On the other, it is also used to refer to a basic orientation of the whole person, more closely akin to trust, confidence or loyalty. The central point of this paper is that faith in God is necessary to the creation of a just society given either meaning of 'faith'.

Is Faith in God Necessary?

Common Human Experience

By 'common human experience' I mean to point to some aspects of human existence which are relatively pre-understanding, pre-thematized, pre-reflective. I have no illusion that it is possible to get behind experience to the raw data of experience, much less to talk about that. All thought and language introduce elements of interpretation. It is not as though we have experience, then think about it, then talk about it. From the onset, experiencing involves its interpretation, interpretation which is shaped not only by human biology but by culture, by inherited traditions of language and speculative thought, cultural symbols and values, racial, sexual and class bias, and much else. Despite all of these realities, I believe it is useful to attempt to distinguish consciously held beliefs from relatively prereflective and pre-articulate knowledge.

A simple example may help. I think we all *know,* at least at a pre-reflective level, that the present is not only preceded by the past but also causally influenced by it. Some philosophers have convinced themselves and others that there is no such causation, that behind the appearance of causal influence there is only "constant conjunction." Yet, no matter how strongly a philosopher is convinced at the conscious level that there is no causation, his or her own pre-reflective experience of causation remains. He or she too experiences emotions such as anger or guilt; has attitudes about responsibility; and acts as though there are real influences upon him or her, and as though his or her own actions have consequences. Thus, whether or not we believe at a reflective level in causal influence, our lives, attitudes, assumptions, emotions and decisions reveal a pre-reflective knowledge of causal influence. When examples of such knowledge are reflected upon and brought into consciousness, it may be desirable to attempt to justify them through argument. We may, for example, want to assure ourselves that they are consistent with other convictions. But our basic acceptance of them is a matter of self-evidence. "Mothers," Whitehead said, "can ponder many things in their hearts which their lips cannot express. These many things, which are thus known, constitute the ultimate religious evidence, beyond which there is no appeal."[1]

To say that such initially inarticulate beliefs are self-evident is not to say that they are equally obvious to everyone. To the contrary, ability to conceive previously unrecognized elements of experience is rare. Once someone has recognized them, and brought them to a level of verbal expression, they can be recognized by others. The verbal expression elicits a believing response because the matter is obvious; that is, self-evident.

Theology

For this reason theology, or at least fundamental theology, should not be *primarily* a matter of argument. First of all, it should attempt to reflect on common human experience so as to elicit in others a responsive recognition or sensitive awareness of their own experience. In a sense, theology is an attempt to make sense of the obvious, to make the obvious more obvious.

By giving this kind of priority to pre-reflective experience, I do not mean to suggest an anti-intellectualism which holds that articulation, conscious belief, argumentation, and the quest for clarity are unimportant. This would follow only if our conscious beliefs had no bearing on felt experience, emotions, attitudes and actions. But all kinds of evidence suggests just the opposite: that conscious beliefs have serious consequences in the development of who we are and what we do. Indeed, they partially shape pre-reflective experience. "Each individual moment of experience involves a complex mutual adjustment of its aspects, and consciously held beliefs play their part in this adjustment. Beliefs about matters of ultimate concern held with deep conviction over a long period are particularly efficacious in shaping one's character, purpose, and general emotional-attitudinal-behavioral stance."[2]

This is one reason it is vitally important that the conversation which is theology be very broad in its composition. A certain richness of experience is required to insure that the conceptions and symbols emergent in a particular stream of history are not mistakenly assumed to be the only way to comprehend common human experience. The location of theology in a genuinely ecumenical, worldwide perspective, leads to a richer, fuller conversation, in which the experience of women, of Afro-Americans, Africans, Asians and Latin Americans, of the handicapped and of the less schooled, is blended with the predominantly intellectual, doctrinal emphasis and approach of European and American males, and those who have been strongly influenced by their traditions.

Is Faith in God Necessary?

Human Faith

I take it that faith, or at least something which can reasonably be designated by 'faith', is a common human experience. It certainly is not the only common human experience. Everywhere one finds human experience corresponding to such terms as 'fear', 'love', 'hope', etc.

"At the base of our existence," says Whitehead, is the "sense of 'worth'."[3] Faith is the primordial experience of one's life as meaningful. It is the deeply felt assurance that my life—what I make of it, how I respond to my environment, what I do—makes a difference, is important. However much I may be restricted or oppressed by circumstances beyond my control, I know that I contribute my bit to the struggles and joys of life. This fundamental faith, I believe, is universal. It is one of the common human elements that underlie all religious traditions. It is this assurance, or faith, that religious traditions re-present in an enormously rich variety of myths, stories, symbols and theologies. Such faith is *saving* faith because it sustains us from ultimate despair, from feeling that nothing could possibly make any difference. To say that such faith is universal is not to say that it is inevitable. Certainly there are times when each of us has doubts, when we think that it's all for nothing and life is not worth living. Some will be led by experience to feel that their lives are without significance or meaning, that nothing they could do could possibly have any significance.

We know that ultimate meaninglessness and despair are possible. The experience of Americans in North Korean prisoner-of-war camps is instructive. The captors set up a system through which every source of faith and trust was systematically eroded. Lectures and testimonies were used to discredit faith in country. Selective censorship of mail and other news from the United States served to discredit loved ones at home. A carefully contrived system of camp informants and arbitrary rewards and punishments made it impossible to trust anyone in the camp itself. Almost no prisoners sought to escape. They had nowhere to which to escape. Few committed suicide, because that would not have been a meaningful act of retaliation. What did happen, in a syndrome not unknown in American hospitals, is that prisoners became radically withdrawn, closed in upon themselves, without resources for relating to anyone or anything. And in some cases, otherwise healthy, reasonably well-fed, physically unabused men went into some corner to die by simply ceasing to live. Such depth of alienation is extreme and uncommon. The fact that it is possible, however, tells us that human faith is not inevitable. The possible transformation of faith into ultimate meaninglessness, the threat of such meaninglessness, is part of what gives rise to religions. They provide assurance that life can be trusted, not necessarily trusted to turn out alright, but trusted to make my life meaningful, to have it count. They do this by representing in myriad ways what we already know in our hearts—that you, and I, are somebody.

Faith and God

Is such common human faith properly understood as faith in God? Clearly, it need not be understood this way to be efficacious. Surely atheists and Theravada Buddhists, and others for whom a conception of God is either unnecessary or pernicious, are not, on that account, left without human faith.

What process theology claims is that one very good way, and perhaps the conceptually most adequate way of understanding such faith, is in relation to God. Against traditions which have taught us to understand God as the Absolute, as the immutable, passionless, controlling power and ground of the status quo, process theology names God as the objective ground of human faith. In this vision, God is conceived to be one whose interest is all interests, whose love encompasses all, who struggles with us to create a fuller, richer life for all, who suffers with us the pain and misery and evil of the world, and who receives into herself all that we create of our world and of ourselves. By insisting that the primary appropriate function or use of the term 'God' is to refer to that in reality itself which grounds our assurance of the worth of our existence, we can make genuinely intelligible how it is that our common human faith is compatible with the creative process which is reality itself. Because God is understood as affected by all that we are and do, the future to which we contribute is understood to be neither merely our own nor merely that of others as limited as ourselves, but also the everlasting future of God's creative becoming. It is God's life that is ultimately enhanced or diminished by all of our finite purposes and acts. It is enhancement of divine life that finally inspires us to maximize the richness of life and joy in the world.

Common human faith is, I believe, properly conceived as faith in God; but it may also be experienced and conceived in other ways.

Thus, it does not entail belief in God or use of theistic language. Theology or theistic language may serve to enhance or reinforce such faith, but faith is initially given to us without such interpretation. Those who find theistic interpretation helpful must never suppose that the "godless" are actually without God or faith. Their faith may actually be as strong as any "believer's." Thus, on this account, there is one sense in which faith in God is necessary, not only for the creation of a just society but for human life generally; however, belief in God is not required.

The Encompassing Ideal

Human society consists of individuals in groups. There are, of course, many kinds of groups: nations, cultural and language groups, racial groups, groups created by religious affiliation, professional groups, and many other special interest groups. Sometimes such groups are communities; sometimes they lack sufficient commonly felt identity to be properly regarded as communities.

If any group is not to be a mere competition of interests against interests, at least one common assumption is required: basically the belief that all purposes and actions are finally to be assessed in the light of some encompassing ideal. Individuals and communities pursue their own interests. For such individuals or communities to be part of a larger community, there must be a good which is more inclusive than the good of the individual members. In order for you and I to be a genuine us, we must have some common purpose or ideal which transcends our individual self-serving purposes. This does not imply that there must be agreement about the substance of such an encompassing ideal—only that there be a belief or assumption that there is some wider good, some larger set of interests. Indeed, within any community, conflicts may arise over different perceptions of what the common good is. But that there is some common ideal, in the light of which all actions are to be judged, is something that cannot consistently be doubted. Actually it is probably better, more conducive to community, if everyone assumes that the encompassing ideal cannot be known, or at least cannot be known definitely. Because every finite individual's conception of the good will be biased by that individual's limited perspectives and interests, and by that individual's necessary ignorance of the perspectives and interests of others, no individual can know the larger good. It must always be something beyond grasp, not only beyond concrete realization but beyond conceptual grasp.

Such wider, encompassing, community ideals require a widest possible all-inclusive, all-encompassing ideal. One might have a family in which the members are obedient to some vision of justice relative to the members of that family, but which is unjust relative to the wider civic community of which the family is a part. It would remain a significantly unjust family. Similarly, nations and other large communities must be judged in the light of some ideal for humanity. But even humanity is finite in relation to the whole range of creatures. Thus, what is needed finally is some notion of a widest possible, all-encompassing ideal. In theistic traditions this might properly be named the will of God, or the kingdom of God.

Explicit Faith

Is belief in some all-encompassing ideal a kind of faith? Although it is not the faith discussed earlier in this paper, i.e., felt meaningfulness, it is, it seems to me, a kind of faith. It is a kind of faith more akin to intellectual assent or belief. I do not mean to imply that such faith is merely intellectual. I don't think any understanding of faith holds that it is merely intellectual. But I do mean to suggest that such faith functions very significantly as belief or assumption. It is something which to be effective must become a matter of public consciousness. For example, for Cicero a republic was a large group of people associated through agreement on the character of justice and pursuit of the public good. And at the same time they established religious pluralism in America, the founders of the American republic recognized the importance of what Benjamin Franklin called essential religious truths. Without some degree of explicit understanding of such notions as public interest and human good, the latter become mere cynical and rhetorical costumes for special pleading, used to give an aura of moral respectability or superiority to limited interests.

Is such faith properly construed as faith in God? Here again it is apparent that the term 'God' is not necessary. What is required is some conception of other, of transcendent purpose, where 'transcendent' is understood to mean all-encompassing. Thus, what cannot be dispensed with is that to which, for many, the symbol 'God' points—that there is a higher or wider or larger purpose or ideal or interest to which all individuals, nations, and communities are finally responsible.

Reality as Relational

Against traditional Western metaphysical views which would have us understand final realities to be independent, individual substances, process theology reaffirms the ancient Buddhist insight that we are largely products of the influences of all kinds of others, including past states of ourselves. We, in turn, are real ingredients in the lives of others. This is a vision of reality as fundamentally social. In contrast with the individualism of the classical liberal tradition of social and political thought, process theology understands each individual and community as existing within a context of relationships which are constitutive of its being.[4] This "structure of experience"[5] is an enormous inheritance which relates each one of us to all that has been in our past, not only to other humans but to all other creatures. It is a depth of our experience, culturally transmitted, which relates us as events to all other existent events. It is a depth which relates us finally to that encompassing reality properly understood as God. Accordingly, political association, political life, the pursuit of human community and the like are not mere conveniences or accidents of our existence, but are an expression of the nature of the reality which defines what we are, creates us, and to which, we contribute and help create.

In contrast to the tradition of individualism rooted in substance philosophy and an absolute distinction between self and others, process thought is a philosophy of interdependence. Instead of justifying authoritarianism and patriarchy through glorification of non-relational power, process theology provides a way of understanding the intrinsic value of each member of society, and the concomitant importance of sensitivity, responsiveness, and mutual caring. In this view, life simply is nothing but enjoyment of relations with others. Thus, healthy self-interest is always other regarding, always to some degree a concern for the welfare and happiness of others, of some public.

The widest possible public is the divine life. In this sense politics and religion cannot be relegated to entirely separate spheres. To be religious is to please God, and to please God is to contribute positively to the creation of a good society. But, if this is so, it is equally the case that to contribute positively to the creation of a good society is to please God—whether or not this is done from a "religious" perspective, the word 'God', is used, or even the existence of God recognized. God can, no doubt, get along quite well without "God."

Contributionism

What process theology asserts and clarifies is how it is that articulate belief in God enhances our understanding of our lives in relation to the widest conceivable good. Rather than stress the immutable character of God, what is emphasized is the ongoing life of God, the sense in which God enjoys and suffers the contributions we make to the divine life by our choices and acts. In this view, every individual receives an inheritance from the past, including past states of the self. This inheritance creates the individual; that is, determines what the individual is. But the determination is not complete. Every individual also always contributes to its own self-creation; that is every individual is self-creating. While such acts of becoming are always valued for themselves, they also always involve some aim or purpose beyond the immediate self. Each occasion, says Whitehead, "arises as an effect facing its past and ends as a cause facing its future. In between them lies the teleology of the Universe."[6] Acts of self-creation are also contributions to the future, to future states of the individual, to other individuals, to a whole range of communities of influence. The one receives from the many and contributes to the many.

The many to which each contributes can be wider or narrower. At its widest, this community is all that God experiences or knows. Just as every finite individual is partially created by others, God is partially created by us. That is, divine experience, therefore divine life, therefore divine being, is shaped by what is included in it. Thus, emphasis on divine receptivity is not merely a way of wriggling out of the theodicy problem, but the most useful way of conceiving how we are related to the most inclusive good.

We may suppose, and I for one do suppose, that such an understanding of ourselves as contributions to the divine life may enhance our ability to make appropriate contributions. We may suppose that conscious attempts to think about the character of divine will, for us may enhance our ability to do God's will. But those of us who choose to use God's language should never suppose that a good life, for an individual or for a community, is not possible apart from some such understanding. For many the term "God" has rightly become problematic, or even repulsive. This is precisely because it has been used against God to promote the interests of various dominant individuals and groups, that is, used to support and sanctify tyranny, sexism, racism, narrow nationalism, etc. Faith in "God," we could say, has too often served the creation of unjust societies.

Creation of a Just Society

I turn now, more briefly, to the third term of our topic—'creation'. The main point I want to make can be put quite simply: neither faith in God, however conceived, nor in anything else, however conceived, can contribute to the creation of a just society unless there can be real creation. Unless what we experience and think and do (and, therefore, are), makes a real difference to the world and to God, talk about creating a just society (or anything else) is just so much fostering of grand illusions. If all that we do is determined by God, if God is the only center of power, if, in this sense, God is all-powerful, then there is no creation except what is solely God's creation. At most we could have an illusion of contributing something to the creation of a just society. And, while such illusions might serve to enhance our lives in some way, we could not in fact contribute to the creation of a just society; or, for that matter, could not contribute to the creation of any kind of society, or anything whatever.

The same is true in principle of divine omniscience. If the future is entirely known by God, if the future is entirely knowable in principle, then what will be will be, and we have at most the illusion of contributing to it. Thus, not only does the idea of absolute divine providence prohibit any notion of contributing to a just society, so does any kind of absolute, i.e., complete, determinism. By helping us to understand that divine omnipotence must not mean that God has all power, but rather that God contributes to all creation, and that divine omniscience cannot mean that God knows all future states of affairs, but rather that God knows all that can be known, process theology makes it possible for us to have a rational understanding of ourselves as genuine creators, and, therefore, as creators of the divine life.

This is why, for Whitehead, creativity is an ultimate. Every feeling or experience, every act, every becoming, involves some degree (generally very minimal) of creativity. The future, accordingly, is radically different from the past. The past is settled, fully determined, unchanging, matter of fact. It is what we have to work with, and as such largely determines what we can become, and, therefore, what the future will be. But the future is unsettled, not yet fully determined, a range of possibility yet to be made definite. An infinite number of choices, including each of our choices, will continue to mark the transition from past to future. From some perspectives, such choices will appear as chance, i.e., as that which cannot be completely predicted from knowledge of previous events. From other perspectives, such choices will appear as freedom or creativity, that is, acts of self-determination. From still other perspectives, they will appear as contributions to the lives of future others, to the public. From the widest possible perspective, they will be seen to be contributions to the divine experience or life.

Conclusion

I have claimed that process theology is one way to understand how faith in God is necessary for the creation of a just society. Apart from a fundamental trust in the meaningfulness of our own lives, we could not live at all. Without assuming that beyond our own narrow interests and purposes there is some transcendent good, we would not work toward a just society. And unless our view of things allows for genuine freedom on the part of creatures, we cannot consistently think of ourselves as contributing to the creation of anything.

But none of these claims can be rationally sustained without making some radical departures from traditional ways of thinking about reality in general and about God. So long as static being is thought to be highest in both reality and value, so long as the real is conceived of as essentially non-relational, so long as freedom is taken to be a mere illusion or ignorance, so long as we think that the future is in principle no different than the past, our faith will in fact be mere superstition, our pursuit of justice mere illusion, our supposed creations mere repetitions.

Thus, our faith in the meaningfulness of existence, our pursuit of a just society, our reality as contributors to an all-encompassing purpose is grounded in and made intelligible by what is fundamentally a secular understanding of sacred reality. Perhaps no philosophy can create a religious tradition. Certainly no philosophy can sustain religious faith. But process theology, I believe, can make intelligible how it is that nothing can wholly or ultimately separate us from the care of God and, therefore, from that in the universe "whereby there is importance, value, and ideal beyond the actual."[7]

NOTES

1. Alfred North Whitehead, *Religion in the Making* (New York: MacMillan, 1926), 65.
2. John B. Cobb and David Ray Griffin, *Process Theology: An Introductory Exposition* (Philadelphia: Westminster Press, 1976), 33.
3. Alfred North Whitehead, *Modes of Thought* (New York: MacMillan, 1938).
4. For very helpful discussions of these matters see Franklin I. Gamwell, "Happiness and the Public World: Beyond Political Liberalism," *Process Studies* 8(1) (1978): 21–36 and "Religion and the Public Purpose," *Journal of Religion* 62(3) (1982): 272–288.
5. See Bernard E. Meland, *Faith and Culture* (New York: Oxford University Press, 1953), 98 ff.
6. Alfred North Whitehead, *Adventures of Ideas* (New York: MacMillan, 1933), 249.
7. Alfred North Whitehead, *Modes of Thought,* 140.

13
Liberation and Pluralism: Two Values For a Postmodern Christianity
JAY McDANIEL

Liberation theologies and other activist perspectives within Christianity suggest that there is an integral relationship between faith in God and the quest for social justice. Faith is understood as openness to God's call toward the kingdom and as acceptance of God's demands to serve the poor and oppressed.[1] For many liberation thinkers this understanding of faith implies not simply that authentic faith involves a quest for justice, but also that an authentic quest for justice involves faith. At times, the rigor with which this implication is unpacked obscures the fact that there are many in the world who, while not believing in God, nevertheless seek social justice in quite significant ways. Humanists and Marxists are among them, as are many Buddhists. How might the liberationist respond to this situation? Should it be assumed that faith in God is not existentially necessary for an authentic pursuit of justice? If so, some of the motivational thrust and cognitive content of liberation theology is undercut. Or, by contrast, should it be assumed that something like faith in God is present in the self-defined nontheist, albeit in an implicit and un-thematized way? If the latter is assumed, can arrogance be avoided?[2]

These questions have relevance beyond mere academia. As Harvey Cox and others suggest, a new, liberation-oriented, postmodern church is emerging in the Third World among the heretofore voiceless, and in the First World among those who theologize in explicit solidarity with the voiceless.[3] If, as many expect and rightly hope, this church becomes a strong and influential social movement within the global community, it will inevitably face the issue that the Western church has so often and so unsuccessfully faced: the problem of religious pluralism. Indeed, in Southeast Asia the new church is already facing this issue in its encounter with Buddhism.[4] Here and elsewhere, postmodern Christianity must come to grips with the fact that there are, and will

Liberation and Pluralism

continue to be, many who do not share some of its deepest convictions concerning the nature of reality, including its conviction that there is a liberating God. Will the new church accept pluralism and welcome diversity? Or will it respond defensively as did its Western predecessors, thus extending a tradition of tragedy and persecution under which too many have already suffered? The question of how the liberation Christian interprets nontheistic activism must be understood in this broader historical context.

The purpose of this essay is to suggest one way that a liberation theology might interpret such activism. The following passage from Rosemary Radford Ruether, herself a postmodern Christian with a liberation orientation, sets the stage for discussion. Concerning Christian claims to universal truth, Ruether writes:

True universalism must be able to embrace existing pluralism, rather than trying to fit every people into the mould of religion and culture generated from one historical experience. Only God is one and universal. Humanity is finally one because the one God created us all. But the historical mediators of the experience of God remain plural. To impose one religion on everyone flattens and impoverishes the wealth of human interaction with God. In order to be truly catholic, Christians must revise the imperialistic way they have defined their universality.[5]

My aim in this essay is to further Ruether's call for a revised image of God's universality by dealing with a peculiarly difficult example: that of the nontheist.

By 'nontheist' I mean anyone who, from his or her own perspective and given his or her understanding of the word 'God', does not believe in the existence of God. In order to avoid the temptation, perhaps common to many theists, to choose images of nontheism that are less than charitable, I will focus on the example of the nontheist of good will—say a Theravada Buddhist monk in Southeast Asia—who actively works toward many of the same ends as the liberation-oriented Christian. My argument is that nontheistic activism in fact involves an unthematized faith in what the Christian calls God; that such faith can and should be distinguished from 'belief' in God; and that Christians can make this claim, and indeed in some instances attempt to persuade the nontheist of its truth, without the kind of arrogance that has haunted much of the Christian past.

I approach these issues from a particular and somewhat new theological perspective that is emerging for the most part in North

America. It can be called 'process/liberation theology' or, alternatively, 'process/political theology', because it involves a synthesis of (a) process (Whiteheadian and Hartshornian) understandings of the world and God with (b) the social concerns and biblical emphases of liberation and political theologies. To date this theology has been articulated most systematically by John B. Cobb, Jr. and L. Charles Birch in their jointly authored work *The Liberation of Life,* and by Cobb, individually, in *Process Theology as Political Theology.*[6] Other thinkers such as Schubert Ogden, Marjorie Suchocki, Delwin Brown, and Sheila Greeve Davaney have also made significant contributions, as has, in a unique and particularly promising vein, the North American black theologian Archie Smith.[7] This essay is a brief contribution—in this instance on the part of a white male in North America—to the continued development of this emerging liberation tradition.[8]

The essay is divided into three sections. In the first, I spell out more clearly what, from a process/liberation point of view, the appropriate ends of contemporary Christian activism are. In the second, I discuss the relation between faith and activism, suggesting that the nontheistic activist displays faith without belief. In the third, I discuss the problem of Christian arrogance.

The Appropriate Ends of Christian Activism

What are the appropriate ends of Christian activism? In light of the nuclear arms race, many Christians in the First World are tempted to say "peace"; and given the stakes, they are not wrong. Yet, as many peace activists recognize, a preoccupation with disarmament alone misses the more concrete needs of many in the third world and not a few in the first and second worlds as well. If the word 'peace' is to name the appropriate end of Christian striving at this stage in history, it must mean more than the absence of nuclear weapons. Rather, it must mean, as it does in the Jewish sense of *shalom,* the presence of the fullness of life for each and every human being on the planet. 'Peace' must mean, among other things, *justice.*

From a process/liberation perspective, as outlined by Birch and Cobb, the word 'justice' rightly implies three things: (1) economic well-being and equality, (2) social participation, and (3) personal freedom. A just world is one in which economic goods such as food, clothing, and shelter are distributed fairly so that basic needs are met; it is one in which individuals and groups are allowed to play significant roles in the social decisions, both political and economic, by which their lives are affected; and it is one in which individuals and groups are allowed to express dissenting perspectives, think freely, practice religious perspectives of their own, and otherwise enjoy personal freedoms. To embody a living faith in God, so a process/liberation perspective suggests, is to seek justice in each and all of these three manifestations. Through active political involvement, nonviolent resistance, and experimentation with alternative lifestyles, it is to strive for a maximum balance of economic well-being, participation, and freedom both locally and globally.[9]

Of course, the Christian activist must realize that trade-offs are sometimes required among the three dimensions of justice. In instances in which one must choose between economic well-being, participation, and personal freedom, the needs of survival—and hence of economic well-being—take precedence.[10] Yet the reality of trade-offs should not be accepted too quickly. In many instances a symbiosis of desirable goals is possible. When the rights of women to education and employment are recognized, for example, birthrates often decline, therein reducing problems of population and hunger. Here the goals of social participation and personal freedom for women are combined with that of economic well-being for the population as a whole. The task of the Christian activist is to think creatively about how the three dimensions of justice can be jointly realized through novel public policies and transformed social systems.

As Birch and Cobb suggest, however, justice is not enough. In the interests of the fullness of life, ecological *sustainability* must also be sought.[11] In terms of public policy, 'sustainability' implies a conservation of precious and relatively nonrenewable resources such as petroleum and topsoil, a responsible management of renewable resources such as timber and water, a minimization of pollution and toxic waste, an emphasis on permanence rather than inbuilt obsolescence in manufactured goods, and the employment of appropriate technologies in such basic industries as agriculture, transportation, and energy-production. In terms of cultural attitudes, 'sustainability' further implies an acceptance of ecological limits, a transcendence of the modern, industrial impulse to dominate the whole of nonhuman nature, a recognition of the rights of nonhuman life, and, once basic needs are met, an emphasis on quality rather than quantity. The appropriate social ideal for the contemporary social activist is not for justice or sustainability alone, but rather for joint realizations of justice and sustainability.[12]

In short, if the word 'peace' names the appropriate end of Christian activism, then it must mean not only nuclear disarmament and an end to violence, but also justice and sustainability. The Christian who seeks peace in its fullest sense seeks justice and sustainability. At a personal level, there are, of course, other appropriate ends: the reconcilation of broken relationships, the discovery of healthy self-love, the transcendence of greed and envy, the acceptance of divine forgiveness, and the cultivation of spiritual depth. From a process/liberation perspective, social liberation and personal liberation are both important. A whole planet depends on whole people, and vice versa.

Faith in God

As the Christian seeks a more just and sustainable world, in what way is his or her striving empowered by faith in God? The answer depends on how God, divine power, and faith are understood.

In process/liberation theology, God is understood as a living subject who is both receptive and active in relation to the world. As receptive, God feels the feelings of worldly beings, suffering with their sufferings and sharing in their joys. As active, God lures worldly beings toward wholeness and growth relative to what is possible in each situation. While God, as thus understood, may not resemble the unmoved mover of Aristotle, the omnipotent determiner of Augustine, or the *esse ipsum* of Aquinas, the argument of process theologians is that this God does resemble the living God of the Bible: a God who calls prophets to speak God's will, who suffers along with the people of Israel, and whose relational character was significantly revealed in the life, death, and resurrection of Jesus.

From a process perspective, as from that of many but not all biblical traditions, the power of God to influence the world, including human life, is persuasive rather than coercive. Human beings experience God not as a force that compels but rather as a power that invites; not as a push from behind but rather as a pull from ahead; not as the compulsion of an efficient cause but rather as the beckoning of a final cause; and not as an already-determined past but as a not-yet determined future. As biblical texts suggest, divine invitation can sometimes be experienced as a threat or demand—that is, as something one is inclined to resist—rather than as an attractive ideal to which one is automatically drawn. Even in such instances, however, the presence of God is inviting rather than manipulating. It is inviting because, as with any invitation, we may or may not respond to it, and because, if we do authentically respond, our own best interests, as well as the interests of others, are served. From a process/liberation perspective, the power of God is that by which and through which both we ourselves, and those we influence, can be guided into the fullness of life.

Technically speaking, this power lies in what process thinkers call *initial aims*. These are *possibilities* for the fullness of life, both personal and social, relative to situations at hand. At a social level, at least for most adults, these aims are for justice and sustainability. They are directly experienced as "lures," that is, as inwardly felt goals that beckon for realization in thought, feeling, and action. They cannot be reduced to static legal codes or formalized prescriptions for conduct; and sometimes—in cases of civil disobedience, for example—their content may directly traverse such codes and prescriptions. The possibilities are apprehended through reason, imagination, and intuition as each person is stimulated by other human beings, historical traditions, physical realities, myths and stories, and concrete social situations.

An analogy from artistic experience can clarify the nature of initial aims. In the same way that an artist is dimly aware of possibilities for creative self-expression that beckon for realization, almost as if they are given by a divine muse, so most adults are dimly aware of possibilities for justice and sustainability that beckon for realization, and that indeed *are* derived from a divine muse. From a process/liberation perspective, artistic inspiration and ethical inspiration spring from a single, divine source. This course is not, and cannot be, all-determining. From God we derive possibilities for justice and sustainability; but it is up to us, not God, to actualize them. The efficacy of God's power in the world depends on the faithfulness of our response.

Although God is present within each human life, not all humans orient themselves around God. The dominant life-orientation in the United States and perhaps in other industrialized countries as well, for example, revolves around the ideal of success understood as fame, fortune, and power. The "still small voice" of God within ordinary experience is obscured by a "still louder voice" that weaves its way into the psyche through advertising and the media, education and the churches, family and friends. Indeed, as Paul

Tillich observed, material success is the ultimate concern of many in North America and perhaps in other industrialized nations as well.

That which either explicitly or implicitly functions as one's ultimate concern is that in which one has "faith." And faith, understood in this sense, is not an act of intellectual belief. It is not an act of consciously assenting, when questioned, to the proposition 'God exists', or to some analogous proposition. Rather, it is an ongoing act of ultimate concern, an ongoing act of *trust* in something that one takes to be ultimately important, ultimately demanding, and ultimately satisfying. One may believe in God consciously and intellectually, and yet not trust God in the sense of taking God as one's ultimate concern. This is the situation with many among the ostensibly religious in industrial nations who have actually given their lives to the ideal of success. Conversely, one may trust God without believing in God. This is the situation with those who give their lives to the ongoing, and perhaps unnamed, spirit of what Henry Nelson Wieman called "creative good," but who do not believe in God in any orthodox way. In the context of our discussion of the relation between faith in God and authentic social activism, the latter possibility requires further elaboration.

Taking Tillich's lead, let us say that faith is a state of ultimate concern in which the very spirit of God is that by which one's life is guided. To have God as one's ultimate concern is: (a) to trust that God is present even when not readily apparent, (b) to be open to God's presence as it avails itself, and (c) to be responsive to that presence as it calls for certain forms of objective behavior. Faith as *trust* involves subjective attitudes of hope, confidence, and expectation; faith as *openness* involves a willingness to be accepting of new possibilities and a reluctance to rest in past achievements; and faith as *responsiveness* involves objective forms of behavior that yield justice and sustainability.

Let us say further that each of these three aspects is necessary to an authentic faith, and that none alone or in twofold combination are sufficient. And let us further affirm that few people, if any, embody unlimited authentic faith. For the vast majority, authentic faith occurs in degrees and modalities. In some ways and to some extent people are genuinely trustful of and attuned to the call of God; and in other ways they are not. Whether they are or are not fully faithful is partially a result of decisions they make, and partially a result of social and physical circumstances. The existential ideal for authentic faith is for a maximum of trust, openness, and responsiveness relative to what is possible in the circumstances at hand. In this context we can ask: Can the person who does not believe in God, either by virtue of choice or the necessity of circumstances, nonetheless exhibit some degree of authentic faith?

Given a process/liberation perspective, it should be clear that a nontheist—a person reared in Marxist China, for example, or a Buddhist activist—may well exhibit a significant degree of faith in its second two aspects. If the person is open to the lure of initial aims for justice and sustainability relative to his or her situation, and if the person is responsive to those possibilities in actual behavior, then indeed from a process perspective we see two of the three seeds of faith. It matters not that the woman or man does not believe in God intellectually; the power of God is at work in the person's life. Of course, nontheism does not guarantee openness and responsiveness to God. The atheist can be just as closed to God as the believer. But nontheism does not prevent these qualities either.

What should be less clear is how the third aspect—trust—pertains to the situation of the nontheist. Does the Buddhist or Marxist, who does not "believe in God," and who pursues a more just and sustainable world, exhibit a confidence in God's presence? I submit that, in an unthematized way, he or she does.

Characteristic of most activism—say that of a Theravada Buddhist monk in Sri Lanka who is active in land reform programs—is an attitude of trust. He trusts that, in light of given situations of injustice and unsustainability, possibilities for justice and sustainability are nevertheless available, and that these possibilities, if actualized, can offer a genuinely improved state of affairs. In many instances it is by no means obvious to others that this trust is justified. To them the situation in its own right looks relatively hopeless. Still the monk hopes, and he encourages others to do the same. He invites them to draw upon their imaginative, intuitive, and rational capacities, and to seek out those possibilities for social wholeness and growth that can bring wholeness out of chaos. He does not claim that such possibilities will inevitably be actualized; but he claims that they are available for discovery and actualization. He is trustful—and in this sense he has faith—that new things are possible.

Of course, the monk will not think about the ontological source of new possibilities in the same way that the process/liberation Christian will. He will not believe that the possibilities to which he is attuned, and in the efficacy of which he has trust, are manifestations of God. Buddhism is a nontheistic tradition in its origins, which means that most Buddhist monks who are familiar with those orgins do not "believe in God." Nevertheless the process/ liberation Christian can discern in the monk's attitudes an implicit trust in God, for to trust God is to trust that, even when situations seem hopeless, possibilities for hope are available for discovery and actualization. In the language of process theology, the monk may not believe in God, but he nonetheless trusts in the reality of initial aims.

In all probability the monk will, if asked, come up with a very different interpretation of his trust than that of the process/liberation Christian. He may say that the possibilities in which he has confidence are human projections and that alone; that they are in no way derived from a transhuman source. And on this, the Christian can and should admit that the monk may be right. In a postmodern Christian theology that is sensitive to religious pluralism, there can be no dogmatic certainty. There can only be honest and thoughtful interpretation. The postmodern Christian is free to interpret the Buddhist activist as embodying a trust, which when combined with openness and responsiveness to initial aims, is rightly named "faith."

Avoiding Arrogance

Should the Christian attempt to persuade the Buddhist monk that in fact God is at work in his life, and that in fact he (the monk) already has an unthematized faith in God, even though the monk thinks the contrary? The abusive way in which such persuasion has often been carried out easily inclines us to say no. In *Beyond Dialogue: Toward a Mutual Transformation of Christianity and Buddhism*, John Cobb suggests a different line of approach.[13] Cobb suggests that interreligious discussions are best served when dialogue is joined with debate: that is, when attempts to understand are joined with attempts, not to dominate, but to persuade. Only when we attempt to persuade others of the truths we believe we apprehend, and, equally as important, only when we open ourselves to the possibility of being persuaded by them, can the kind of creative transformation occur that is at the heart of human growth.

In many instances, of course, religious practitioners of diverse orientations have attempted to persuade one another of the truth of their respective perspectives for reasons that are destructive rather than constructive. As the neo-Jungian psychologist James Hillman points out, monotheists have been particularly at fault here.[14] All too easily a monotheistic religious orientation within Christianity has yielded a "monotheistic psychology" that seeks to reduce the world to oneness and sameness, and that fails to appreciate pluralism and diversity. The Christian who exemplifies this psychology is bent upon remaking the world in his or her own image, transforming it so that all people will be reflections of his or her ego. The prevailing assumption on the part of the Christian who adopts this stance is that there is one and only one path to God, and that Christianity is that path. The working maxim is "one God, one way, my way."

If attempts to persuade others of the truth of one's own perspective reflect the kind of religious imperialism of which Hillman speaks, then, of course, persuasion is inappropriate for the contemporary Christian. There is certainly the danger, within and outside process and liberation theologies, that such attempts are accompanied by precisely the motivation that Hillman criticizes. But it is possible that persuasion can be done in a somewhat different spirit. After all, Hillman, too, seeks to persuade the reader of the truth of this perspective, as do Buddhists and many others. The type of persuasion envisioned by Cobb proceeds from a different, more Hillmanian spirit.

This different spirit is grounded in the assumption, characteristic of almost all process theologies, that diversity is a good thing. Process theology envisions God as a pluralist rather than a monist. Within the general parameters of justice and sustainability, the lure of God calls individuals and groups toward a realization of different values—different ways of being human—relative to needs and circumstances. The ultimate priority of God is not that all people adopt the same point of view or the same belief system, but rather that all people enjoy those ways of being human that are best for their situations and circumstances. This means that God may well call some people to be Buddhist rather than Christian, and, indeed, that the history of Buddhism reveals a unique and distinctive way of authentically responding to God. When or if a just and sustainable world arrives, there will be and ought to be many religious ways. In biblical terminology, when or if "the kingdom of God" of which Jesus speaks arrives, and the will of God is done "on earth as it is in heaven," not all participants in the kingdom will be, or need think of themselves as, Christian.

Indeed, the process/liberation interest in pluralism is still more radical. From a process/liberation perspective, it follows that when or if the kingdom comes, not all participants may believe in God. All may have *faith* in the sense defined in the previous section, but not all may have, or need *belief*. Not all need assent to the proposition 'God exists' or some equivalent. The appropriateness of belief is relative to the situation of the individual person. If intellectual assent to the idea that God exists can in fact enhance that person's capacity to be open to God, and hence open to possibilities for realizing the fullness of life, then belief might be appropriate. But if intellectual assent is irrelevant to, or perhaps even detracts from, that person's capacity to be open to possibilities for life's fullness, then it is inappropriate. From a process/liberation perspective, the will of God is that the fullness of life be realized on earth. If in some instances "belief in God" might hinder a realization of that fullness, then God may well call certain individuals not to believe in God.

This insistence on the value of religious pluralism helps assure that when a process/liberation Christian engages in dialogue with a nontheist, arrogance can be avoided. The Christian need not assume that the ultimate stakes of such discussions are heaven or hell. Conversely, the Christian can assume that his or her partner in dialogue, even while not believing in God, may be open to God in ways that transcend traditional Christian practices and in ways from which there is much to learn. Even as the Christian endeavors to persuade the nontheist of the reality of God, the Christian can realize that the nontheist may be more open to that reality than is the Christian herself or himself. And, of course, the Christian must be open to the possibility that, after all, the nontheist is correct, that there is no God in the first place. In dialogues that involve efforts at mutual persuasion, both parties must be open to possibilities for creative transformation, agreeing that the truth—whatever it is—is that to which both are ultimately committed.

But why endeavor to persuade at all? Why not simply allow the nontheist to rest in his or her perspective? Sometimes such allowance may indeed be the most appropriate response. In the future, the Christian tradition must not relax its commitments to justice and sustainability, but it can and should relax its tendency toward dogmatism. When, however, the attempt at persuasion stems from a genuine love of the other person as informed by an assessment of that person's actual needs, and when it is itself open to creative transformation in the context of dialogue, persuasion may be appropriate. If, as the postmodern Christian of a process/liberation orientation believes, there really is a living Subject in the depths of people's experience who calls them toward personal wholeness and toward social action, it may sometimes be the case that people's conscious acknowledgement and recognition of that Spirit can enhance their own ability to be open to it. From a process/liberation perspective, such acknowledgement and recognition constitutes "belief in God." It may be in people's own interests to shift from a perspective of unbelief to belief. In such instances, which cannot be predicted in advance and which can only be recognized on a case by case approach, the attempt at persuasion is itself appropriate, because it is motivated by love.

By contrast, when persuasion stems from an impulse to remake the world in one's own image, and when it is itself closed to the possibility of creative transformation, it is arrogant. Persuasion in the interests of love is healthy; persuasion in the interests of the will-to-power is destructive. The line between the two is often difficult to draw, but it is incumbent that the postmodern Christian attempt to draw it. Arrogance *can* be avoided in the Christian future, but only by those who are willing to question their own motives for persuasion. Whenever there is an interest in persuasion, the postmodern Christian must ascertain, to the best of his or her abilities, that the attempt to persuade stems from an actual concern for the other person's and society's well-being rather than from the impulse to dominate. Furthermore, the Christian must be open to the possibility of being persuaded by the other person, and the Christian must be willing to "agree to disagree" if persuasion fails. For the postmodern Christian, there are, after all, more important things than belief in God.

I suggest, then, that in the future postmodern Christianity can and should jointly realize two ideals that have often been thought mutually exclusive: *commitment to liberation* and *tolerance of diversity.* Postmodern Christians can be committed to the liberation ideals of justice and sustainability, and to the idea that faith in God is an essential element in the much-needed pursuit of such ideals. Yet they can also be tolerant of those who disagree. The tolerance at issue is not one of condescension or pity. It is one of genuine openness to the other as other, originating with a realization that the other may be right to disagree both intellectually and in terms of the circumstances of his or her life. If the future of Christianity lies in the liberation-oriented, postmodern church that sees an essential connection between faith and justice, and if this church is to accept the reality of religious pluralism, then commitment and tolerance must be synthesized. The ideas articulated in this essay indicate one path for achieving this synthesis.

NOTES

1. Representative examples of this perspective from within Latin America include Gustavo Gutierrez, *The Power of the Poor in Human History* (Maryknoll, New York: Orbis Press, 1983), Leonardo Boff, *Liberating Grace* (Maryknoll, New York: Orbis Press, 1979), and Juan Luis Segundo, *The Liberation of Theology* (Maryknoll, New York: Orbis Press, 1976). An example from Southeast Asia is Tissa Balasuriya, *The Eucharist and Human Liberation* (Maryknoll, New York: Orbis Press, 1979). Examples from North America include James Cone, *The God of the Oppressed* (New York: Crossroads, 1978), and Rosemary Radford Ruether, *Sexism and God-Talk* (Boston: Beacon Press, 1983).

2. One Latin American thinker to deal with this question in a constructive and non-arrogant way is Antonio Perez-Escalarin. See his *Atheism and Liberation* (Maryknoll, New York: Orbis Press, 1978).

3. Harvey Cox, *Religion in the Secular City: Toward a Post-Modern Theology* (New York: Simon and Schuster, 1984).

4. See John May "Christian-Buddhist-Marxist Dialogue in Sri Lanka: A Model for Social Change in Asia?" *Journal of Ecumenical Studies* 19(4), (1982).

5. Rosemary Radford Ruether, *To Change the World: Christology and Cultural Pluralism* (New York: Crossroad, 1981), 39.

6. John B. Cobb, Jr. and L. Charles Birch, *The Liberation of Life* (London: Cambridge University Press, 1981). John B. Cobb, Jr., *Process Theology as Political Theology* (Philadelphia: Westminster Press, 1982).

7. Ogden Schubert, *Faith and Freedom: Toward a Theology of Liberation* (Nashville, Tenn.: Abingdon Press, 1979); *Process Philosophy and Social Thought,* edited by John B. Cobb, Jr. and W. Widick Schroeder, Chicago: Center for the Scientific Study of Religion, 1981); *Feminism and Process Thought,* edited by Shiela Davaney (New York: Edwin Mellen Press, 1981); Delwin Brown, *To Set at Liberty; Toward a Theology of Liberation* (Maryknoll, New York: Orbis Press, 1980); Marjorie Suchocki, *God-Christ-Church: A Practical Guide to Process Theology* (New York: Crossroads, 1982). See also, Archie Smith *The Relational Self: Ethics and Therapy from a Black Church Perspective* (Nashville, Tenn., Abingdon Press, 1982). See page 212 for the reference to Hartshorne. Although Smith does not speak of himself as a "process" thinker, he is nevertheless influenced by the Hartshornian understanding of God, and he draws heavily from the process-oriented perspective of George Herbert Meade.

Liberation and Pluralism

8. There is an important difference between (a) a theology that is done by the poor and oppressed, or by those in persistent and direct contact with the disfranchised class, and (b) a theology that is done in solidarity with the poor and oppressed, even though articulated by those who are members of the dominant social class (usually white and male). Sometimes the phrase 'liberation theology' refers to the former and 'political theology' to the latter. In light of this distinction, the perspective I am adopting would best be called a process/political theology. However, because in contemporary Christian parlance the word 'liberation' is coming to have connotations that include both types of theology, I will use the term in this more general and inclusive sense, thus identifying my own point of view as a "liberation" perspective. Clearly it is an instance of the second rather than the first type of activist theology, and clearly there are many respects in which the first type is immensely more relevant to the concrete needs of liberation.

9. While not dismissing violence as a last resort, a process/liberation perspective is inclined toward nonviolent modes of social change whenever possible. See Cobb, *Process Theology as Political Theology*, 160.

10. The current situation in China provides an illustration. In order to assure sufficient food and comfort in the future, families in the present, particularly in urban settings, are strongly encouraged and in many ways forced to have only one child. The Chinese government has decided that the goal of general subsistence in the future is preferable to that of a certain sort of personal freedom in the present. As a prerequisite for general survival, economic equity takes precedence over personal freedom.

11. For an analysis of this need on a global level, see *The Global Report to the President: Entering the Twenty-First Century*, (Washington, D.C., 1980) Vol. 1, *passim*.

12. Here, too, a symbiosis of goals is possible. In many instances responsible forms of agriculture are best achieved, not by the wealthy absentee landowner who farms for short-term profit, but rather by the rural farmer who lives on his or her land and who cultivates subsistence rather than cash crops. In the same way that sustainable population policies and justice for women can go hand in hand, so sustainable forms of agriculture and justice for the rural poor can be united.

13. John B. Cobb, Jr., *Beyond Dialogue: Toward a Mutual Transformation of Christianity and Buddhism* (Philadelphia: Fortress Press, 1982).

14. James Hillman, *Inter Views: Conversations with Laura Pozzo on Psychotherapy, Biography, Love, Dreams, Work, Imagination, and the State of Culture* (New York: Harper and Row, 1983), 75–92.

14
The Rational Society and the Future of Religion
RICHARD L. RUBENSTEIN

If one were to identify the dominant characteristic of the modern world, at least in the West, it could fairly be described as the progressive rationalization of ever-greater areas of human enterprise. Max Weber has described this development with both clarity and brevity:

The fate of our times is characterized by rationalization and intellectualization and above all by the disenchantment of the world.[1]

According to Weber, the world is disenchanted when:

One need no longer have recourse to magical means in order to master or implore the spirits, as did the savage, for whom such mysterious powers existed. Technical means and calculations perform the service. This above all is what intellectualization means.[2]

We can perhaps excuse Weber his cultural provincialism in referring to those who live in a religiously enchanted universe as savages. In so doing he was no worse than were the majority of his scholarly contemporaries throughout Europe and America. For our purposes, it is important to note that Weber equated disenchantment and intellectualization with civilization.

The rationality to which we refer is very different from rationalism, which is a philosophic doctrine concerning the nature of knowledge. Weber has defined the process of rationalization as "the methodical attainment of a definitely given and practical end by means of an increasingly precise calculation of adequate means."[3] Modern rationality is a preeminently practical trait. It is also *wertfrei*, that is value-neutral. Aiming at the solution of problems, it normally excludes all consideration of questions of good and evil from its calculations. It has for that reason frequently been referred to as instrumental rationality.

Adam Smith was one of earliest social thinkers to realize the revolutionary character of instrumental rationality as applied to the processes of production. In the well-known passage with which he begins *The Wealth of Nations,* Smith observed: "The greatest improvements in the productive powers of labour . . . seem to have been the effects of the division of labour."[4]

Although some measure of *specialization* of labor is inherent in human biology and is prevalent in all societies, the division of labor discussed by Smith was a radically new historical development. In most societies roles were specialized. In eighteenth century England the complex processes of production were broken down into their simplest components. By virtue of component simplicity, work which previously required skilled artisans could be distributed among a number of unskilled workers. Moreover, the unskilled workers could produce a far greater output than had the artisans. Smith illustrated the power of this rationalized division of labor by describing a pin-making factory in which a few unskilled laborers, each working at one component of the process of production, together were able to produce 48,000 pins a day. Under the old system the same number of laborers, each working by himself, would have been unable to produce more than twenty pins each.

The Wealth of Nations was first published in 1776 at the very beginning of the Industrial Revolution in England. Although Smith alluded to the ability of machines to enhance productivity, his primary emphasis was upon the rationalization of the way work was *organized* rather than upon the substitution of machines for human beings. By emphasizing the division of labor rather than the substitution of machines for human labor, Smith anticipated, albeit unintentionally, the bureaucratic rationalization of the economy, society and politics which has been so decisive a feature of the modern world. It is especially noteworthy that Smith realized the potentiality of rationalized production, even before machines began seriously to displace human labor.

Unlike the great writers on economics who came after him, Smith was optimistic about the social consequences of the triumph of rationality. We find no such optimism in Thomas Robert Malthus and David Ricardo, the great economic and social thinkers of the generation that followed Smith. Moreover, Smith's optimism was based upon the paradoxical conviction that the unvarnished egoism and self-interest of the individual economic actors would yield the greatest good for society as a whole, a position enthusiastically affirmed by the New Right in America.[5] Instead of seeing economic egoism as socially destructive, as had almost all previous social and political thinkers, Smith took the revolutionary position of regarding it as the cornerstone of public good. Among the passages in which Smith expressed this opinion are the following:

A revolution of the greatest importance to the public happiness was in this manner brought about by two very different orders of people who had not the least intention to serve the public. To gratify the most childish vanity was the sole motive of the great proprietors. The merchants and artificers, much less ridiculous, acted merely from a view to their own interest, and in pursuit of their own pedlar principle of turning a penny wherever a penny was to be got. Neither of them had either knowledge or foresight of the great revolution which the folly of the one, and the industry of the other, was gradually bringing about.[6]

The division of labour, from which so many advantages are derived, is not originally the effect of any human wisdom, which foresees and intends that general opulence to which it gives occasion. It is the necessary, though very slow and gradual consequence of a certain propensity in human nature which has in view no such extensive utility; the propensity to truck, barter, and exchange one thing for another.[7]

Smith observed that this "propensity to truck, barter, and exchange" is rooted in naked self-interest:

Man has almost constant occasion for the help of his brethren, and it is in vain for him to expect it from their benevolence only. He will be more likely to prevail if he can interest their self-love in his favour, and show them that it is to their own advantage to do for him what he requires of them. Whoever offers to another a bargain of any kind, proposes to do this. Give me what I want, and you shall have what you want....[8]

Unfortunately, Smith could not foresee the tragic predicament of an age in which tens of millions of men and women would be incapable of saying to each other "Give me what I want, and you shall have what you want," because they have nothing to give and lack the means of acquiring anything of value. This is not the place to explore the causes of a paradoxical contemporary condition which is far more bitter than the paradox to which Smith referred. This writer has attempted to do that elsewhere.[9] For our purposes, it is sufficient to note that the fundamental cause of the worldwide

The Rational Society and the Future of Religion

phenomenon of mass poverty and unemployment has been the triumph of the same revolution of rationality concerning which Smith was so optimistic. Moreover, out of respect for a great mind, we must acknowledge that in his own time Smith had reason to be optimistic concerning the revolution of rationality. He could not foresee that reason's revolution would so lower the value of unskilled human labor at a time of rapidly expanding population growth—itself a further consequence of that same revolution—that tens of millions of human beings would be condemned to live without hope of ever finding gainful employment or of improving their condition.

While Smith did not foresee this crisis in human affairs, Karl Marx did. He foresaw that those who own the means of production would be compelled by competition drastically to reduce labor costs, either by reducing wages or by employing laborsaving machinery. In our era, the cost of labor can also be reduced by transferring manufacturing operations from countries where labor costs are high, such as the United States, to those where they are low, such as the developing nations. Without discussing Marx's opinion that capitalism was destined to self-destruct as a result of its own inner contradictions, it is important to note that Marx predicted that (a) an ever-greater proportion of the labor force would cease to be self-employed because of the ever-increasing capital requirements for maintaining a successful business enterprise, and that (b) laborsaving machinery would have the result of creating a large population of men and women whose subsistence needs would be wholly dependent upon their ability to sell their labor power under conditions in which there would be ever-fewer purchasers.

Marx's gloomy predictions concerning the collapse of capitalism have not been fulfilled. Nevertheless, Marx did identify certain problems in the capitalist system that have periodically returned to plague it. Moreover, a principle reason why capitalism did not collapse was the fact that no government has permitted pure, *laissez-faire* capitalism to function. To some extent, the human consequences of such a system have always been taken into account.

As is well known, Marx's solution to the problems of capitalism was a revolution in the economy and society through which the producers would jointly come to possess the means of production. According to Marx, when this condition came to pass, the producers would no longer be compelled to submit to the expropriation of their product by a non-producing class. Marx did not, of course, spell out the details of his proposed system, save by vague indication. Nevertheless, he was convinced that the socialist society he advocated would involve a further advance in economic rationality. Although bourgeois society represented an enormous advance in rationality over feudalism, its tendency toward periodic economic crises, and mass unemployment arising out of unprecedented affluence, appeared to Marx as expressions of the ultimate irrationality of capitalism. *According to Marx, the ills of a rationalized society could be cured only by further rationalization.*

It is important to note that Marx saw important parallels between what he regarded as the irrationality of religion and the irrationality of bourgeois, capitalist society. According to Marx, in religion people enslave themselves to their own immaterial product, failing to grasp that the product, namely God, is merely the objectified expression of human self-alienation. In capitalist economics, again according to Marx, the laborer produces products, commodites, which are expropriated by the capitalist and with which the capitalist achieves an overwhelming economic advantage over the worker. Utilizing the worker's own product, which the workers in their alienation fail to recognize as their own, the capitalist compels the worker to accept conditions of work and life infinitely inferior to his own. In the final act of the capitalist drama, the workers are rendered entirely superfluous by their own material product, namely, automated machinery, and the sum total of capital stock, which has been expropriated from them by the capitalist.

Thus, Marx's twin calls for atheism in religion and for communism in economics and politics are in reality two aspects of a single demand: that producers recognize and reappropriate as their own both material and immaterial products. The rationalist motif in Marx's revolutionary program should be clear. Marx calls for an end to self-negation and self-alienation as the preconditions of humanity's non-alienated material and spiritual life. Recognizing its true essence for the first time, humanity will, according to Marx, finally be able to devote its energies to its own improvement and benefit.[10]

It was Goya who was reported to have said that "the dreams of reason bring forth monsters." Goya's remark has certainly been an appropriate comment on most of the twentieth century attempts to implement Marx's dream of a rational social order. As horrendous as has been the number of people murdered by National Socialist

The Rational Society and the Future of Religion

Germany, that number has been more than equaled by those killed in the Soviet Union since the Russian Revolution, especially, but by no means exclusively, under Stalin. It is conservatively estimated that in the great political purges of the nineteen-thirties, the forced collectivization of Soviet agriculture, the deportations and massacres of "unrealiable" nationalities, ethnic groups and former Russian prisoners of war, the abusive slave-labor camps, the squandering of life in excess of all requirements of military necessity during World War II, and the persectuion of intellectuals, religious believers (Jewish, Christian, Moslem and Buddhist), and other dissidents, no less than 80,000,000 Soviet citizens lost their lives as a result of the policies of their own government. No other state in history has ever initiated policies which have resulted in the elimination of so many of its own citizens. Yet, what is most incredible, is that the violence was legitimated as a series of measures necessary for the creation of a fully rational society![11]

For our purposes, a particularly striking example of the use of mass violence ostensibly to foster a rational society can be seen in Stalin's attempt to compel the collectivization of Soviet agriculture. In 1930 Stalin initiated a program of the sudden and total collectivization of the Soviet Union's small agrarian holdings. This was, of course, in accordance with communism's goal to abolish private property. It was also an attempt to rationalize Soviet agriculture. Stalin understood that, as long as agriculture remained in the hands of 25,000,000 small, inefficient producers, it would be impossible to create a modern economy in the Soviet Union. The same movement toward the consolidation of small holdings had manifested itself in the West, save that in Western countries the pressure upon smallholders came from the market place rather than from the police powers of the state.

Stalin believed that a rationalized economy required centralized control over agricultural production, enhanced productivity, and the achievement of economies of scale through consolidation and the use of scientific agricultural techniques. Moreover, an industrialized economy in relatively backward Russia would require a greatly enlarged industrial working force that could only come from displaced rural workers whose services on the land had been rendered redundant by consolidation and collectivization. To achieve his objectives, Stalin was willing to sacrifice the lives of millions of Russians. Those who stood in the way of economic rationality and "progress" were regarded as class enemies who deserved to be liquidated. Neither Stalin nor his close followers had any qualms about mass slaughter. With the restraints of religion removed, large-scale slaughter had become simply a method of rational problem-solving. Both Lenin and Marx had taught that the members of the bourgeoisie, both *grande* and *petite,* were part of a dying class doomed by history to elimination. Stalin demonstrated one of the forms elimination would take. "Class enemies" were not to be regarded as members of the same moral community. Their elimination was legitimated by Stalin's reading of Marxist ideology. Stalin stated succinctly the nature of his agricultural program: "The liquidation of the kulaks as a class."[12]

Stalin's program involved the forcible seizure of the property of millions of Russian peasants. Five months after its inception, over half of all peasant households had been collectivized. However, the rationality of Stalin's program was not apparent to the target group, which saw the communist state as involved in a program of expropriation of infinitely greater scope than either the feudal nobility or the capitalist bourgeoisie had ever attempted. Millions of peasants resisted, killing their own livestock rather than permit them to become state property. This resulted in a man-made famine which compelled Stalin to retreat temporarily. Nevertheless, by 1932 he had broken the back of the country's peasantry.[13] During World War II Stalin admitted to Churchill that 10,000,000 peasants had to be "dealt with" in the crisis and that the "great bulk" had been "wiped out."[14] As Solzhenitsyn has pointed out, millions of peasant families were uprooted from their agrarian holdings and condemned to enforced proletarianization, abusive slave labor, or death. Stalin had achieved his objectives. Millions of kulaks and less prosperous peasants had been liquidated "as a class." It is now estimated that 22,000,000 died as a result of Stalin's attempt to rationalize Soviet agriculture.[15]

It has, of course, been argued that Stalinism represents a perversion of Marxism and that one cannot judge Marxism by so gross a caricature. There is some truth in the apology insofar as Marx devoted far more energy to his analysis of the social reality he could observe, nineteenth century English capitalism, than in offering a concrete blueprint for a socialist society which had yet to materialize. Nevertheless, no human being ever had the unimpeded power to concretize the communist dream as did Stalin, and we are, therefore, not unfair in judging communism, at least partially, on the basis of his record.

The Rational Society and the Future of Religion

An important conclusion that emerges from an examination of Stalin's record is that *when morally neutral functional rationality is used to create an economic and social order, such rationality ultimately becomes the handmaiden of power.* In the case of Stalin, whether one assumes that the dictator was corrupted by power and sought only his own aggrandisement, or that he would tolerate no impediment to the creation of a communist society, the results were the same: *Nothing prevented him from bringing about the death of millions of Soviet citizens and inflicting extraordinary misery on even more millions.* The horror was ultimately carried out in the name of reason, and reason provided the method of implementation. Whatever may have been the capacities of reason, it did not have the ability to limit itself.

Unfortunately, when we turn from the record of communism to that of bourgeois capitalism, we find that the dream of a rational society is not without its negative side as well. Obviously, the bourgeois capitalist conception of a rational society is very different from the Marxist version. Fundamental to bourgeois rationality is the market economy. Such an economy is both rationalizing and desacralizing. It is rationalizing insofar as it aims at the universal quantification of all of the goods, services and experiences of value to humanity. A market economy is also desacralizing. In a perfectly rational money economy, no religious or moral value can function as a restraint upon the free functioning of the market place. It is for that reason that in the West the Roman Catholic Church was traditionally hostile to unfettered capitalism. Only with the advent of Calvinism was it possible for the commited Christian to feel at home in a market economy.

Max Weber has given expression to the morally neutral and depersonalized aspect of the market economy:

The market community as such is the most impersonal relationship of practical life into which humans can enter with one another. . . . The reason for the impersonality of the market is its matter-of-factness, its orientation to the market and only to that. Where the market is allowed to follow its own autonomous tendencies, its participants do not look toward the persons of each other but only toward the commodity; there are no obligations of brotherliness or reverence, and none of the spontaneous human relations that are sustained by personal unions. They all would just obstruct the free development of the bare market relationship. . . . Market behavior is influenced by rational, purposeful pursuit of interests.[16]

Concerning such a system, Weber offers the following comment:

Such absolute depersonalization is contrary to all the elementary forms of human relationship. . . .

The "free" market, that is, the market which is not bound by ethical norms . . . is an abomination to every system of fraternal ethics. In contrast to all other groups which always presuppose some measure of fraternal relationship or even blood kinship, the market is fundamentally alien to any type of fraternal relationship.[17]

In a purely market economy, even the participants' willingness to honor business promises is not based upon moral but instrumental considerations. Without this modest form of self-limitation, there would be no possiblity of continuous trade. Yet, even that form of behavioral constraint is not always observed. Among the recent examples of the subordination of ethical to purely instrumental values was the decision of the Ford Motor Company to permit the continued manufacture of some lines of their automobiles which were known to have defects of sufficient gravity to result in the loss of life. This decision was actually based upon the calculation that the cost to the company in law suits resulting from loss of life would be less than the cost of correcting the defect. Ford did not give their customers any indication that its products were defective.[18] Regrettably, such behavior is frequently found in the contemporary business world.

There are, of course, fundamental differences between the rationalization of the economy and society under communism and in free societies. Under normal conditions, citizens of a free society need not fear that they have been targeted for elimination simply because they are perceived to be un-assimilable to the existing political system. Millions of people have suffered that fate under communism. Nevertheless, the fact that a market economy is in no sense bound by ethical norms and is wholly depersonalized means that a society in which a market economy is permitted unrestricted reign is one in which the bonds uniting persons will tend to be instrumental rather than moral. In reality no such society could exist for very long. Without some degree of self-limitation and even civic altruism, any society would disintegrate into a congeries of self-aggrandizing atoms wholly indifferent to each other's fate.

Thus, there is a fundamental tension between the requirements of a pure market economy and the values necessary to maintain a community. Put differently, in spite of the modern tendency toward the progressive rationalization of the economy and society, no community can survive on the basis of pure rationality alone. Every community requires some measure of altruism and self-limitation on the part of its members. One of the most important reasons the business class was regarded as of low status in almost all pre-capitalist societies was because its pursuit of economic self-aggrandizement was recognized as in tension with the requirements of a well-functioning community.

The real difficulty with the values of a market economy in our era is that such values offer no credible rationale—save the maintenance of public order—by which society could be effectively concerned with the fate of its disadvantaged members, should they find themselves politically or vocationally redundant as a consequence of the revolution of rationality. The seriousness of this problem becomes evident when one considers that, of the 100,000,000 men and women in the U.S. work force, it is estimated that forty-five percent will experience job displacment in the next two decades as a result of automation of the office and the factory.[19] This does not mean that all of the displaced workers are fated to be permanently unemployed. Nevertheless, it is fair to assume that many millions of those who lose their jobs will never find new ones. Nor is this condition restricted to the United States. In many respects, Europe is likely to be faced with an even graver employment problem than the United States.

In the past, emigration constituted the principal humane solution to the problem of vocational redundancy. There have been, of course, infinitely less humane ways of solving the problem of eliminating target populations deemed vocationally superfluous or otherwise unwanted.[20] In many parts of the world emigration still constitutes the most important humane method of solving this problem, as witnessed by the flood of immigrants from the Caribbean and Central America to the United States. Nevertheless, emigration has its limits, and no society can stretch its absorptive capacities beyond a certain point. For several centuries the United States was the solution to the surplus population problems of other societies. The problem is now American. Undoubtedly, the current political discontent of the American black community is largely rooted in the inability of American society to solve the problem of large-scale, relatively permanent black unemployment. This discontent is one of the elements in the very strong support that community gave the Reverend Jesse Jackson's 1984 presidential campaign.

At present, the problem of mass unemployment is troubling in the United States and Europe, but it has yet to reach crisis proportions. Should it do so in the future, the United States and other non-socialist nations will require more than economic rationality to work out a humane solution. As noted above, pure economic rationality depersonalizes human relations and strips them of all ethical content. In an economic crisis, those who are capable of economic survival are likely to reject as irrational any sense of obligation to those who are without resources and, hence, cannot enter into the only relationship that retains meaning in a market economy, namely that of the market place. Without a commitment to shared obligation and shared community, only the cruelest versions of Social Darwinsim and Neo-Malthusianism will appear as plausible ideologies.

In *The Age of Triage* this writer concluded his historical survey of the long-range consequences of (a) the problem of mass vocational redundancy and (b) state-sponsored programs of population elimination in modern times with the observation that absent some credible adherence to religious values within society, we would be unable to meet the human crisis brought about by the ongoing revolution of rationality. Although some critics saw this as the least convincing part of the book, this writer is compelled to reiterate that observation on this occasion. Nor have his reasons for insisting upon a new religious consensus changed since writing that book. He argued that *"a purely secular, rationalistic approach to our social problems is unlikely to produce the collective altruism our situation demands."*[21] It should be noted that the observations concerning a religious consensus were offered within the context of a single nation, the United States.

The reasons were simple. Even in an advanced industrial country like the United States, the revolution of rationality threatens to render millions of human beings economically helpless by virtue of the fact that there is likely to be little need for their labor. This could easily lead to radical social polarization between those whose labor is needed and those who can find no work. Having no hope of gaining society's rewards, the latter group would have little reason to be bound by society's behavioral constraints. In Western Europe the problem has been somewhat disguised by the presence of foreign workers, who are usually the first to be dismissed in hard times. In the United States a segment of the black and Mexican working force plays a role not unlike that of Europe's *Gastarbeiter*.

The Rational Society and the Future of Religion

Unfortunately, current levels of unemployment may be a foretaste of things to come, not only for minority and foreign workers but for the population as a whole.

There is, of course, an available ideology which can legitimate the radical dichotomization of society and even the use of state-sponsored violence to control or eliminate unwanted or unneeded sectors of the population. I refer to Social Darwinism and Neo-Malthusianism. That ideology has already been used to legitimate the murderous destructiveness of National Socialism. In the long run, a dichotomized society is likely to be a terror-ridden society. No matter how well protected the haves may be, they will live in fear of assault and theft by the have-nots, who will have no rational motive for respecting moral norms. Without legally and socially acceptable means of earning a living, the more resourceful of the have-nots will be tempted to turn to crime, drug-vending and prostitution. Nor will the have-nots be free from terror under such circumstances. In all probability they will be subject to draconian police control. An overworked police force will act as the interface between the haves and have-nots. Both the economic frustration and vocational uselessness of the have-nots will tempt the police to abuse of authority. The worst fear of the have-nots will be the temptation of state authorities to eliminate them altogether. In past societies the underclass could at least find useful roles through the institution of slavery. In a time of automated production, slaves would only be so many useless mouths to feed. Social Darwinsim could easily become a self-fulfilling prophecy as the polis gives way to the law of the human jungle. As a matter of fact, the scenarios we project are already visible to some extent in many advanced industrial societies. These extrapolations are not based upon fantasy but on already existing conditions.

The alternative to the dichotomization of society is the credible affirmation of a universe of moral obligation which includes every member of society. Secular rationalism simply cannot provide any such universe of obligation. Much of the appeal of racism in the twentieth century has been its affirmation of common origin as the basis of moral obligation in a period in which religion had lost much of its credibility for large numbers of men and women. As we know, racism is ultimately destructive of moral obligation in a complex multi-ethnic society. Far from ending the radical dichotomization of society, it intensifies it.

Only religion has offered men and women a way of establishing an enduring universe of moral obligation that transcends ethnicity and class. Indeed, it may have been one of the functions of the world religions to establish newer and broader universes of moral obligation when communication and human interchange made older, narrower moral universes parochial and inadequate to the social requirements of each new historical epoch. In the West, this has been true of Judaism, Christianity and Islam respectively. This development begins for the biblical religions with Judaism. Although Judaism is often thought of as essentially the religion of a single nationality, contemporary biblical scholars now regard it as having had its beginnings in the imperative requirement of tribal groups of diverse religious and ethnic origin to establish themselves as a unified community at the time of the exodus from Egypt. In the ancient Near East only shared religion could provide the basis of such a community. Without common origins, and sharing only the experience of Egyptian slavery and liberation therefrom, the diverse peoples who participated in the exodus under Moses became one people by affirming a common loyalty to the God who was the author of their shared experience. That God's demand that the united tribes serve Him alone, can be seen as the resolute determination of the new community to put aside those ancestral gods which in the past had divided them into mutually exclusive moral universes, and to render their wholehearted fidelity to the God who had liberated them and transformed them into a single moral community.

The same process is visible on a much larger scale in the founding of both Christianity and Islam. In each case, the new religion was able to create a new community which transcended older tribal ties of loyalty and obligation. An important expression of the creation of a new and larger moral universe is to be discerned in the observation of Paul of Tarsus:

For as many of you as were baptized into Christ have put on Christ. There is neither Jew nor Greek, there is neither slave nor free, there is neither male nor female: for you are all one in Christ Jesus. And if you are Christ's, then you are Abraham's offspring, heirs according to promise. (Gal. 3:27–28)

Paul proclaimed a new universal community in which the old divisions would be healed. As is known, neither Christianity nor Islam entirely succeeded in healing the old divisions or preventing the rise of new sources of discord. Nevertheless, more often than

The Rational Society and the Future of Religion

not, both religions had a certain restraining effect on the worst elements of human destructiveness. Secular critics of religion have often argued that it separates men and women from each other and can lead to violent conflict. Insofar as each religion constitutes a solipsistic moral universe, there is truth in this complaint. Nevertheless, the worst excesses of religious conflict cannot compare in brutishness or mass destructivness to the excesses of those political movements of the twentieth century which have regarded themselves as wholly liberated from all religiously defined moral constraints. Indeed, radical secularization was an indispensable precondition to most of the mass excesses of the twentieth century.

The last two decades have witnessed the growth of a worldwide market place of unprecedented scope, as well as the rise of East Asia to a place of economic and technological primacy among the nations of the world. It may be that, as the growth of the Roman Empire rendered obsolete many of the earlier small communities based upon tribal and kinship bonds, so too the rise of Asia and the world marketplace calls for a new and more broadly based moral community than has previously existed. The rise of the Holy Spirit Association for the Unification of World Christianity and the techings of the Reverend Sun Myung Moon can be seen as an important response to that need. This development was especially evident in the mass wedding of some 4,000 members of the Unification Church at Madison Square Garden on July 1, 1982, an event which was the object of considerable media criticism. Older ties of loyalty and moral obligation were transcended, though not negated, by the marriages in which young men and women from every corner of the earth married outside of their inherited religious and tribal boundaries, and shared in a new common religious experience.

It is, of course, easier to point to the shortcomings of unrestrained, morally neutral rationality and the need for a new religious consensus than it is to produce one. That task cannot be performed by an historian of religion or a theologian. If the new consensus is to arise, it will do so as a consequence of truly inspired religious leaders and a population prepared to receive their teachings. This writer is fully aware of the profound difficulties that can easily hinder the successful development of a religious consensus within a single nation and, most certainly, in the world at large. Moreover, he has no blueprint for its implementation. Nevertheless, he is aware of the need and he knows that where such a need has arisen in the face of past crises of civilization, it has providentially been met.

NOTES

1. Max Weber, "Science as a Vocation," in *From Max Weber: Essays in Sociology*, H. H. Gerth edited by C. Wright Mills (New York: Oxford University Press, 1946), 155.
2. Weber, "Science as a Vocation," 138.
3. Weber, "The Sociology of the World Religions" in *From Max Weber: Essays in Sociology*, 293.
4. Adam Smith, *The Wealth of Nations*, edited by Andrew Skinner (Harmondsworth, Middlesex: Penguin Books, 1969), Chapter I, 109.
5. See Jerome L. Himmelstein, "The New Right: in *The New Christian Right*, edited by Robert C. Liebman and Robert Wuthow (New York: Aldine Publishing Company, 1983), 16ff.
6. Smith, *The Wealth of Nations*, 515.
7. Ibid., 117.
8. Ibid., 118.
9. See Richard Rubenstein, *The Age of Triage: Fear and Hope in An Overcrowded World* (Boston: Beacon Press, 1983).
10. For a useful study of some of Marx's leading ideas, see Shlomo Avineri, *The Social and Political Thought of Karl Marx* (Cambridge: Cambridge University Press, 1968).
11. See Richard Grenier, "The Horror, The Horror," in *The New Republic*, 26 May 1982; Robert Conquest, *The Great Terror: Stalin's Purge of the Thirties* (Harmondsworth, Middlesex: Penguin Books, 1974), 699–713.
12. Adam Ulman, *Stalin: The Man and His Era* (New York: Viking/Compass, 1973), 423.
13. See Ulman, *Stalin*, 289ff; Alan W. Gouldner, "Stalinism: A Study in Internal Colonialism," *Telos* 34 (Winter 1977–78).
14. Winston S. Churchill, *The Second World War*, Vol. 4 (London: Cassell, 1951), 447–448.
15. Grenier, "The Horror, the Horror," 28; Solzhenitsyn estimates that 15,000,000 died. See Alexander Solzhenitsyn, *The Gulag Archipelago Three* (New York: Perennial Library, 1976), 350.
16. Max Weber, *Economy and Society: An Outline of Interpretive Sociology*, edited by Guenther Roth and Claus Wittich (New York: Bedminister Press, 1968), Vol. II, 636.
17. Weber, *Economy and Society*, Vol. II, 637.
18. See "Ford Study: Death, Injury Cheaper than Fixing Cars," *Tallahassee Democrat* 14 October 1979. This was a *Chicago Tribune* wire service dispatch.
19. See "The Speedup in Automation," *Business Week* 3 August 1981.
20. See Richard Rubenstein, *The Age of Triage*.
21. Richard Rubenstein, *The Age of Triage*, 232.

15
On The Creation of a Good Society
THOMAS WALSH

Introduction

We have been asked to explore not merely the relevance, not merely the function, but the necessity of "faith in God" for the "creation of a just society." Now it seems obvious that "faith in God" is necessary for the creation of a Christian society, indeed a just Christian society; and the same holds true for the creation of a Unification society. That is, having faith in God is somehow constitutive of one's being at all Christian or Unificationist, not to mention Jewish or Muslim. However, it seems less obvious that "faith in God" is necessary for the creation of "a just society," with society being understood in a generic sense. There are any number of ways to articulate a theory of justice independent of theology and/or theism. In fact, that has been a primary pursuit of most modern theorists of justice, beginning (and restricting myself narrowly to the locale of Western European and American thought) with Kant, through Marx, to the more recent work of John Rawls: to seek a rational and universally valid ground for a theory of justice binding on all persons regardless of theological convictions, thus securing a basis for the legitimation of law in a society which lacks theological consensus.

Modern, non-theological theories of justice may be understood as attempts to secure a foundation for justice, and concomitantly law, without appeal to any particular theological perspective. After all, given the sheer multiplicity of theological perspectives, and hence the sheer multiplicity of theological theories of justice, there seems little hope of securing either consensus or compliance if justice requires a theological grounding. The heterogeneity of theories of the God in which one might have faith, has dampened the prospects for anchoring a theory of justice, which is to be valid within a pluralistic society, by appeal to theology. On the contrary, if justice is to prevail, while the gods are nevertheless at war, then it would seem that justice must have autonomy from theology. Here we have, I would argue, the warrant for both Marxist and liberal-democratic non-theological—and in the case of Marxism, anti-theological—theories of justice.

I do not intend to argue that faith in God is necessary for the creation of a just society. Rather, I will argue, or suggest, that a merely just society which views the "faith in God" issue as a matter of indifference, an optional choice as liberalism teaches us, or a regressive choice as orthodox Marxism claims, may not only be an impoverished society, but an impersonal and vicious society as well. That is, a theory of justice which does not appeal either to a system of meaning such as theology may provide, or to a particular vision of the good life, can indeed eventuate in a society which is both just and meaningless, and which, moreover, militates against the promise of achieving a good society. In sum, a just society is not necessarily a good society, and may in fact be devoid of character and community.

Furthermore, given the heterogeneity of even non-theological theories of justice, i.e., the incommensurability of the criteria in terms of which justice is to be understood, it stands to reason that what may be perceived as justice from say within the Politburo is patently unjust when viewed from Washington, and vice versa. And since it seems to be the case that the implementation of justice requires power and domination administered in regard for what are perceived to be generalizable interests—for example, the implementation of equality may require the domination of liberty—it is possible to say that a just society is not necessarily, nor even probably, free of domination. And if justice as the right is determined prior to any consideration of the good, then a just society might also be an unhappy society. In sum, I contend that it is not wholly unintelligible to assert that a just society may be characterized by both domination and misery; such is the price that one may be obliged to pay for the implementation of some particular theory of justice.

Faith in God, while it may not be necessary for the creation of a just society, may be necessary for the creation of a good society. Stating the thesis less theologically, a theory of justice or rights that lacks any determinate theory of the good life, also lacks the substance on which the fullness of a human life—both individual and social—depends. By 'substance' I refer to the realm of meaning and its important role in the formation of character, community, and a vision of history.

I will initially focus on what may be called the liberal theory of justice, a non-theological and non-teleological theory of justice. Some mention will also be made of a Marxist theory of justice. I will attempt to be both descriptive and critical of the non-theological theories of justice, and critical in general of the attempt to view justice as prior to any substantive and determinate theory of the good. I will seek backing for my position by appeal to Michael Sandel, Alasdair MacIntyre, and Bernard Williams. Having made my protest, I will attempt to show the importance (if still not quite the necessity) of theology for a theory of justice. Some mention will be made of Paul Tillich, and H. Richard Niebuhr, and their attempts to establish, respectively, an ontological and anthropological ground for theological justice. These more abstract theological approaches will be contrasted, in a final section, with an exploration of Unificationism as a practical theology, which—unlike conventional Neo-Marxist notions of praxis as protest, critique and rebellion—represents a more classical notion of practice. I will argue that given this approach neither theology nor practice is reduced to justice, and yet justice emerges as a necessary concomitant of a theological vision of the good life.

On the Autonomy and Priority of Universal Principles of Justice: A Signal of the Erosion of Meaning, Character and Community

"Modern moral philosophy" understands itself as autonomous; morality is believed to be independent of religion and theology. However, if G. E. M. Anscombe is correct in her assessment of the problematic that is "modern moral philosophy," then the concept of obligation which moral philosophy presumes, is really an historical accomplishment—one might say a virtue—derivative from divine-command, i.e., theistic ethics. Obligation, as modern moral philosophy would have it, represents "the survival of a concept outside the framework of thought that made it a really intelligble one."[1] We have a "law conception of ethics" without a lawgiver, God.[2]

Perhaps the key figure in presenting a "law conception of ethics" without a lawgiver is Kant. For Kant the lawgiver is pure practical reason, his foundation for ethics, autonomy, and theology. According to Kant the moral law is characterized by universalizability and independence from any theory of, or pathological inclination toward, the good. Morality is severed from telos, utility, and human purpose. The "right" is defined prior to the "good," and is independent of the good. That is, a notion of justice or rights may be obtained without any consideration of such matters as: the meaning of life, its purpose and value, what a human being ought to aspire to achieve in a full human life, and what constitutes human fulfillment. Such is the nature of Kant's deontological ethics—a rejection of incipient utilitarianism and teleological (consequentialist) ethics. And Kant, as a forerunner of liberalism, develops an ethics which is only derivatively theological, and which celebrates formal rationality, impartiality, and universalism.

In his work, *Liberalism and the Limits of Justice,* Michael Sandel characterizes liberalism's preoccupation with the right and justice, at the expense of the good, as "deontological liberalism."

'Deontological liberalism' is above all a theory about justice, and in particular about the primacy of justice among moral and political ideals. Its core thesis can be stated as follows: society, being composed of a plurality of persons, each with his own aims, interests, and conceptions of the good, is best arranged when it is governed by principles that do not in themselves presuppose any particular conception of the good; what justifies these regulative principles above all is not that they maximize the social welfare or otherwise promote the good, but rather that they conform to the concept of right, a moral category given prior to the good and independent of it.[3]

A key point here is the notion of society as an irreducible plurality, particularly as regards theories of the good life, or we might say, particularly as regards theories of substantive meaning and theories of how one ought best to live one's life. Given pluralism, and given the desire for a peaceful society, ethics searches for bottom lines and generic principles, while bracketing substantive questions. Hence we have the preoccupation with rights, as the bottom line of political and social ethics. And, as Sandel points out, "given its independent status, the right constrains the good and sets its bounds."[4] For a contemporary example one may look to the way questions of rights come to the fore in such institutions as marriage and family. While the concern with rights seems at first glance to be an advance, a preoccupation with rights as applied to marriage and family can also be a trojan horse. And while I do not wish to gainsay the problems of child and spouse abuse, it may be that a theory of the rights of persons is not an adequate solution, and is more a symptom of distrust rather than a means of reconciliation. Apart from marriage and family there is also a kind of imperialism of impartial justice, that in the name of neutrality *vis-à-vis* churches, may seriously hinder the work of churches.

Rights and obligations in most modern moral philosophy are generic features of human beings considered as such, regardless of their character, their commitments, and their community. These generic rights and obligations are derived by removing oneself—alienating oneself from the particular historical situation, thus achieving through the virtue of alienation, autonomy—from one's particular commitments and imagining oneself in an "original position" free from the constraints of history.[5] As one reflects on fundamental rights of persons and universally valid principles of justice—universally valid in being non-dependent on particular theories of meaning which are not widely shared—one often finds oneself at odds with historical manifestations of the good. Sandel continues:

Bound up with the notion of an independent self is a vision of the moral universe this self must inhabit. Unlike classical Greek and medieval Christian conceptions, the universe of the deontological ethic is a place devoid of inherent meaning, a world 'disenchanted' in Max Weber's phrase, a world without an objective moral order. Only in a world empty of telos . . . is it possible to conceive a subject apart from and prior to its purposes and ends.[6]

Furthermore:

To see ourselves as deontology would see us is to deprive us of those qualities of character, reflectiveness, and friendship that depend on the possibility of constitutive projects and attachments.[7]

What I am suggesting, with Sandel's help, is that the way to a just society seems inherently at odds with the way to the good society. To achieve a theory of justice one is required to subordinate systems of meaning, including theology, and to put aside what Bernard Williams refers to as "life projects."[8] The virtue of practical reason, embedded in tradition and community, is rejected in favor of a theory of virtually ahistorical rationality; practical reason seeks to be pure and impartial, unsullied by either time or purposes. Such is the potential tyranny of the impartiality ideal—impartiality with regard to any particular relationship, commitment, or goal—that undergirds contemporary liberal theories of justice. While we are wont to regard impartial procedures of justice as an index of the quality of life; quite the reverse may be the case. There may be a direct ratio between concern with justice and rights, and loss of meaning and social solidarity within a society. The exponential growth of practitioners in the legal profession evidences this point. Quoting Sandel again:

> Where justice replaces injustice, other things being equal, the overall moral improvement is clear. On the other hand, where an increase in justice reflects some transformation in the quality of pre-existing motivations and dispositions, the overall moral balance might well be diminished.[9]

The point here is that "the exercise of justice in inappropriate conditions will have brought about an overall decline in the moral character of the association."[10] Justice becomes wholly a matter of law rather than a matter of virtue. As Alasdair MacIntyre has said of law:

> The nature of any society therefore is not to be deciphered from its laws alone, but from those understood as an index of its conflicts. What our laws show is the extent and degree to which conflict has to be suppressed.[11]

In liberalism, due to the recognized heterogeneity of the good, justice is defined independently of any theory of the good. Justice is defined formally, in terms of procedures, principles and laws that hold for all persons. As questions of justice take on increasing importance, questions of substance and meaning take on marginal status. They are *adiaphora*; matters of indifference. At the same time, and perhaps most importantly, questions of substance and meaning are known to be consensus-forming and identity-forming factors at the local level, but contention-forming factors at the global level, e.g., interminable religious wars. For this latter reason also, substantive concerns are bracketed when attempting to provide grounds for a theory of justice. Nevertheless, the substance of life, and we might say with Bernard Williams, that which makes life worth living, is duly privatized and becomes a matter of choice, a reflection of subjective partiality. Williams, however, questions this trend.

> There can come a point at which it is quite unreasonable for a man to give up, in the name of the impartial good ordering of the world of

On the Creation of a Good Society

moral agents, something which is a condition of his having any interest in being around in that world at all.[12]

And furthermore:

Life is to have substance if anything is to have sense, including adherence to the impartial system; but if it has substance, then it cannot grant supreme importance to the impartial system, and that system's hold on it will be, at the limit, insecure.[13]

Substance, as I interpret the term, entails meaning. Not merely in the sense of chosen meaning, as one chooses a suit of clothing, but meaning in the sense of destiny and commitments. Substance implies meaningful history, both in terms of the past as well as the future. Where we have been and where we are going, and what we are aiming for, that is, the good, becomes determinative even of a theory of justice. Consider MacIntyre's comment on an Aristotelian theory of justice:

Justice, on an Aristotelian view, is defined in terms of giving each person his or her due or desert. To deserve well is to have contributed in some substantial way to the achievement of those goods, the sharing of which and the common pursuit of which provide foundations for human community.[14]

Liberal justice operates in accord with what Rawls has called a "thin theory of the good,"[15] or what also may be called teleological minimalism as applied to character and community. Ethics is reduced to the theory of justice and rights understood independently of a theory of the good. Hence the lack of attention given to concerns having to do with the formation of character and community, and the transmission of tradition. Finally, as the concern with character, community, and tradition is marginalized, and as these factors become less operative in society, the greater the need for consideration of rights and justice, often to correct the lack of social solidarity. Justice, under the conditions of such character and community erosion, is what obtains between strangers who share no common vision of the good life; justice defines our distance from one another.

A Word on Orthodox Marxism's Anti-Theological Theory of Distributive Justice

Marxism, unlike liberalism, does not espouse neutralism and impartiality in its theory of the right. However orthodox Marxists do claim to have neutrally and impartially (i.e., scientifically) formulated what justice requires. But like liberalism, Marxism views justice (i.e., economic equality) as the centerpiece of ethics, a sufficient condition for the creation of an ideal society, and in this sense Marxism, like liberalism, is deontological. Marxism is also antitheological insofar as theism and religion are viewed as twin ideologies which blind one from the concrete realities of economic inequality. And, having rejected even practical theology (e.g., Christian socialism) Marxism becomes practical sociology.

Marxism reduces justice to its economic component—justice is only distributive justice rigidly fixed on insuring equality of result—and in so doing reduces politics to the task of meting out economic equality, often with a vengeance. Whereas liberalism may be described as relatively noninterventionist, Marxism is interventionist, taking control of the wheel of justice, and exemplifying the paradigm of a just society which is totalitarian, a veritable tyranny of justice. Furthermore, with Marxism, to an extent much greater than with liberalism, meaning is generally viewed as a threat to justice, especially when meaning systems (e.g., religion) take priority over a party-defined theory of the right. The persecution of religion and the social premium placed on atheism evidences the need to evacuate all substance from society—e.g., religiosity, ethnicity, and tradition—in order to effectively serve the program of justice.

In order to eliminate the domination of economic oppression, i.e., to legalistically institutionalize a theory of distributive justice, another form of domination is required: cultural and political domination. This, of course, creates a new form of injustice. We might consider the Soviet Union a just society, given its definition of justice, but not a good society—at least not in the sense that the common good of its citizens is preferred to the universalization of economic equality.

Of course, liberal democratic societies, while not anti-theological like a society governed by a communist party, are nevertheless destructive of the good in their own way. The neutrality principle itself militates against the idea of accenting a theory of the good as a basis for a theory of justice. And as the kind of social unity that derives from the sharing of a common project and a common meaning recedes, the gap is filled by laws, lawyers, litigation, and interminable conflicts. Law, and bottom-line justice, are the only stuff of which community is made. The courts, instead of being a measure of a nation's justice, are a measure of a lack of solidarity. On top of this, most capitalist societies manage to systematically undermine, particularly through the medium of advertising, meanings and traditions which are not conducive to consumer hedonism and materialism.

Theological Justice: A Brief Look at Two Modern, Western Christian Thinkers

Can a distinctly theological theory of justice be more than merely a local theory of justice, relevant only to those who share in a particular theological language game or religious form of life? It seems clear that a theologically grounded theory of justice, requires theological commitment if the theory of justice is to be at all intelligible. Hence, while one might claim that faith in God is necessary for the creation of a just Christian society, or a just Unification society, or a just Muslim society, one cannot say simply that faith in God is necessary for the creation of "a just society." As mentioned above the Soviet Union, given its own definition of justice, may be understood as just, and certainly "faith in God" does not enter into that self-understanding. Nevertheless, it seems in order to point out that a kind of faith is operative in the Soviet or any non-theological society. The conflict between say church and state in Poland is not best understood as one of faith versus unfaith, but rather as a conflict between incommensurable faiths. The individuals and groups involved have different faiths and different theories of justice.

In twentieth century Christian thought H. Richard Niebuhr and Paul Tillich both attempted to articulate fundamental theological perspectives which illustrate the universal or public relevance of Christian categories for social and political theory. In so doing they attempted to formulate theories of justice which are attentive to the theological dimension they believed constitutive of human existence. While Niebuhr attempted a kind of anthropological approach to justice, Tillich took an ontological approach.

Niebuhr argued that "faith" is a constitutive feature of human existence, and not merely a feature of an explicitly religious mode of existence. In an essay entitled "Faith in Gods and in God," he says:

Now it is evident, when we inquire into ourselves and into our common life, that without such active faith or such reliance and confidence on power we do not and cannot live. Not only the just but also the unjust, insofar as they live, live by faith.[16]

Faith is thus not a matter of choice, but is a condition of being human. It is only the object of our faith—for Niebuhr either God or a god—which constitutes our distinctiveness. Niebuhr also suggests that not only is faith a constitutive feature of being human, but so too is the call to locate a "center of value," and in this sense, faith in one God/god or another is generic. Pressing the point we might say, therefore, that faith in God, for Niebuhr, is necessary for the creation of a just society.

Niebuhr espoused monotheistic faith as a basis for his ethics of responsible openness to all being. Only a transcendent God, standing above all human constructions can serve to redeem us from idolatry and defensiveness. This faith, however, is not natural, but derives from revelation or from a story which gives meaning to history and which provides a warrant for trusting in being/God. This story, for Niebuhr, is the Christ event, an expression of love which allows us to conclude that God/being is good and worthy of trust. According to Niebuhr, without such a warrant for trust we are condemned to defensiveness and distrust of all being, i.e., an ethics of suspicion. Hence, for Niebuhr, faith in God does seem necessary for the creation of character and communities of trust. And faith in God seems necessary to an agent's capacity to discern the fitting or just act, in any given context. In other words, for Niebuhr, the sensibility for, and the motivation to do, justice, derives from a fundamental orientation to God/being. This fundamental orientation, intimately related to the biblical narratives, enhances one's capacity to see what a situation calls for, viz., that which would enhance being.

This theory of justice is theological and aesthetic insofar as faith in God serves the cause of seeing the particular in a universal context so that one may respond justly or proportionately. It is in this sense that Niebuhr's ethics of the fitting is inclusive of a theory of justice, and in many respects this perspective—absent the universalism and the Christology—mirrors the Aristotelian notion of *phronesis* or practical wisdom. But, whereas for Aristotle *phronesis* is acquired through education and habituation according to the model of the good man (the *phronemos*), for Niebuhr practical wisdom is grounded in an experience—in this case the Atonement—of the goodness of being or God. While Niebuhr offers a theory of faith grounded in a philosophical anthropology, i.e., a theory of the human being, he does not develop either a theory of social justice or a theory of the good. In this sense Niebuhr's ethics remains rather abstract and, finally, somewhat disappointing. Niebuhr's brother, Reinhold, was much more attentive to the need for a Christian theory of social justice, which he formulated as the approximation of love under the conditions of history. Reinhold, however, seems essentially to argue that Protestant (Lutheran) Christian faith is fundamentally compatible with liberal democracy.

Paul Tillich, like Reinhold Niebuhr, viewed justice as an expression of love in social situations where love is not a sufficient condition for mutual well-being. Tillich saw "creative justice" as "the form of reuniting love."[17] That is, justice represents an ontologically grounded thrust toward reconciliation. More specifically, Tillich's "creative justice" seeks, "fulfillment within the unity of universal fulfillment. The religious symbol for this is the Kingdom of God."[18] While Tillich does not specifically say that "faith in God" is necessary for the creation of a just society, he does argue that there can be no adequate theory of justice which does not ground itself ontologically in a theory of fundamental being, a condition which requires theological reflection. And in this sense Tillich does argue the necessity of faith in God—though he might not use such language—for the creation of a just society.

Given Tillich's ontological theory of justice and H. Richard Niebuhr's anthropology of faith, one can find warrant for connecting faith in God and justice. One might even argue for there being a necessary connection between faith, at least in something, and an adequate theory of justice. Furthermore, if we are to push to the roots in grounding a theory of justice, Niebuhr and Tillich remind us that we hazard a theological turn. But it remains to be seen whether such attempts to ground a theory of justice within the context of a fundamental theology or philosophical theology are not overly abstract, and lacking in the substance requisite for concrete community and social practice. This, I believe, is the challenge posed by contemporary political and liberation theologians who attempt to "fuse the horizons" of Christian faith and Marxist practical social theory. Another challenge, but of a thoroughly different nature, issues from such Christian communitarians as John Howard Yoder and Stanley Hauerwas, who I suspect would argue that the theological perspectives, which Tillich and Richard and Reinhold Niebuhr provide, represent little more than a capitulation to liberalism's requirement that theology make itself presentable, i.e., in attenuated form, if it is to be uttered in mixed company.

How might a theology of justice be formulated which neither gives too much authority to liberal culture, thereby losing any determinate grounding in a theology of the good, nor becomes too enchanted with being critical in a Marxist manner, thereby enshrining a determinate protest idiom as adequate for speaking about justice? Both of these options, if my preceding argument has been persuasive, face the perils of either deontological liberalism or anti-theological Marxism. Under the constraints of deontological liberalism, theology must either be bracketed altogether or else phrased in a manner that is intersubjectively valid within a pluralistic community. Needless to say, this blunts the edge of theology. Under the constraints of anti-theological Marxism, theology is called on to give way to social praxis and critical activity. In the bargain theology is tamed by a theory of justice that derives from a particular social theory, so that sociology governs theology. Furthermore, as I argued earlier, a society, characterized by either deontological liberalism-cum-theology or anti-theological Marxism-cum-theology (i.e., critical or negative theology) may nevertheless be a society lacking in meaning, solidarity, and human fulfillment, and thus may not be a good society.

It is this problematic which gives rise to the appeal of a more classical teleological and communitarian framework for developing a theory and theology of justice. Within such a framework, one which accents a theory of the good, justice is understood in the context of a fundamental vision, a model of character or virtue, and in view of traditions or concrete activities and practices which contribute to the creation of the good society. This view, I suggest, is most compatible with the more conservative, and at the same time radical, types of intentional religious communities. Such a tendency also characterizes certain newer religious movements like the Unification Church, which although theologically heterodox, is in terms of practice quite compatible with various forms of conservative and radical sectarian Christianity. In the following section I consider Unification theology as a practical theology which departs from the contemporary tendency to reduce and utterly politicize the notion of practice.

On the Creation of a Good Society

Theology of Practice as Theology of the Family

I have argued that the modern preoccupation with justice, either in the form of deontological liberalism or anti-theological Marxism, does not hold much promise for the creation of either a good or *de facto* just society. I have also attempted to demonstrate, speaking through Niebuhr and Tillich, the relevance of theism for the creation of a just society. At this point I shall move from these theoretical considerations to more practical ones, focusing in particular on a notion of practice which operates outside the paradigms of either deontological liberalism or anti-theological Marxism.[19] In essence, I will attempt to show that whereas justice may not be good, goodness may entail justice.

Any contemporary political and/or liberation theologian will be dissatisfied with the distinct paucity of justice themes in Unification theology. Unlike most political/liberation theologies, Unificationism does not sublate theory with the praxis of justice; and although Unification theology may indeed be understood in the mode of practical theology, justice is not the sole criterion for practice. Obviously, then, justice is not the central category for Unification theological ethical reflection. However, this is not to be confused with a failure to underscore the importance of human responsibility in the transformation of human society; nor should this be confused with the privatization of faith. Responsibility is a major aspect of Unification's theological anthropology; just as political and economic activism are a part of its social teachings. The goal of responsibility and activism, however, is understood less in terms of justice than in terms of goodness. And in this respect, practice is not understood in terms of ideological critique or subversive social activity, but in terms of the creation of goodness. Furthermore, the central paradigm for understanding goodness is the family. In this respect Unification practical theology is a theology of the family. Unification theologian Young Oon Kim evidences this point:

Unification theology takes into account man's relatedness and responsibility by using the family as a model. . . . As individuals we live and grow in the matrix of the family. . . . Only if these kinship relationships are positive and creative is it possible to manifest the full give and take of love with God and our fellowman.[20]

Kim also points to similarities between the Unification theology of practice and the Confucian notion of *jen,* or "humanheartedness." To practice *jen,* Kim argues, "means to treat all men humanely" and "to live for the welfare of society."[21] Such a practice is cultivated in the family, but is not kept there, for it becomes the foundation for what might be called one's vision of the world.

At this point, Unification thought is at odds with most contemporary Christian social ethics, not only in its accent on the family as the central category for ethical reflection, but in its view that social ethics can be essentially an ethics of love, rather than one of justice. For example, Reinhold Niebuhr's "moral man, immoral society" thesis argues that the love which is operative at the face-to-face level, or that selfless love which was exemplified on the Cross, can never serve as a basis for a social ethics, except at a distance in the form of a regulative principle. Unification's ambition, on the other hand, is for a family ethics that is socially relevant at the political and economic level. Consider the comment by Unificationist philosopher Sang Hun Lee:

> The ideal family represents the fulfillment of God's ideal for the creation and the place where His love is realized. Family ethics are the foundation for all ethics such as business and national ethics.[22]

In other words family ethics is the basis for social ethics.

Normally a family ethics indicates an espousal of tribalism, or a form of particularism that closes itself off from others. Family or tribal economics and family or tribal politics means preferential treatment for tribe members, and the exclusion of others who live beyond the pale of the moral community. Family justice thus allows for a very narrow scope wherein justice could be said to apply. Justice, therefore, is not owed to non-family members. Family ethics also suggests a kind of organic and totalitarian solidarity: coerced consensus with exile and dispossession handed out to the dissenter. Such is the ethics of *Gemeinschaft.* Unification theology, however, aspires to create a family ethics which is universal in its vision, i.e., that is detribalized, deracialized, and denationalized. Inter-tribal, inter-racial, inter-national, and inter-religious marriages provide a key to a universalist ethics of the family.

Just as one might argue that certain basic ego-strengths are foundational to the capacity for moral action, Unificationism suggests that a qualitatively enriched family environment can become the basis for the formation of a mature moral agent. This position is, of course, very similar to the one taken by Horace Bushnell in *Christian Nurture*.[23] The theological backing for the stress on the family derives from the interpretation of the doctrine of God and christology: God as both male and female is the parent of humanity; and following from this the fullness of Christ, or Incarnation, is represented in "the marriage supper of the lamb," interpreted as the need for a married messiah, that is, for True Parents.

Family ethics has generally been eclipsed in modern philosophical and theological ethics. Either individual ethics or macro-social ethics has been accented. Given the premium placed on autonomy and objectivity, ethics comes to deal only with principles and procedures that are binding between strangers. Justice is the obligation that strangers, autonomous and anonymous agents who do not share a common vision of the good life or of truth, owe to one another. Idealistic in its approach, Unification thought seeks to embed its social ethic in a theory of love. Not in an abstract theory of love as such, but in a theory of family as the locus of God's love.

At the center of this project is the view that rationality, as it operates in the modern world, can be transformed so as to move beyond both positivistic instrumental rationality and beyond its converse (namely, critical or negative dialectical rationality), not to a form of irrationality or obscurantist relativism, but to a form of substantive rationality or theistic rationality which is particular and concrete, and yet inclusive and respectful of all being. Unification theological ethics suggests that theocentric rationality or theocentric consciousness can be operative not only at the sectarian level of social existence (i.e., the community set apart from the world) but at the global level. Furthermore, it is believed that the family can operate as the basis for the cultivation of such a globally sensitive substantive rationality.

As I see it, the logic or justification for the lack of a justice theme in Unification theology derives from its trust that goodness—both the goodness of God and the goodness of "restored" human beings—requires justice. Justice is then sublated by practice, governed by a vision of the good identified with a way of discipline, and by devotion to a family ideal, and service to others. It might be said that for the Unificationist, justice is achieved by way of a benevolent form of double effect, whereby the intention for goodness is believed to be inclusive of justice. Of course, for most people this represents either a very unsatisfying option, or else a merely curious one undeserving of a second look. Deontological liberals will argue that they would prefer objective justice to the imposition of a Unification interpretation of goodness; critical Neo-Marxists will protest, and rightfully, that goodness has historically been inclusive of injustice, with theories of goodness functioning as ideological covers for systematic oppression. Such arguments must be respected. And certainly it remains to be seen whether or not Unificationism can continue as a community—particularly if it is to move with increasing complexity from the simplicity of a tribe or sect of the religiously gifted to a differentiated society accepting of the religiously ungifted—without thematizing more explicitly its theology of justice, particularly if there is to be any hope to communicate or even survive in the West. It is perhaps this concern, more than any other, that encourages this attempt to explore the theology of justice latent within Unificationism. That is, if a Unification-like theology of goodness is to establish itself as a viable option, then it must be demonstrated that beneath the practice of goodness there does not lurk—either malevolently as some surmise, or benevolently—a sociology of oppression and injustice. In other words, it must be demonstrated that goodness does not require injustice.

There seems to be a pressing need, in fact, for Unificationists to begin to reflect on the adequacy of a literally understood family ethics as a basis for order in a post-tribal society or nation. How, for example, is wealth to be distributed in Unification businesses? Or, as philosopher Gene James has phrased the question:

Can the values upon which the family is based, even if it is a family centered on God, be generalized to society as a whole? Are the duties and obligations we acquire from our relations with our parents and friends appropriate for governing urban societies in which most of our interaction with others must be brief and impersonal? . . . Should we look upon government leaders as wise parents who know better than all the rest of us what should be done for our own good?[24]

If, as seems to be the case, the preferential love that is inherent in family relations cannot manifest itself in any concrete way in larger differentiated communities, then some supplemental basis for attending to the common good must be established. In this case the family model may serve as a regulative ideal for the larger society, while at the same time a codification of law, a constitution and bill of rights, as well as a theory of justice must be formulated. Though perhaps unnecessary at the level of family, these are required to insure order and fairness in the absence of immediate familial love. Of special significance here will be the passing on of the movement's spiritual parents, the Reverend and Mrs. Moon. These accommodations added in admission of the limits of the adequacy of a simple familial model for a larger and twenty-first century Unification society, do not undermine the social relevance and even primacy of the family for the creation of a good and just world.

From the perspective of theologians informed by either deontological liberalism or anti-theological Marxism, the family practice of Unificationism misses the point that people are suffering due to economic and political exploitation. Hence, the move to translate theology into a publically relevant form of political and economic discourse. Perhaps no other term more aptly describes theologically sublated praxis, especially that of the political and liberation theologians, than the term 'democratic socialism'. Contemporary practical theologians, most of whom remain indebted to conversations with Marxists and Neo-Marxist social theorists, not only tend to reduce practice to justice, but also tend to reduce justice to democratic socialism. Authentic praxis involves democratic socialist activity, which also entails being critical of democratic market societies.

While Unificationism seems to be committed to socialism (in the long run), as well as to a society where there is equality of prosperity and opportunity, Unificationism presents its own unique theory of the "carrier" of this liberating social praxis. That is, Unificationism disputes the claim that a Marxist-Leninist informed clergy or vanguard-church will lead the world to a society of "justice with a human face." Rather, Unificationists trust that justice will be achieved only on the foundation of a kind of reconstructed Christian practice, reconstructed not in light of Kantian individualism or Marxist sociology, but in light of Unificationism's theology of the family. Hence, Unification social thought can be seen as deferring to the primacy of cultural factors, as opposed to political and economic factors, in its theory of social change. And yet, unlike various forms of cultural Marxism, Unificationism views the creation of a new culture (not merely a counterculture defined in terms of what it reacts or protests against) as the practice most necessary for the creation of goodness and justice. The creation of culture, however, is very different from the attempt to politically or economically engineer society. The creation of a culture as the carrier of a good society requires practices embedded in an ethics of character, family, and tradition.

Conclusion

In this essay I have addressed forms of non-theological (liberal), anti-theological (Marxist), fundamental theological (Niebuhrian, Tillichian) and practical theological (Unificationist) justice. The first stresses political justice and accents the criterion of freedom. The second stresses economic justice, and reduces justice to equality (of economic result). The third focuses on the philosophical foundations for a theological theory of justice which affirms the universality and intelligibility of Christian truth claims. In essence this position implies that faith in God is inescapably relevant to the creation of a just society. The fourth, characterized as a theology of practice in a more classical, non-Neo-Marxist mode, accents the primacy of family as the entrée into the good society; here again faith in God is a sine qua non.

I have tried to show that liberalism seeks to secure a non-theological theory of justice in order to preserve justice in the face of theological chaos and religious wars. The incommensurability of theologies gives rise to the quest for a theory of justice and rights grounded in some generic feature of human beings. However, the attempt to ground a theory of justice in some formal feature of human beings does not necessarily solve the problem of pluralism. Theories of justice, theological or not, are also denominationally defined, and there exists many a war among the just, who happen to have competing views of what constitutes justice. And religious believers, like theorists of justice, can be dogmatic and moralistic.

I have also tried to make a persuasive argument that the just society is by no means necessarily a good or desirable society. There are tyrannies of justice. Certainly, communist societies are, for the most part, tyrannies of justice; and liberal societies are impoverishing themselves with a pursuit of justice that overlooks character, community, and the meaning of life. Of course, there are also instances of tyrannies of goodness, that is, societies with a vision of the good which is imposed ruthlessly on even the unreceptive. In such cases justice is denied, while injustices are legitimized by appeal to the inviolability of the good. For this reason, there is a need for theories of universal human rights, and for critical principles which are not merely circularly related to some parochial theory of the good. "Good" societies that espouse a type of slavery based on race or ethnicity are abominable.

I do not pretend to have proven that faith in God is necessary for the creation of a just society. This, after all, was never my goal. I have argued that a theory of goodness is an ethical category that stands prior to, though inclusive of, justice. My basic claim has been that justice is made both intelligible and achievable when embedded within a theory and practice of goodness.

NOTES

1. G. E. M. Anscombe, "Modern Moral Philosophy," in *The Journal of the Royal Institute of Philosophy,* Vol. XXXIII (124) (January 1958), 6.
2. Ibid.
3. Michael Sandel, *Liberalism and the Limits of Justice* (New York: Cambridge University Press, 1982), 1.
4. Ibid., 2.
5. The term 'original position' comes from John Rawls' *A Theory of Justice* (Cambridge, Mass: Harvard University Press, 1971). It refers to an original contract situation where the parties enjoy a kind of noumenal existence.
6. Sandel, 175.
7. Ibid., 181.
8. The term "life projects" is taken from Bernard Williams' essay "Persons, Character and Morality," in his *Moral Luck* (Cambridge University Press, 1981).
9. Sandel, 32.
10. Ibid., 35.
11. Alasdair MacIntyre, *After Virtue* (South Bend: Notre Dame Press, 1981), 235. I must admit a great deal of indebtedness and appreciation for MacIntyre's thought, though, of course, he should in no way be held responsible for whatever weaknesses characterize this document.
12. Bernard Williams, 14.
13. Ibid., 18.
14. MacIntyre, 188.
15. Taken from John Rawls', *A Theory of Justice.*
16. H. Richard Niebuhr, *Radical Monotheism and Western Culture* (New York: Harper & Row, 1970), 117.
17. Paul Tillich, *Love, Power, and Justice* (Oxford University Press, 1980), 67.
18. Ibid., 65.

19. David Tracy, "Theologies of Praxis," in *Creativity and Method,* edited by Matthew Lamb, (Marquette University Press, 1981), 35–51. Tracy distinguishes two types of practical theology. One, characterized by such thinkers as Bernard Lonergan and Eric Voegelin, employ a "fundamentally classical, usually Aristotelian" notion of practice, emphasizing "the constant need for personal transformation and 'conversion'." The other, characteristic of the political and liberation theologians, employs "some variant of Marxian social analysis for understanding the social praxis." Tracy's distinction I find very illuminating, although I am suspicious of the apparent compatability or "collaboratability" he sees between the two options. I see the two as being seriously at odds, just as I would view Aristotle and Marx as being at odds. I understand the Unification theology of practice as having an affinity with the more classical notion, and as being at odds with tendencies in a Marxist notion of practice.
20. Young Oon Kim, *Unification Theology* (HSAUWC, 1980), 78.
21. Ibid.
22. Sang Hun Lee, *Explaining Unification Thought* (New York: Unification Thought Institute, 1981), 236.
23. Horace Bushnell, *Christian Nurture* (Basic Books, 1979).
24. Gene James, "Family, Spiritual Values and World Government," in *The Family and the Unification Church,* edited by Gene James, (Rose of Sharon Press, 1983), 265.

Notes on Contributors

Deane William Ferm, Author, Gettysburg, Pennsylvania.

James Gaffney, Professor of Ethics, Loyola University, New Orleans, Louisiana.

Olusegun Gbadegesin, Lecturer, University of Ile-Ife, Nigeria.

Vitaliano R. Gorospe, Professor of Theology, Anteno De Manila University, Quezon City, Phillipines.

Ilhan Güngören, Author and Publisher, Istanbul, Turkey.

Gene G. James, Professor of Philosophy, Memphis State University, Memphis, Tennessee.

William R. Jones, Professor of Religion, Florida State University, Tallahassee, Florida.

Jay McDaniel, Assistant Professor of Religion, Hendrix College, Conway, Arkansas.

Gene Reeves, Dean, Meadville/Lombard Theological School, Chicago, Illinois.

J. Deotis Roberts, Professor of Religion, Eastern Baptist Theological Seminary, Philadelphia, Pennsylvania.

Richard L. Rubenstein, Professor of Religion, Florida State University, Tallahassee, Florida.

Abdulaziz A. Sachedina, Associate Professor of Religious Studies, University of Virginia, Charlottesville, Virginia.

Shivesh C. Thakur, Professor of Philosophy, University of Northern Iowa, Cedar Falls, Iowa.

Doboom Tulku, Director, Tibet House, New Delhi, India.

Thomas Walsh, Adjunct Professor of Ethics, Marist College, Poughkeepsie, New York.

Index

Abhidharma texts, 124
absolutes, *x*, 94
Achebe, Chinua, 54
'adl (justice), 110
Age of Triage, The (Rubenstein), 188
ahimsa, 36
ahl al-sunna wa al-jama'a (people of the custom and community), 111. *See also* Sunnites
Ahlstrom, Sidney, 5
ajogun (malevolent spirits), 66
alewilese (he who can not only say but can also do), 59
Alingal, Father Godofredo, S.J., 47
al-qist (justice), 101
anawim, 31
"animal pain," 17
Anscombe, G. E. M., 195
apocalypse, 132
Aquino, Sen. Benigno S., Jr., 28, 39
ara (body), 61, 63
Araya, Victorio, 7
Aristotle, 107, 135–138
arrogance, avoiding, 172-176
Asharites, *xi*, 105
Atiba, Alaafin, 61
authority, Islamic sources of, 110
Avatamsaka Sutra, 119

bahala na attitude, 31
Bakolori massacre, 57
Barth, Karl, 6, 9; neo-orthodoxy of, 2–3; on righteousness of God, 11
Basic Christian Communities (BCC) movement, 40, 46
belief, as different from faith, 174
Berger, Peter, 90, 94
Berkovits, Eliezer, 92, 93

Beyond Dialogue: Toward a Mutual Transformation of Christianity and Buddhism (Cobb), 172
Bhalas, 125
Birch, L. Charles, 166–167
Black Muslims. *See* Nation of Islam
black theology, 7–8
Bodhisattva, *xi*, 128–129
Bodhisattva Bhumis, 125
Bodhisattva discipline, 127
Bodhisattvayana, 124
Bonhoeffer, Dietrich, 3, 4–5
Bonino, Jose Miguez, 79
Books (revealed messages), 103
Brown, Delwin, 166
Brunner, Emil, 3, 6, 9
Buddha: as omnipotent, 125–126; as omnipresent, 125; as omniscient, 124–125
Buddhism: and initial aims, 172; Tathagata, 123; Theravada, *xi*
Buddhist Trinity, 123
Burkle, Howard, 95
Bushnell, Horace, 206–207

Carroll, John, 39, 42, 43–44
Carter, Pres. Jimmy, 25
Catholic church in Philippines, *viii-ix*
causal influence, 153
causality, 116. *See also* karma
Chandrakirti, Acharya, 125, 126
Chandrapradin Sutra, 123
character, importance of in Yoruba religion, 64–65
charismatic movement, 7
Christian activism, 166–168
Christian love, as subversive, 76–77
Christian Nurture (Bushnell), 207

Index

Christian perspective: sociological, 36–47, 48; theological, 29–36, 48–49
"Christian realism," 43–44
Christianity, 54, 190. *See also* Church
Christians and the Great Economic Debate (Wogaman), 30
Church: challenge to, 44–45; as institution, 37–47; as political force, 39–41; transcendence of, 46–47
Church Dogmatic, Vol. II (Barth), 11
church growth thesis, 23
Cicero, 158
Cobb, John B., Jr., 166–167, 172
Cobb, William D., 92–93
coercion theory of social change, 43
colonialism, 24, 54–55
community, *xviii,* 157–158, 186–187
compassion, 125
"comrade," 140
Cone, James, 7–8
Conference for Human Development, 41
conservatism, 2
"constant conjunction," 153
"contractocracy," 56
contributionism, 160–161
conversion, 74, 132
cooperation in community, 34, 46
"corrective justice," 135
"Council of Reconciliation," 41
counter violence, *xviii*
Cox, Harvey, 6, 164
creation: Christian doctrine of, 31–33; as ongoing process, 32–33; metaphysical sense, 130; popular sense, 130
creative transformation, 174–176
creativity, 161-162
Creator, what is the, 126
Cry Justice (Sider), 11
culture, creation of a, 209

Davaney, Sheila Greeve, 166
death-of-God theology, 6
deconstruction, theological, 85
democratic socialism, justice as, 209
Democratic Socialist regime, 149, 150

deontological liberalism, 204
de-sanctification, 93
despair, 155–156
destiny, 65–68. *See also* predestination
determinism, *xi–xii*
Dhammapada, 117
Dharma (correct path), 123
Dharmakirti, Acharya, 124–125
dialectical theology, 104–105
Dialogue for Peace, A, 38
Dickens, Charles, 20
dikaiosune (justice), 136
disciplines, Buddhist, 127
disenchantment of the world, 178
diversity, tolerance of, 175
domination, and injustice, 200
doubt, as ingredient of faith, 4
dualism, Greek, 70, 73

economic exploitation, 7, 11–13, 24–25
Ekpu, Ray, 52
emi (life-breath), 61–62, 63
emigration, 187
encompassing ideal, 157–158
esp, *ix–x;* defined, 82
esp oppression, 85–88. *See also* oppression
evangelicalism, 8
Evangelicals and Development. Toward A Theology of Social Change (Sider), 11
evil, and God, 18–19
Exhortation Against Violence, 38
Exodus story, 73
explicit faith, 158–159
exploitative relationships, 55. *See also* economic exploitation

fairness, 137–138
faith: as belief, *xiv, xv–xvi;* in Biblical sense, 72; childlike, 19; as commitment, *xiv, xv–xvi;* as conceived in West, *xii;* and cooperative action, *xv;* existential ideal for, 170–172; Filipino, 29; and God, 156–157; and "good" society, *xviii;* in liberation theology, 69–81, 164; need for

Index

worldwide, *xvii*; Tillich on, 4; universal definition of, *xiv*
faith in God: conceptions of, 131–134; and creation of good society, 194; as experienced by many, 134; and legitimating just society, 82–96, 140–141, 143–144, 210; and process theology, 152–163; as useful tool, 151; Western concept of, 152
family, as locus of God's love, 207
feminist theology, 8
Ford Motor Company, 186
Foucauld, Charles de, 77
Fourth Great Awakening, 5
Franklin, Benjamin, 158
free will, *xi*
freedom, 19–20, 135, 162
Fundamentalist Theocratic regime, 149, 150

Gastarbeiter, 188
Gaudium et spes, 71
Gemeinschaft, 206
generosity, and just society, 140
genocide, *xvi*, *xix*
gist, 110
God: Asian Christian concept of, 9; Biblical concept of, 10–11; black theology's concept of, 7–8; exalted status of, 121; feminist theology's concept of, 7–8; as Great Liberator, 6, 7; as immanent activist, 7; Indian concept of, 9; as justice, 10–13; liberation theology's concept of, 7, 11–12; in mainstream Christian theology, *vii–viii*; Minjung theology on, 12; as a pluralist, 173; process theology on, 156, 160–161, 168, 169, 175; restore image of in man, 33; Roman Catholic concept of, 5; as symbol, 158–159; Tillich on, 4; Yoruba concept of, 58–59
"God-intoxicated," 142
Golden Rule, 137–138
good society, creation of, 193–210. *See also* just society
goodness, and injustice, 208
Goya, F. J., 182

greed: economic, *xviii*; as social sin, 18
guidance: divine, in Qur'an, 102–107; universal or natural, 105–107
Gutierrez, Gustavo, 12

Hallen, Barry, 62
Hauerwas, Stanley, 203
Hillman, James, 173
Holy Spirit Association for the Unification of World Christianity, 191
Honest to God (Robinson), 6
human condition, 20–22
human dignity, 38
human experience, common, 153–154
human faith, 155–156; as faith in God, 156–157
human rights, 25–26, 147; and idea of divine grace, *xiv*; and national pride, 25–26; need for theories of universal, 210
human suffering, 15–20
humanocentric theism, 92–95
humanism, 92
Hunger for Justice: The Politics of Food and Faith (Nelson), 12–13

idolatry, *viii*, 9–10
Ifa religion, 58–68
Igbo (tribe), 53
ijma (jurists), 109
ijtihad (human reasoning), 108
Imam (messianic leader), 99
Imami Shi'ism, 100
individualism, tradition of, 159–160
inequalities: trans-generational, 86; in theocratic society, 147
initial aims: process liberation on, 169; and nontheists, 171–172
injustice, 90–91
integration theory of social change, 42–43
intellectualization, 178
Islam, 100, 190
iustitia (justice), 136

James, Gene, 208
Jane Eyre (Bronte), 89, 91

Index

jen (humanheartedness), 206
Judaism, 190
just society: Buddhist view of, 116–122; fundamental rights of, 145; identifying marks of, 145; meaning of, 84; as not necessarily good society, 194, 210; ontological base for, 95; process theology on, 152–163; Western secular concept of, 135
justice: on autonomy and priority of universal principles of, 195–199; in the Bible, 29–31; Church's promotion of, 37–38; corrective, 135; as democratic socialism, 209; divinely sanctioned standard of, 102; as evolving concept, *xiii*; and faith in societies, 144, 150–151; and human intention, 143–144, 148–149; as initial aim, 169, 171–172; and knowledge of God, 10–13; in liberation theology, 69–81; Marxist concept of, *xvii*, 199–201; modern capitalistic concept of, *xvii*; natural, 107; non-theological theories of, 193–195; and pluralism, 210; process/liberation perspective on, 166–168; and the Prophet, 113; qur'anic notion of, 101–107; as requiring divine intervention, 143, 147–148; and righteousness, 136; in theocentric sense, 143, 146–147; theological, 201–204; three dimensions of, 167; Unification view of, 207, 208; varying concepts of, *xii–xiii*
"justice with a human face," 209

Kant, Immanuel, 195–196
karma, 116, 119–120
karuna (compassionate heart), 121
Kelley, Dean, 8
Kennedy, Pres. John F., 5
Khaldun, Ibn, 114
Kim, Young Oon, 205–206
King, Martin Luther, Jr., 77
Kurada, S., 120
Kurunmi, 61

labor: division of, 179; specialization of, 179–181

land tenure system, 55
Lee, Sang Hun, 206
Letters and Papers From Prison (Bonhoeffer), 4–5
Liberal Democratic regime, 149, 150
liberalism, 1–2
Liberalism and the Limits of Justice (Sandel), 196
Liberation of Life, The (Cobb and Birch), 166
liberation theology: on counter violence, *ix*; faith in, *ix*; and God equals justice theme, 11–13; insights of, *ix–x*; justice in, *ix*

MacIntyre, Alasdair, *xviii*, 195; on law, 198; on justice, 199
McLoughlin, William, 5
Madhyamaka literatures, 125
Madhyamakavatara (Chandrakirti), 125, 126
Mahayana, 127
Mahayana Buddhism, 119
Mahayana doctrine, *xi*
Mahdi, 97–98, 100
Malthus, Thomas Robert, 179
Mantrayana, 124
market economy, 185–186
martial law, 38–39
Marx, Karl, 181–182, 199–201
mass unemployment, 187–188
Mays, Benjamin, 88
meaninglessness, ultimate, 155–156
merit, 70–72, 135
messianism, Islamic, 97, 98–99
mind, as ultimate factor, 123, 129
Minjung theology, 12
Miscellaneous Charismatic regime, 149, 150
mizan (scale), 110
Mohammed, Bala, 57
Mohammed, Gen. Murtala, 56
monotheistic doctrine, 109
"monotheistic psychology," 173
Moon, Rev. Sun Myung, 191
Moral Majority, 23–24
moral obligation, 189–190
Muhammad, Prophet, 98
Muhammed, Elijah, 87–88

218

Index

Mutazilites, *xi*, 104–105
muttaqi (godfearing), 104

Nam-dong, Suh, 12
Nation of Islam, The, 87–88
"natural injustice," 145
Nelson, Jack, 12–13
Neo-Malthusianism, *xvi*, 188, 189
neo-orthodoxy, 2–3; demise of, 6; resurgence of, 7, 8–9
New Right, 179–180
Niebuhr, H. Richard, 195, 201–204
Niebuhr, Reinhold, 3, 6, 9, 203, 206
nihilism, 83–85, 94
niratma, 128
Nirvana (Buddhahood), 126
nontheist, 165, 171–172
nonviolence, 36
Novak, Michael, 79

obligation, moral philosophy on, 195
Ogden, Schubert, 166
Ogud (god of iron), 61
Olodumare: and character, 64; as dispenser of justice, 60; as God, 58–59, 67; and predestination, 61, 65; as theological doctrine of despair, *ix*
omnipotence, divine, 161. *See also* Buddha
omniscience, divine, 161
On The Boundary (Tillich), 3
"one-dimensional religion," *viii*, 22–23
Ongpin, Jaime, 38
ontological priority, 94–95
openness, faith as, 170–172
oppression: dual nature of, *x*; mechanism of, 88–90; nature and operation of, 85–88; and quietism, 88–90, 91, 93, 95
ori (personal spirit), 62–67
original sin, 33–34
orisa (divinities), 58, 60
Orisanla (arch-divinity), 59, 61, 63
orthopraxis, 78
Orunmila (god of divination), 59, 62, 63; divining power of, 66
Osu (social segregation), 53

paramita (perfections), 128–129
paschal mystery, 35–36
pasyon, 35
peace, meanings of, 166–168
persuasion, and creative transformation, 174–176
phronemos (good man), 202
phronesis (practical wisdom), 202
Plato, 135
political independence, 55–58
polytheism, 59
Pope John XXIII, 5
Pope John Paul II, 37
postmodern Christianity, 164–177
power, and oppression, 87
Pramanavartikakarika, 124–125
predestination, *xi*; and social injustice, 65–68; Yoruba belief in, 61–65
"primary goods," *xiv*, 145–146
prisoner-of-war camps, 155–156
privileges, unequal access to, 87
Process theology: on faith in God/just society, 152–163
Process Theology as Political Theology (Cobb), 166
proportional equality, 135–138

Quebedeaux, Richard, 8–9
QUESTION, 82–96
quietism, 88–90, 91, 93, 95

racialism, 87–88
racism, *xix*, 7–8, 11; as national sin, 21–22; and racialism, 87–88
rational society, 178–192
rationalist objectivism, 105
rationality: as basis for just society, 148; functional, 183–184; instrumental, 178–179; modern, 178; revolution of, 180–182; substantive, 207
"rationalization," *xvi*, 178
Rawls, John, 147, 193, 199
reality: Buddhist vision of, 159; liberation Christian interpretation of, 165; objectivated, 90; objective, 90; process philosophy on, 159; as relational, 159–160; Western metaphysical view of, 159

Index

reconciliation (doctrine), 79
religion, future of in rational society, 178–192
religious commitment, need for, *xviii*
religious imperialism, 173
religious pluralism: in America, 158; increasing, 9; and justice, 210; problem of, 164; process theology on, 173–174
responsiveness, faith as, 170–172
revolutionary violence, 77–78
Ricardo, David, 179
righteousness, and justice, 136
Robinson, Bishop John, 6
Romero, Bishop Oscar, 47
Ruether, Rosemary Radford, 8, 165

St. Augustine, 139
St. John, 32
St. Paul, 32
St. Thomas Aquinas, 70
salvation: Buddhist view of, 119; Islamic doctrine of, 98, 113; and karma, 119–120; liberation theology concept of, 75; Lutheran doctrine of, 2; Old Testament concept of, 73; Shi'ite concept of, 112
samadhi, 127
Samartha, Stanley, 9
samsara (the round of birth and death), 118
Sandel, Michael, 195, 196, 197, 198
Sangha (spiritual community), 124
Santayana, George, 6
Saoshyani (Messiah), *xi*, 97
Sarvagyan (All-Knowing), 125
satyagraha, 36
Schaeffer, Francis, 83
Secular City, The (Cox), 6
secularism, 5, 6
secularization, radical, 191
Segundo, Juan Luis, 70–72
self, 118, 120
Sexism and God-Talk (Ruether), 8
Shari'a, 107–109
Shi'ism, 99. *See also* Imami Shi'ism; Shi'ites
Shi'ites, 99, 111–113

shunyata, 128
Sider, Ron, 11
"silent majority," *viii*
sin, concept of, 73–74
Sin, Jaime Cardinal, 41–42
Smith, Adam, 178–181
Smith, Archie, 166
social analysis, 78–79
social change, 42–43
Social Darwinism, *xvi*, 188, 189
social injustice: dimensions of, 53–58; and predestination, 65–68
social justice: Buddhism and, *x*, *xi–xii*; Muslim view of, *xi*
social order, creation of a just, 97–115
social sins, defined, 34
Socialist Collectivist regime, 149, 150
society, dichotomization of, 189
Song, C. S., 9
soul, 118–120
Soviet Union, 182–185
spiritual life, 74–75
spirituality, for social justice, 36
Sravakayana, 124
Stalin, Josef, 183–185
stewardship, man's, 32
substance, meaning of, 199
success, concept of, 169–170
Suchocki, Marjorie, 166
Sunna (model pattern of behavior), 108
Sunnites, 111
sunyata (emptiness), 118
sustainability, 167–168, 171–172
suum cuique, 135–136

talakawa (peasants), 67
Tale of Two Cities, A (Dickens), 20
taqwa (life of uprightness), 104
Tathagata Buddha, 123
tathata (suchness), 118
"Theatre of the Absurd," 149, 151
theism, *x*, 83, 205
theistic subjectivism, 105
theocentric theism, 90–91
theocracy, 110
theodicy, 15, 160

Index

theology: and deontological liberalism, 204; of family, 205–209; liberation theology on, 78; location of, 154; and *orthopraxis*, 78; as "second act," 78
Theravada Buddhism, *xi*
Things Fall Apart (Achebe), 54
Tillich, Paul, *xv*, 3–4, 195; on material success, 169–170; on justice, 203
Tolstoy, Leo, 139
Torres, Camillo, 77
Traditional Feudal regime, 149, 150
transcendence, 3
trust, faith as, 170–172
truth, in Biblical sense, 72

Unification Church, 139, 191
Unification theology, 195, 204–209
universalism, 165

Vajracchedika Sutra, 119
Vatican II, 5, 71
violence: Christ's attitude toward, 77; as embodiment of injustice, 151; institutional, 77; issue of, *xviii*; in liberation theology, 69–81; revolutionary, 77–78; Soviet use of mass, 182–185

Wealth of Nations, The (Smith), 179
Weber, Max, 178
We Drink From Our Wells (Gutierrez), 12
wertfrei (value-neutral), 178
Whitehead, Alfred N. 153, 155, 161–162
Why Conservative Churches Are Growing (Kelley), 8
Williams, Bernard, 195, 197, 198–199
Wogaman, J. Philip, 30

yada (to know/to love), 11
Yahweh, 29–30
yathabhutam (reality), 118
"yo-yo" theology, 8
Yoder, John Howard, 203
Yoruba: and concept of God, 58–59
Yoruba Ifa theology, 61–65